CYCLING
LOS ANGELES

CYCLING
LOS ANGELES

BY DON AND SHARRON BRUNDIGE

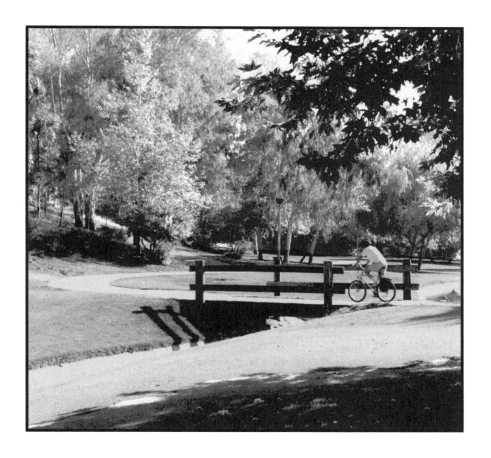

SUNBELT PUBLICATIONS
San Diego, California

Cycling Los Angeles
Sunbelt Publications, Inc.
Copyright © 2007 by Don and Sharron Brundige
All rights reserved
First edition 1989. Second edition 2007

Edited by Jennifer Redmond
Cover design by Kathleen Wise
Composition by W.G. Hample and Associates
Project management by Jennifer Redmond
Photography by Don and Sharron Brundige, unless noted.
Printed in the United States of America by United Graphics, Inc.

Sunbelt Publications, Inc.
P.O. Box 191126
San Diego, CA 92159-1126
(619) 258-4911, fax: (619) 258-4916
www.sunbeltbooks.com

10 09 08 07   5 4 3 2 1

"Adventures in the Natural History and Cultural Heritage of the Californias"
A Series Edited by Lowell Lindsay

Library of Congress Cataloging-in-Publication Data

Brundige, Don.
  Cycling Los Angeles / by Don and Sharron Brundige. — 1st ed.
    p. cm.
  ISBN-13: 978-0-932653-81-9
  ISBN-10: 0-932653-81-2
  1. Bicycle touring—California—Los Angeles—Guidebooks. 2. Los Angeles
(Calif.)—Guidebooks. I. Brundige, Sharron. II. Title.

GV1045.5.C22B78 2007
796.6'409794'94—dc22
                                2007016183

Cover photograph: Long Beach Shoreline Park

DEDICATION

To our family

....Who we love very much

George, Bernice, Don, Pat, Kathie, Jim, Stevie, Rich, Pon, Eric,
Astrid, Zoltan, Kyali, Greta, Sammie, Greg, Mark, Caitlyn, Mandy,
Pete, Diane, Bradley, Michelle, Vlad II, Ayana, and Vlad III.

CONTENTS

71 Trips and 85 Rides

ACKNOWLEDGMENTS

We offer our thanks to family, friends, and bicycling acquaintances who gave us ideas, advice, and plenty of encouragement while we were developing this biking book. This includes a "thank you" to the state, county, and city agencies and individuals who offered their services and publications. Kudos to Sam Nunez, Susan Cohen, Jill Morales, Karen Profet, Walt and Sally Bond, Rich Davis, Anders Ljungwe, Jim Cradduck, and the folks we met on the road, for sharing the tours. We also show particular gratitude to our venerable crew that was kind enough to review and comment on our original manuscript: Jill Morales, Al Hook, and Walt and Sally Bond. Thank you Jackie Broom and Alex Moi for helping us through so many computer crises.

We specifically wish to acknowledge the following individuals and/or organizations who provided some excellent ideas for bicycle trips in the original book: Joel Breitbart of the City of Los Angeles; the folks at CALTRANS District 07; the Department of Transportation of the City of Los Angeles; Al Kovach of the City of Torrance; the Recreation Department of the City of Arcadia; the Public Works Department of the City of Pasadena; the Parks and Recreation Department of the City of Burbank; the Cities of Glendale and La Mirada; and Noelia Chapa of the City of La Habra Heights.

Finally, we want to thank: the East Area Administrative Office for their help in directing us around Elysian Park; Pete Weisser at the California Department of Water Resources, for providing updated information about the California Aqueduct; Ron Milan of the Los Angeles County Bicycling Coalition (LACBC), for acquainting us with the latest additions to marked City of Los Angeles bikeways; Will and Kathi Decker of the *Southern California Bicyclist* magazine, for keeping us on our toes to update our tours; and both Cary Green and Dick Farrar, local cycling enthusiasts, for providing corrections/updates to some of our previous ride descriptions.

INTRODUCTION

As with all our books, we wanted to provide a trip guide that concentrates on trip navigation, contains a large number of well-documented trips, provides the necessary trip maps and elevation contours, and is reasonably priced. Hopefully, again, we have succeeded!

This guide has been developed based on biking trips revisited in 2006 and corrections/updates supplied by book users since the last printing. This is a new edition of our classic *Bicycle Rides: Los Angeles County* in a smaller, handier format, published by Sunbelt Publications.

There are over 1100 <u>one-way</u> bike miles described! The document identifies 71 trips which blanket Los Angeles County. Trips of exceptional length or complexity are broken down into segments or "rides." There is a total of 85 rides described, with each ride written to be as complete and self-standing as possible. The authors and riding buddies used 18-speed bicycles, although the vast majority of trips can be ridden with bikes having fewer gears. We have noted the few rides which are more amenable to hybrid and/or fat-tire ("balloon-tire") bikes (for Trip #70C, they are necessary). In no cases are mountain bikes required.

A cross section of trips is provided. There are some short-length family trips on separated bikepaths, many longer exploratory and workout trips for more experienced bikers on various quality bike routes, and a few "gut-buster" trips on open roadway for the most physically fit and motivated cyclists. The trip domains include cities, parks, beaches, harbors, rivers, lakes, valleys, canyons, mountains, and desert. The trips vary from extremely scenic to somewhat monotonous (e.g., certain stretches of the concrete "wastelands" along the Class I river routes). There is a little something for everybody!

The strong emphasis in this book is "getting from here to there." This navigation is provided using detailed route descriptions in terms of landmarks, mileage, elevation contours, and a quality set of trip maps. Scenery, vistas, and scenic or historic landmarks and sightseeing attractions are regularly noted for each trip, although detailed information about these features must be sought out in other publications. Public restrooms and sources of water are identified on those few trips where these facilities are readily available. Pleasant rest spots are also pointed out. Finally, "wine and dine" spots are noted for two specific circumstances: 1) where places to eat along the route are scarce; and 2) where the establishment is too unique or exceptional not to mention.

HOW TO USE THIS BOOK

There are two ways to use this book: one way is for the person who wants to enjoy the research along with enjoying the bike ride, and another way is for the biker who is just anxious to get out there "amongst 'em."

For the "anxious biker," follow Steps 1 through 5 below and split!

1. Check the "BEST RIDES BY CATEGORY" trip summary, noted on the inside cover, for candidate trips or use the "Master Trip Map" in the "TRIP ORGANIZA-TION" section to select areas of interest for the bike ride. Note the candidate trip numbers. (Another option is to select a trip by using the "INDEX TO LAND-MARKS AND ATTRACTIONS BY TRIP NUMBER" near the end of the book.)
2. Go to the "Master Trip Matrices" in the "TRIP ORGANIZATION" section and narrow down the number of candidate trips by reviewing their general features.
3. Read about the individual trips and select one. Make a photocopy of the trip(s) of interest, subject to the copyright limitations noted on page iv.
4. Read and understand the safety rules described in the "GENERAL BIKING CON-SIDERATIONS" section and review the "CHECKLIST" section.
5. See you later. Enjoy the ride!

For the more methodical folks, continue reading the next chapter. By the time you're through, you'll understand the trip description and maps much better than the "anxious biker."

TRIP ORGANIZATION

This bike book is organized by trip number. Extended length trips are broken down into trip segments by ride number, which is the trip number plus a letter. Thus, Trip #6 is the "Palos Verdes Peninsula Loop," while Ride #6A is the "Palos Verdes Drive North" segment. Trip numbers are in a general sequence governed by whether the tours are coastal, river, inland, or special tours. Refer back to the "CONTENTS" pages for the entire trip list.

The "Master Trip Maps" show the general trailhead location of trips, using a circled reference number (i.e., ⑦ refers to Trip #7). Extended length trips are identified by circled numbers at both beginning and terminal points.

The "Master Trip Matrices" provide a quick reference for selecting candidate trips and for more detailed reading evaluation. The matrices are organized by trip number. The key trip descriptors provided in those matrices are briefly explained in the foot-notes at the bottom of the last matrix. A more detailed explanation of those descriptors is provided in the "TRIP DESCRIPTION/ TERMINOLOGY" section which follows.

MASTER TRIP MAP: SOUTH L.A. COUNTY

FREEWAY / ROADWAY
RIVER / CREEK
COUNTY BOUNDARY
TRIP NUMBER "N"

N
MILES
0 5 10

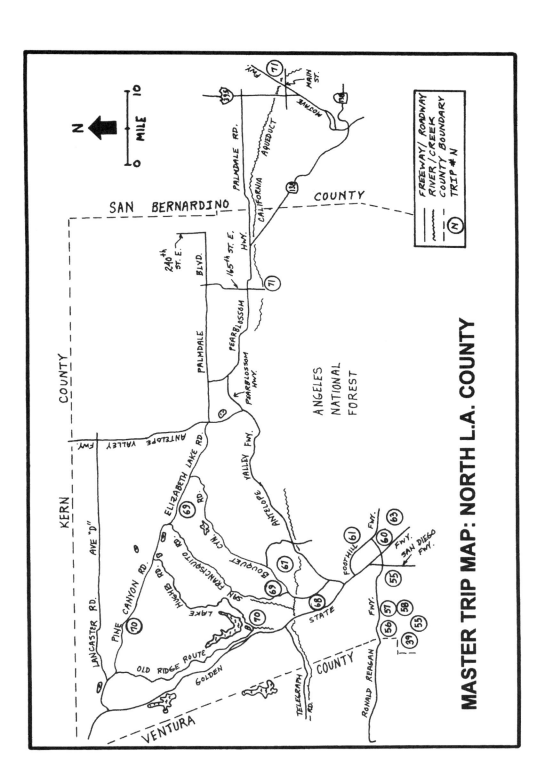

MASTER TRIP MAP: NORTH L.A. COUNTY

MASTER TRIP MATRIX

| TRIP NO. | GENERAL LOCATION | LEVEL OF DIFFICULTY | | | ROUTE QUALITY | | | TRIP CHARACT.[2] | COMMENTS |
		L.O.D.[1]	MILES	ELEV.	BIKE TRAIL (%)	BIKE LANE (%)	OTHER (%)		
1	Redondo Beach-Pacific Palisades	M (1-w) M-S (r/t)	22.0 (1-w)	Flat	90	10	-	S, L, S/A, M	South Bay Bike Trail
1A	Redondo Beach-Manhattan Beach	E	5.4	Flat	80	20	-	S, L, S/A	Southern Segment
1B	Manhattan Beach-Marina Del Rey	E	7.3	Flat	100	-	-	S, L, S/A	Middle Segment
1C	Marina Del Rey-Pacific Palisades	E	9.3	Flat	80	20	-	S, L, S/A	Northern Segment
2	Santa Monica	E (1 loop) M (2 loops)	6.4 11.9	Flat Flat-Mod.	10 40	90 60	- -	S, L, S/A	Santa Monica Loops
3	Westwood	M	6.7-7.5	Flat-Mod.	10	70	20	S, L	Westwood Loops (2 options)
4	Marina Del Rey-Culver City	E (1-w) M (r/t)	6.6 (1-w)	Flat	100	-	-	M	Ballona Creek Bikeway
5	Westwood-Encino	S (1-w) S-VS (r/t)	7.3 (1-w)	Steep	-	50	50	S, E	Old Sepulveda Blvd. (Sepulveda Pass)
6	Palos Verdes Peninsula	S-VS	23.2	Steep	20	80	-	S, L, S/A, E, M	Palos Verdes Peninsula Loop
6A	Rolling Hills	M (1-w) M-S (r/t)	5.8 (1-w)	Mod.	70	-	30	S, L, E	Palos Verdes Drive North
6B	Palos Verdes Estates	M (1-w) M (r/t)	5.1 (1-w)	Mod.	-	20	80	S, L	Palos Verdes Drive West
6C	Rancho Palos Verdes	M (1-w) M (r/t)	5.7 (1-w)	Mod.	-	-	100	S, L, S/A	Palos Verdes Drive South
6D	Miraleste-Rancho Palos Verdes	S (1-w) S-VS (r/t)	6.6 (1-w)	Steep	10	-	90	S, E	Palos Verdes Drive East

1.2 See footnotes on page 12

MASTER TRIP MATRIX

TRIP NO.	GENERAL LOCATION	LEVEL OF DIFFICULTY			ROUTE QUALITY			TRIP CHARACT.[2]	COMMENTS
		L.O.D.[1]	MILES	ELEV.	BIKE TRAIL (%)	BIKE LANE (%)	OTHER (%)		
7	San Pedro	M (1-w) M (r/t)	6.2 (1-w)	Mod.	30	60	10	S, L, S/A	Cabrillo Beach, Point Fermin
8	San Pedro	E (1-w) E (r/t)	6.2 (1-w)	Flat	10	-	90	S, L, S/A	L. A. Harbor Main Channel, Ports O' Call
9	Los Angeles Harbor	E (1-w) E-M (r/t)	9.6 (1-w)	Flat	10	—	90	S, L	East and West Basins
10	Long Beach Harbor	M (1-w) M (r/t)	13.1 (1-w)	Flat	-	-	100	S, L	Cerritos and Back Channels
11	Long Beach Harbor	E (1-w) E-M (r/t)	8.4 (1-w)	Flat	-	-	100	S, L, S/A	Southeast Basin
12	Los Angeles Harbor, Long Beach Harbor	E (E)	6.0 (12.8)	Flat	-	-	100	S, L	Terminal Island Loop (with excursion trip)
13	Harbor City	E (E)	4.5 (5.5)	Flat	60	-	40	S, N	Harbor Regional Park Loop (with campus excursion)
14	Long Beach	E (E)	7.6 (9.0)	Flat	90	-	10	S, L, S/A	L.B. Shoreline Park Loop (with excursion trip)
15	Long Beach, Naples	E (E)	10.9 (12.9)	Flat	50	20	30	S, L	Belmont Shore, Naples Loop (with Marina Park excursion)
16	Long Beach	E	4.3	Flat	100	-	-	S, N, S/A	El Dorado Park Loop
17	Santa Monica Mountains	VS	43.8	Steep-Sheer	-	30	70	S, N, L, E, M	PCH-Topanga Canyon-Mulholland Hwy. Loop
18	Santa Monica-Port Hueneme	M-S (1-w) S-VS (r/t)	44.7 (1-w)	Mod.-Steep	-	80	20	S, N, L, S/A, E, M	Bicentennial Coastal Route
18A	Santa Monica-Malibu	M (1-w) M (r/t)	10.5 (1-w)	Mod.	-	-	100	S, N, L, S/A	Southern Segment

1,2 See footnotes on page 12

MASTER TRIP MATRIX

TRIP NO.	GENERAL LOCATION	LEVEL OF DIFFICULTY			ROUTE QUALITY			TRIP CHARACT.[2]	COMMENTS
		L.O.D.[1]	MILES	ELEV.	BIKE TRAIL (%)	BIKE LANE (%)	OTHER (%)		
18B	Malibu-Sycamore Cove	M-S (1-w) S (r/t)	20.1 (1-w)	Mod.-Steep	-	100	-	S, N, L, S/A, E	Middle Segment
18C	Sycamore Cove-Port Hueneme	M (1-w) M (r/t)	13.7 (1-w)	Mod.	-	70	30	S, N, L	Northern Segment
19-20	El Monte-Long Beach	M (1-w) S (r/t)	28.1 (1-w)	Flat	100	-	-	S, N, L, M	Rio Hondo-L.A. River Bike Trail
19	El Monte	E (1-w) M (r/t)	8.2 (1-w)	Flat	100		-	S, N, L, M	Upper Rio Hondo River Trail
20A	Downey	E (1-w) M (r/t)	9.0 (1-w)	Flat	100	-	-	S, N, L, M	Upper Lario Trail (Rio Hondo & L.A. Rivers)
20B	Long Beach	E (1-w) M (r/t)	10.9 (1-w)	Flat	100	-	-	S, L, M	Lower Lario Trail (Los Angeles River)
21	Southgate-Bell	E (1-w) E (r/t)	5.6 (1-w)	Flat	95	-	5	M	Los Angeles River (northern segment)
22	Seal Beach-Azusa	M-S S (r/t)	39.0 (1-w)	Flat	100	-	-	S, N, L, S/A, M	San Gabriel River (shore to mountains)
22A	Seal Beach-Long Beach	E (1-w) E (r/t)	5.6 (1-w)	Flat	100	-	-	S, N, S/A, M	Ocean to El Dorado Park
22B	Long Beach-Downey	E (1-w) M (r/t)	9.7 (1-w)	Flat	100	-	-	S, N, S/A, M	El Dorado Park to Wilderness Park
22C	Downey-Pico Rivera	E (1-w) M (r/t)	7.7 (1-w)	Flat	100	-	-	S, N, L, M	Wilderness Park to Whittier Narrows/Legg Lake
22D	Pico Rivera-Irwindale	E (1-w) M (r/t)	11.4 (1-w)	Flat	100	-	-	S, N, L, M	Whittier Narrows/Legg Lake to Santa Fe Dam
22E	Irwindale-Azusa	E (1-w) M (r/t)	7.5 (1-w)	Flat	100	-	-	S, N, L, M	Santa Fe Dam to San Gabriel Canyon

1,2 See footnotes on page 12

MASTER TRIP MATRIX

TRIP NO.	GENERAL LOCATION	LEVEL OF DIFFICULTY			ROUTE QUALITY			TRIP CHARACT.[2]	COMMENTS
		L.O.D.[1]	MILES	ELEV.	BIKE TRAIL (%)	BIKE LANE (%)	OTHER (%)		
23	Sea to Mountains to Sea	VS	83.5 (1-w)	Flat	90	5	5	S, N, L, S/A, M	San Gabriel-Rio Hondo-L.A. River Loop
24	Long Beach-Cerritos	E (1-w) M (r/t)	14.0 (1-w)	Flat	100	-	-	S, L, M	San Gabriel River-Coyote Creek
25	Angeles National Forest	M (River) S (Dam)	13.4 (15.0)	Flat (Sheer)	100	-	-	S, N, E	West Fork, San Gabriel River (plus Cogswell Reservoir)
26	Pico Rivera	E	11.2	Flat	100	-	-	S, N, L	Whittier Narrows, Legg Lake Loop
27	Hacienda Heights	M	5.6	Mod.	-	100	-	S	Hacienda Heights Loop
28	San Marino	M	6.8	Mod.	-	-	100	S, L	San Marino City Loop
29	Montecito Heights	E	7.5	Flat	50	50	-	S, N, L	Arroyo Seco Bike Trail (loop)
30	Highland Park	E	7.6	Mod.	10	80	10	S, N, L, S/A	Highland Park City Loop
31	Pasadena	E-M (1-w) M (r/t)	6.8 (1-w)	Mod.	20	80	-	S, N, L	Kenneth Newell Bikeway
32	Arcadia	M-S	29.4	Mod.	-	100	-	S, L, M	Arcadia City Loops
33	Griffith Park	M-S (M)	8.8 (8.2)	Mod.-Steep (Mod.)	-	100	-	S, L, S/A	Griffith Park Loop (easier up and back option)
34	Elysian Park	M-S (E)	6.4	Mod.-steep (Mod.)	-	-	100	S, L, S/A, E	Elysian Park Loop (without Angel's Point Road)
35	Glendora	M	8.3	Mod.	-	100	-	S	Glendora Bikeway (loop)
36	Burbank	M-S	14.8	Steep	-	100	-	S, L, E	Burbank City Loop
37	Encino-Universal City	S (1-w) S-VS (r/t)	13.0 (1-w)	Steep	20	80	-	S, L, E, M	Mulholland Drive

1,2 See footnotes on page 12

MASTER TRIP MATRIX

TRIP NO.	GENERAL LOCATION	LEVEL OF DIFFICULTY			ROUTE QUALITY			TRIP CHARACT.[2]	COMMENTS
		L.O.D.[1]	MILES	ELEV.	BIKE TRAIL (%)	BIKE LANE (%)	OTHER (%)		
38	Encino	E	9.1	Flat	95	5	-	S, L	Sepulveda Dam Bikeway (loop)
39	Chatsworth	E	6.3	Flat	20	-	80	S, L	Chatsworth Tour, Brown's Creek Bikeway (loop)
40	Torrance	M	14.3	Flat	5	55	40	S	Torrance Tour (loop)
41	Gardena	E	12.2	Flat	40	-	60	S, N	Gardena Tour, Dominguez Channel (loop)
42	Diamond Bar	M	10.4	Mod.	60	-	40	S	Diamond Bar Loop
43	Walnut, City of Industry	M	12.9	Mod.-Steep	-	40	60	S, E	San Jose Hills (loop)
44	Pomona, San Dimas	M	8.9	Mod.	30	20	50	S, N, L, S/A	Bonelli Park, Puddingstone Reservoir (loop)
45	San Dimas, La Verne, Claremont	M	22.3	Mod.	-	-	100	S, L, S/A	Baseline Road, San Gabriel Mountain Foothills (loop)
46	La Mirada	E	10.0	Flat-Mod.	30	65	5	S, N	La Mirada City Loop (loop)
47	Los Angeles Civic Center	M	9.8	Mod.	-	35	65	S, L, S/A	Skyscraper Tour (downtown Los Angeles loop)
48	Central Los Angeles	M	9.8	Mod.	100	-	-	S, L, S/A	L.A. Bikeway System, Exposition Park, USC Campus
49	South Bay-Central L.A.-L.A. River-Long Beach-Palos Verdes Peninsula	S	71.7	Mod.-Steep	50	10	40	S, L, S/A, M	Tour de Los Angeles (loop)
50	Avalon, Santa Catalina Island	S	9.7	Mod.-Steep	-	-	100	S, L, S/A, E	Avalon Tour (loop)

1,2 See footnotes on page 12

MASTER TRIP MATRIX

TRIP NO.	GENERAL LOCATION	LEVEL OF DIFFICULTY			ROUTE QUALITY			TRIP CHARACT.[2]	COMMENTS
		L.O.D.[1]	MILES	ELEV.	BIKE TRAIL (%)	BIKE LANE (%)	OTHER (%)		
51	Dominguez Hills	E	3.5	Flat	-	-	100	S, L	California State, Dominguez Hills campus
52	Agoura Hills, Thousand Oaks	M	8.7	Mod.	-	80	20	S	Agoura Hills Loop
53	Westlake Village, Thousand Oaks	E	9.2	Mod.	10	90	-	S, N, L	Westlake Lake Loop
54	Thousand Oaks, North Ranch	M	10.9	Mod.	-	60	40	S	North Ranch Loop
55	Chatsworth, Granada Hills	M	28.4	Mod.	-	30	70	S, M	Chatsworth-Northridge-Granada Hills Loop
56	Chatsworth-Simi Valley	S (1-w) S-VS (r/t)	4.1 (1-w)	Steep	-	-	100	S, L	Santa Susana Pass
57	Porter Ranch	E	3.8	Mod.	80	-	20	S, N	Limekiln Canyon Trail (loop) (some unpaved trail)
58	Northridge	E	3.0	Flat	40	-	60	S, L, S/A	California State Northridge campus (loop)
59	Woodland Hills, Tarzana	M	22.5	Mod.	5	5	90	S, S/A	Woodland Hills-Tarzana Loop
60	Pacoima, San Fernando	E (E)	4.5 (4.1)	Flat (Mod.)	-	-	100	S, N, L	Hansen Dam ride (bottomlands ride)
61	San Fernando	E	2.2	Flat	100	-	-	S, N	El Cariso Park (loop)
62	Glendale, La Crescenta	M (1-w) M (r/t)	9.6 (1-w)	Mod.	-	-	100	S, L	Verdugo Mountains Foothills
63	La Crescenta, Tuna Canyon, Burbank	M-S	23.9	Mod.-Steep	-	20	80	S, L, E, M	Verdugo Mountains Loop

1,2 See footnotes on page 12

MASTER TRIP MATRIX

TRIP NO.	GENERAL LOCATION	LEVEL OF DIFFICULTY			ROUTE QUALITY			TRIP CHARACT.[2]	COMMENTS
		L.O.D.[1]	MILES	ELEV.	BIKE TRAIL (%)	BIKE LANE (%)	OTHER (%)		
64	Duarte	E	5.0	Flat	30	-	70	S, N	Duarte Bikeway (loop)
65	San Dimas	M-S	8.9 (r/t)	Mod.-Steep	-	-	100	S, N, L	San Dimas Canyon Road
66	Claremont	E	4.7 (r/t)	Mod.	100	-	-	S, N, L	Thompson Creek Trail
67	Bouquet Canyon, Saugus, Santa Clarita	S (M-S)	20.3 (12.8)	Mod.-Steep	30	20	50	S, N, L, S/A, E	Canyon Country Tour (loop) (Whites/Plum Cyn. bypass)
68	Valencia	E	7.8	Flat	-	10	90	S, L, S/A	Valencia Loop
69	Santa Clarita, Green Valley / Green & Leona Valleys	VS / S-VS	40.8 / 22.8	Steep-Sheer / Stp.-Shr.	- / -	20 / -	80 / 100	S, N, L, E, M / S, N, E	San Francisquito and Bouquet Canyons (loop) / Rift Zone Loop
70	Castaic, Lake Hughes, Sandberg	VS	68.7	Steep-Sheer	-	10	90	S, N, L, E, M	Lake Hughes, Pine Canyon & Old Ridge Rte. Rds. (loop)
70A	Castaic-Lake Hughes	S-VS (1-w) VS (r/t)	23.5 (1-w)	Steep-Sheer	-	-	100	S, N, L, E, M	Lake Hughes Road
70B	Lake Hughes-Sandberg	S (1-w) S (r/t)	17.2 (1-w)	Mod.-Steep	-	-	100	S, N, E, M	Pine Canyon Road
70C	Sandberg-Castaic	S (1-w) VS (r/t)	28.0 (1-w)	Mod.-Steep	70	-	30	S, N, L, E, M	Old Ridge Route Road (non-maintained section)
71	Pearblossom, Hesperia	M (1-w) M-S (r/t)	27.5 (1-w)	Flat	100	-	-	S, N, L, M	California Aqueduct

1 **L.O.D.** - Overall trip level of difficulty: **VS**-very strenuous; **S**-strenuous; **M**-Moderate; **E**-easy; 1-**w**-one way; r/t-round trip or up and back

2 **TRIP CHARACTERISTICS** - General trip features and highlights: **S**-scenic; **N**-nature trail; **L**-landmark(s); **S/A**-sight-seeing attractions; **E**-elevation workout; **M**-mileage workout

TRIP DESCRIPTION/TERMINOLOGY

The trip descriptors in the "Master Trip Matrices" are described below in further detail. Several of these same descriptors are also used in the individual trip writeups.

GENERAL LOCATION: The general location of the bike trail is provided in terms of a city, landmark, or general area description, as applicable. The "Master Trip Map" may be useful in conjunction with this general locator.

LEVEL OF DIFFICULTY: The rides are rated on an overall basis with consideration for elevation gain, trip distance, and condition of the bike route.

A *very strenuous* trip can be of any length, has very steep grades, and is generally designed for bikers in excellent physical condition. Trips are well enough described such that the biker might plan to ride the easier part of a stressing trip and link up with other easier trips.

A *strenuous* trip has some steep grades and/or relatively long mileage (on the order of 50 miles total). The trip is of sufficiently long duration to require trip planning and strong consideration of weather, water, food, and bike spare parts. Some portions of the trip may be on surfaces in poor condition or on shared roadway.

A *moderate* trip may have mild grades and moderate mileage, on the order of 15-30 miles. The trip is typically of several hours duration and is generally on a well-maintained bike route.

An *easy* trip is on the order of 10 miles or less, is relatively flat, and is generally on well-maintained bike trails or bikepaths.

TRIP MILEAGE: Trip mileage is generally computed for the one-way trip length for *up-and-back* trips, and full-trip length for *loop* trips. *Up-and-back* is specifically used for trips that share a common route in both outgoing and return directions. *Loop* specifically means that the outgoing and return trip segments are on predominantly different routes. *Round trip* is used without distinction as to whether the trip is an *up-and-back* or *loop* trip. In the trip writeups, the mileage from the starting point or "trailhead" is noted in parentheses to the nearest tenth mile, for example, (6.3).

Obviously, the one-way trips listed can be exercised with a planned car shuttle, ridden as an *up-and-back* trip, or biked in connection with another bicycle trip listed in this book. Connections with other trips are noted in the trip text or in a separate subsection for that trip titled, "Connecting Trips."

TRIP ELEVATION GAIN: The overall trip elevation gain is described in a qualitative fashion. *Flat* indicates that there are no grades of any consequence. Steepness of upgrades is loosely defined as follows: 1) *light* indicates limited slope and very little elevation gain; 2) *moderate* means more significant slope requiring use of low gears and may be tens of feet of upgrade; 3) *steep* indicates workout-type grades that require low gears and high physical exertion; 4) *sheer* indicates gut-buster grades that require extreme physical exertion (and a strong will to live!).

The frequency of upgrades is divided into the following categories: 1) *single* for flat rides with a single significant upgrade; 2) *periodic* for flat rides where uphill segments are widely spaced; 3) *frequent* where narrowly spaced upgrades are encountered (e.g., rolling hills).

Elevation contour maps are provided for trips with significant elevation change. A reference 5 percent (*steep*) grade is shown on all such maps.

BIKE ROUTE QUALITY: The trip is summarized with respect to route quality in the "Master Trip Matrices," and a more detailed description is given in the individual trip writeups. The following route terminology (which is similar to that used by CALTRANS) is used:

• *Class I* - off-roadway bike paths or bike trails
• *Class II* - on-roadway, separated (striped) bike lanes
• *Class III* - on-roadway, signed (but not separated) bike lanes

If the route is on-roadway and not signed (i.e., not marked as a bike route), it is arbitrarily referred to as *Class X*. All routes are paved unless otherwise noted.

TRIP CHARACTERISTICS: The overall highlights of the bike trip are provided in the "Master Trip Matrices" to assist in general trip selection. The trip may be scenic (*S*), having sweeping vistas or exciting overlooks or generally providing views of natural or manmade attractions such as cities. Alternatively, the trip may be a nature trail (*N*) or a path through areas which have an abundance of trees, flowers, and other flora. The nature trips or portions thereof are generally on Class I bike routes. The trip may highlight historical or well-known landmarks (*L*) or may have one or more sightseeing attractions (*S/A*). An example of the former is the Whittier Narrows Dam on the San Gabriel River (Trip #22C), while the latter might be the Los Angeles Zoo in Griffith Park (Trip #33). Finally, some trips are potentially good workout trips in that there is significant elevation change (*E*) or lengthy mileage (*M*) if the entire trip is taken. Some trips may provide a mix of these characteristics and are so noted.

Several descriptors are unique to the individual trip writeups. Those descriptors are defined below.

TRAILHEAD: The general location of the start of the bike path is provided for a single starting point. Driving directions to that trailhead and/or directions for parking are included where there is a possibility of confusion. Always check to ensure that parking is consistent with current laws.

Note that for most trails, there are multiple points of entry beyond the primary point listed. For some of the trips in this book (particularly the river routes), alternate bicycle entry points are noted on maps by arrows (✗) along the bike route. Alternate trailheads may be found by using information obtained from other bikers, or from state or local publications for more popular routes.

WATER: In the "Trailhead" description, general statements are provided about water needs. In the "Trip Description," available water along the route is noted where water is scarce. Particular emphasis is placed on public facilities for water and use of restrooms. Stores, shopping centers, and gas stations are sometimes noted, although the availability of water or other facilities in these instances is subject to the policies of those establishments.

CONNECTING TRIPS: Where bike trips can be linked, they are so noted. *Continuation* trips are those where there is direct linkage at the beginning or end of the trip being described. *Connection* trips are either not directly linked (i.e., a Class X connector is required) or the linkage occurs at the interior of the trip being described. A brief "connector" route description is provided.

BIKE TRIP MAPS: Each ride in the book has an accompanying detailed bike map. A summary of symbols and features used in those maps is provided below.

— — — —	Bike trail in trip description (unless otherwise noted).				
• • • • • •	Alternate bike route (unless otherwise noted).				
L.A. RIVER	River or creek when it is a point of interest.		MAIN ST		Roadway
VENICE	Nearby City	Park		☐ 5 ▨ 5	Landmark #5
W	Public Water Source	P	Parking	→	Entry Point to Trail
●—•	Locked Gate/ Limited Entry	Railroad	Crossing or Overcrossing	⌂	School (as a trip point of interest)
⌂	Mission	✕	Gravel Pit	△5%	Reference 5% grade
MAP SYMBOLS AND FEATURES					

GENERAL BIKING CONSIDERATIONS

This is a collection of the thoughts that we've had in the hundreds of miles of biking that we have done:

SAFETY: Use common sense when you are biking. Common sense when combined with courtesy should cover most of the safety-related issues. The four safety "biggies" are: 1) understand bike riding laws; 2) keep your bicycle in safe operating order; 3) wear personal safety equipment as required (helmet is a must, bright or reflective clothes, sunglasses); 4) ride defensively – always assume that moving and parked car inhabitants are not aware that you are there.

Common courtesy is to offer assistance to bikers stopped because of breakdowns. Point out ruts, obstructions, and glass to bikers behind you.

TRIP PLANNING/PREPARATION: We are absolute believers in advance planning. You minimize nasty surprises and have the joy of two trips for one (the anticipated trip and the physical trip itself). Familiarize yourself with the trip ahead of time; start by reading recent tour guides and talking to people who have been there before. For long-distance and/or more remote adventures, we do not recommend going alone.

Plan bicycle trips that are within your (or your group's) physical and technical abilities. Start with less-demanding trips and work your way up the difficulty ladder. Work on physical fitness and technical skills between trips to maintain or improve your abilities. Take rides with professional leaders and/or learn the necessary skills with an accomplished veteran in that activity area. As part of the training, learn first-aid techniques and use of the kit as appropriate for your activity.

The discussion which follows is applicable to both high-difficulty and/or extended-mileage day trips and multi-day tours. Look over the topographic maps and get a feel for the key areas of elevation change and locate the key road junctions. Where relevant, check that the roads/river trails are open and available for public travel by making advance inquiries. Identify contingency routes if there is any doubt as to your ability to follow the nominal plan or if adverse weather or road conditions could require trip alteration.

Once you have identified your outdoor adventure, assess your gear needs for the trip. Work with your group to define individual responsibilities for group gear items. Ensure that you know how to use each piece of activity gear before departure. Maintain your gear, particularly that most critical to safety, and perform a pre-trip check that gear is in design-operable condition.

EQUIPMENT: This subject is covered in great depth in B-D Enterprises' publication, *Outdoor Recreation Checklists*. That reference covers gear needs for about every major outdoor activity, including on-road and mountain biking for both daytime and multi-day trips.

The discussion which follows focuses on day trips. The minimum biking equipment includes a water bottle or two, a tire pump, a tool kit — typically tire irons, wrench(es), and screwdriver(s) — a patch kit, and (sorry to say) a bike lock. For longer day trips, add a spare tube and a bike repair manual. We recommend a bike light even if there are no plans for night biking.

Necessary cyclist apparel includes a helmet, sunglasses, and clothes which will fit pessimistic weather conditions (particularly for longer trips). On all-day, cool or wet winter outings, we carry a layered set of clothes (this includes long pants, an undershirt, a long-sleeve shirt, a sweater, and a two-piece rain suit). Padded cycling pants and biking gloves are a must for long trips. Modern day, warm-when-wet clothes are light and extremely functional. For cool and dry days, we may drop the rain suit for a windbreaker (look for a windbreaker that folds up into a fanny pack). For other conditions, our outfits are normally shorts, an undershirt, a long-sleeve shirt, and a windbreaker. Laugh if you must, but wait until you find yourself biking home at night, in mid-winter, along a beach with a healthy sea breeze after you spent the day biking in the warm sun (an example of poor trip planning, we admit).

Bring a first-aid kit. For urban tours, our packaged, baggie-sealed kit has the following: sunscreen (15 SPF or greater), lip salve, aspirin, and band aids. For trips where help may not be so readily available, we add gauze (roll), ace bandage (roll) and butterfly clips, small scissors, moleskin, a needle, and an antiseptic such as hydrogen peroxide or iodine. Think about insect repellent if you think conditions may warrant.

If you are going to get your money out of this book, **get an automobile bike rack**! The cost of bike racks is cheap compared to most bikes. Besides, it just doesn't make sense to bike fifty miles to take the planned twenty-mile bike trip.

GENERAL INFORMATION: A collection of seemingly random, unconnected, and useless comments which we actually think are "gems of wisdom," based on hard experience, is provided:

- Develop and follow a checklist for a pre-trip bike examination (tires, brakes, cables, etc.) and equipment (water, food, clothing, tools, spare parts, etc.). It's embarrassing to start a trip and realize that you've forgotten your bicycle! (Strongly consider purchasing the B-D Enterprises *Outdoor Recreation Checklists* reference book.)
- Check the weather (including smog conditions in urban areas) before going on an extended trip. Select trips and plan clothing accordingly.
- Plan the trip timing to ensure that there is a "pad" of daylight. Night biking just isn't as fun when it wasn't in the original plans. Night biking without the proper equipment is dangerous!
- Trip timing should include allowance for finding parking, trailheads, or connector routes. You never can fully trust authors of bike books!
- Trip conditions and routing are subject to change as a result of weather damage, building and highway construction, bikepath rerouting, etc. Especially for long trips, research these key elements before departing.
- Plan for afternoon headwinds when heading toward the beach (particularly west-facing beaches). "Pain" is what you feel when the last several miles of your fifty miler is spent bucking the sea breeze.

- Stay out of riverbeds, even concrete ones, unless one is marked part of the route. It may be a very long way to the next exit and it may also rain.
- Some marked river and creek trails flood out during heavy rains, particularly at river crossings and underpasses. More than likely, these areas will be closed off in inclement weather. Don't take these trips after heavy rains unless you are willing to plan on many route detours.
- Portions of the river trails are isolated and an increasing incidence of theft and assault has been reported. Bike in daylight, with a partner.
- Take water, no matter how short the trip. Bring enough to provide for the contingency that "guaranteed" water spots may be dry. Having water available provides a feeling of security. Being thirsty creates a bad attitude.
- The best time of day for most trips on busy thoroughfares is before the rush-hour morning traffic. Morning is also best for rides on narrow country roads. With few exceptions, the best time of the week is the weekend, particularly Sunday.
- The best season for some trips depends on the person. If you want camaraderie, ride the more popular routes in the summer. If your pleasure is free-wheeling and wide-open spaces, save these routes for other seasons.
- Bring snacks for longer trips. Snacks provide needed energy and attitude improvement when the going gets tough. Having snacks available also allows more flexibility in selecting a "dining out" stop.
- Walk your bike through heavily glass-strewn areas. Lift your bike onto and off of curbs. Trips are more fun when you can ride your bike!
- Bring a map for trips that are not on well-marked bike routes. Once off the prescribed route, it is amazingly easy to lose the sense of direction.
- Maintain a steady pace when taking a long bike ride. For pleasure trips, the pace is too fast if you cannot carry on conversation while biking.

THE COAST

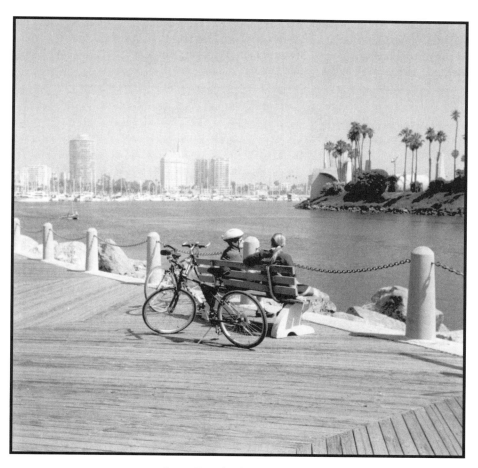

Long Beach Shoreline Park

TRIPS #1A-#1C - SOUTH BAY BIKE TRAIL

It is appropriate that the book should start with the most popular bike route in Los Angeles County. The moderate-to-strenuous level South Bay Bike Trail (44-mile round trip) travels the beachfront from Torrance Beach to Will Rogers State Beach. This trail is a segment of the Pacific Coast Bicentennial Bike Route.

Trip #1A starts at Torrance Beach, explores King Harbor and Hermosa and Manhattan beaches, and ends at the Manhattan Beach Pier. Trip #1B leaves that pier and continues north through Manhattan and Dockweiler beaches, Playa Del Rey, and the Del Rey Lagoon, terminating at Marina Del Rey. Trip #1C cruises the periphery of Marina Del Rey, visits Venice Beach and the Venice Pavilion, passes the Santa Monica pier, and ends at Will Rogers State Beach.

TRIP #1A - SOUTH BAY BIKE TRAIL: REDONDO BEACH TO MANHATTAN BEACH

GENERAL LOCATION: Redondo Beach - Manhattan Beach

LEVEL OF DIFFICULTY: Up and back - easy
Distance - 5.4 miles (one way)
Elevation gain - essentially flat

HIGHLIGHTS: The southern segment of the Class I South Bay Bike Trail cruises Torrance, Redondo, and Hermosa beaches. This segment includes the Redondo Beach Pier and the King Harbor area where there is plenty of sightseeing, as well as shopping spots and eateries. The path also visits Hermosa Beach Pier and passes near several small parks. The views south to the Palos Verdes cliffs and north along the Los Angeles County beaches are spectacular. Water is plentiful and several bike parking racks are placed strategically along the route.

TRAILHEAD: From Pacific Coast Highway in Torrance/South Redondo Beach, turn south toward the ocean at Palos Verdes Boulevard. Continue about half a mile and turn right at Calle Miramar. In a few hundred feet, veer left on Via Riviera and continue 0.1 mile to the terminus at Paseo De La Playa. Find free parking on this street, but subject to local parking regulations.

Bring a light water supply; this segment is well stocked with water and restrooms.

TRIP DESCRIPTION: **Redondo Beach.** Near Via Riviera and Paseo De La Playa, follow the asphalt path down the small bluff to the South Bay Bike Trail origin on the beach. There is a great view of the Palos Verdes cliffs south and Santa Monica and intervening beaches north. Bike north past the walkers, skaters, bathers, model airplane flyers, metal detector searchers, and other bikers along one of several lovely beaches on this segment. In about one mile, the trail passes a half-mile stretch of condominiums built up along the beach path.

At condomania's end is a small grassy rest area which is part of Veteran's Park (1.8). Just beyond is Monstad Pier and a host of restaurants and shops. There is a walking entry (i.e., no biking) into this area which leads left to the pier and straight ahead into a parking structure. Our route leads into the structure where bikers can remount and ride through, exiting the garage at Fisherman's Wharf. This scenic structure was partially destroyed by high seas in the winter of 1987 and a disastrous fire in the spring of the following year. There is shopping, sightseeing, and munching for the easily sidetracked.

The path continues alongside Redondo Beach Village, Basin No. 3 with its fishing boat moorings, and then the Redondo Beach Marina (2.1). In 0.2 mile at Beryl Street, the route crosses Harbor Drive and continues north on a Class II path. There is a diversion trip west on Beryl Street (which becomes Portofino Way) that leads to inner King Harbor and a swimming lagoon. However, we continue north past a series of beachfront restaurants/watering holes which includes the Cheesecake Factory. Continue past Marina Way and the steam power plant to Herondo Street (2.9).

**TRIP #1A - SOUTH BAY BIKE TRAIL: REDONDO BEACH TO
MANHATTAN BEACH**

Redondo Beach Village area

Hermosa Beach. Cross Herondo Street and follow the bikepath to the Hermosa Beach Strand. This is a shared pedestrian/biker path alongside the local residences. For the next mile, the city has a 10-mph speed limit, and flashing lights during busy periods which require cyclists to walk their bikes. The bikeway passes more great beach, volleyball courts, and one-after-another residences until it reaches the Hermosa Beach Municipal Pier and the Tim Kelly Memorial (3.7). Just beyond are rental shops (surfboards, bikes) and several beachfront eateries. A favorite is La Playita, just off the path, which dishes up some mean Mexican and Gringo dishes.

The path returns to residential beachfront and continues 0.9 mile before jogging away from the beach. The trail temporarily ends at 35th Street at a small series of steps where bikes must be carried a short distance. An option is to turn right three blocks earlier, at Longfellow Avenue, then left at The Strand and follow the marked bike route.

Manhattan Beach. The route continues on Class I bikeway along Manhattan County Beach, passing more beach and volleyball country. Though still crowded together, the beachfront homes in this area are more stately and architecturally varied. There is a fine view back to the Palos Verdes Peninsula from this area. Continue 0.6 mile from 35th Street to reach the Manhattan Beach Municipal Pier (5.4). There is some interesting sightseeing at the pier and there are some local rest stops just up the hill on Manhattan Beach Boulevard. Take a break before starting the return trip.

CONNECTING TRIPS: 1) Continuation with the South Bay Bike Trail to Marina Del Rey (Trip #1B) - continue north from the Manhattan Beach Pier; 2) connection with the bike routes along Palos Verdes Drive North (Trip #6A) and Palos Verdes Drive West (Trip #6B) - from the trip origin, return to Palos Verdes Boulevard and turn right (south), continuing another 0.8 mile to the three-way junction in Malaga Cove.

TRIP #1B - SOUTH BAY BIKE TRAIL: MANHATTAN BEACH TO MARINA DEL REY

GENERAL LOCATION: Manhattan Beach, El Segundo, Playa Del Rey,
Marina Del Rey

LEVEL OF DIFFICULTY: Up and back - easy
Distance - 7.3 miles (one way)
Elevation gain - essentially flat

HIGHLIGHTS: The middle segment of the Class I South Bay Bike Trail, this route tours Manhattan and Dockweiler beaches. The segment starts from the Manhattan Municipal Pier, includes a pass below the Los Angeles Airport runway, and visits the Del Rey Lagoon of Playa Del Rey, Ballona Creek, and Fisherman's Village in Marina Del Rey. There are excellent views into Santa Monica Bay and the Santa Monica Mountains, and a great boat-watching vista along the Marina Del Rey entrance channel. Water is available at strategic spots along the way.

TRAILHEAD: From Sepulveda Boulevard in Manhattan Beach, turn west at Manhattan Beach Boulevard and continue about a mile. Find parking, subject to local parking laws, on Highland Avenue, Manhattan Avenue, or The Strand, most likely south of Manhattan Beach Boulevard. From the San Diego Freeway, exit west on Manhattan Beach Boulevard and proceed about 2.5 miles to the parking area discussed above.
   Bring a light water supply. There are scattered sources along the way.

TRIP DESCRIPTION: **Manhattan Beach.** From the Manhattan Beach Pier at the foot of Manhattan Beach Boulevard, follow the curved, marked bikepath to the right as it separates from the pedestrian walkway. There is a view across Santa Monica Bay in this area. Continue north past the tournament volleyball courts, playgrounds, and the expensive residences above the pedestrian walkway. One-half mile from the pier, there is a great view of the city of Santa Monica. The houses come in all shapes, styles, and sizes up to the point where the path reaches the foot of Rosecrans Avenue at "Volleyball City" (1.2).
   El Segundo. The path cruises El Porto Beach, then swings west and passes alongside the fenced-off power generating station (1.6). There is a narrow, exposed bike strip for the next 0.3 mile. There are large rocks on the seaward side, and the signs warn of sand on the path, testifying that this strip can be very exciting and possibly dangerous in rough weather. Next is a small breakwater and probably the most secluded section of beach along the bikepath (2.0). In 0.2 mile is the Grand Avenue automobile entry to the beach, and 0.4 mile further is the northern end of the fenced-in plant (2.6).
   The beach widens and the bikepath twists and winds, then climbs to some bluffs which are one of the favorite local hang-glider training spots (3.0). Next is the Imperial Highway beach entry and a water stop in the middle of the only dry stretch on the trip.

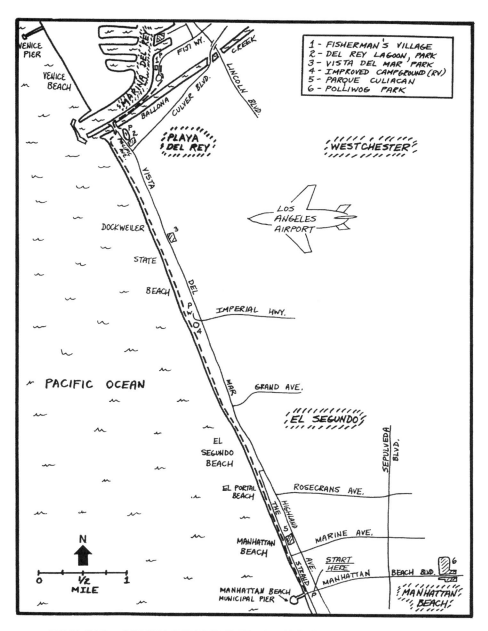

**TRIP #1B - SOUTH BAY BIKE TRAIL: MANHATTAN BEACH TO
MARINA DEL REY**

In another 0.4 mile, there is a small rise and a nice view down the beach to Santa Monica (3.6). For the next 0.3 mile, the path winds under the busy Los Angeles Airport flight path. Stop and watch the air traffic from an unusual vantage point.

Playa Del Rey. The route passes an automobile access road (4.0) and a large playground area with several sculptures (4.5). With the small bluffs to the landward side, the path reaches a pleasant palm-tree-lined rest and watering area near the residential edge of Playa Del Rey (5.2). In 0.4 mile, the bike route passes residences built near the bikepath. The bikeway transitions from beach to strand and passes near Del Rey Lagoon Park and the Del Rey Lagoon. The trail then swings north along Ballona Creek (6.2) and continues to a small bridge across the creek in 0.1 mile. There are views of the creek and of the exit channel and marina for the next half mile.

Marina Del Rey. Once across the bridge, the bikepath follows a levee between Ballona Creek and the exit channel. Because of the winds, this is a "bear" of a bike segment when heading west in the late afternoon! There are unique views of the Westwood and Century City skyscrapers from the levee (northeast direction), as well as a peek into the Ballona Wetlands to the south.

The trail reaches a junction point with the Ballona Creek Bikeway just beyond the end of a single apartment complex (7.0). Turn left at the junction, passing through a fence and biking 0.1 mile to the Fiji Way cul-de-sac. In 0.2 mile north on Fiji Way is the Fisherman's Village (7.3). This is a fine place to stop and take a munchie break or to do some sightseeing before returning.

CONNECTING TRIPS: 1) Continuation with the South Bay Bike Trail to Redondo Beach (Trip #1A) - at the trip origin, head south; 2) continuation with the South Bay Bike Trail to Santa Monica (Trip #1C) - at the trip terminus, continue north; 3) connection with the Ballona Creek Bikeway (Trip #4) - at the junction discussed above at (7.0), take the right-hand junction along Ballona Creek.

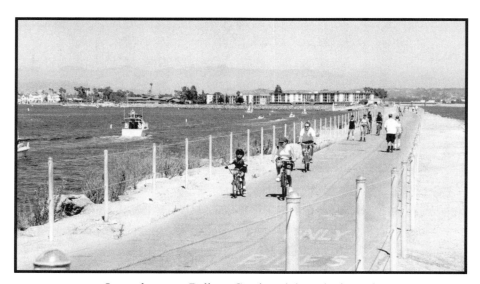

Levee between Ballona Creek and the exit channel

TRIP #1C - SOUTH BAY BIKE TRAIL: MARINA DEL REY TO PACIFIC PALISADES

GENERAL LOCATION: Marina Del Rey, Venice, Santa Monica, Pacific Palisades

LEVEL OF DIFFICULTY: Up and back - easy
Distance - 9.3 miles (one way)
Elevation gain - essentially flat

HIGHLIGHTS: The northern segment of the Class I South Bay Bike Trail starts from scenic Marina Del Rey and visits exceptional Venice Municipal Beach, Santa Monica State Beach, and Will Rogers State Beach. This segment includes Venice Pier, Venice Pavilion, the Venice Beach Carnival, and Santa Monica Pier. The tour through Marina Del Rey includes scenic views of the marina and pleasure boats of all types. A passage through Venice Pavilion includes a visit to individualism at its finest, or the other side of Mars, depending on your outlook. Be prepared for unusual flea markets, a guitar-playing swami on skates, mimes, sidewalk preachers, and other surprises.

TRAILHEAD: Follow the Marina Freeway to its terminus and continue west to Lincoln Boulevard. Turn left (south) on Lincoln Boulevard and continue about one-half mile to Fiji Way. Take Fiji Way to the parking area at Fisherman's Village or use the overflow parking lot between the village and Lincoln Boulevard.

Bring a light water supply. There are plentiful sources along the route.

TRIP DESCRIPTION: **Marina Del Rey.** Pedal north past Fisherman's Village with its shops and restaurants and pass a yacht dealership. In 0.5 mile, just before reaching Admiralty Way, follow the signed path left into the boat storage and repair area. The route parallels Admiralty Way and passes Mindanao Way (0.8); to the left, a short spur path leads to Burton Chase Park where there is an elevated platform for harbor viewing. Our route crosses Bali Way (1.0) and passes behind the Marina Library, then turns sharply right and follows the library parking lot to Admiralty Way.

Cross the street and follow the bike route along Admiralty Park. There is an interesting Class X spur trip along Admiralty Way and south on Via Marina; however, our route continues along the park past the Marina Towers and Duck Pond (1.7). This pond is one of the last remnants of the Ballona Wetlands in this area and does have a fair number of friendly inhabitants. The route crosses Washington Boulevard and follows that street toward the ocean, on a Class II bikepath. The path crosses a small Venice Canal (2.6) and in 0.1 mile passes a couple of outdoor bistros.

Venice. At the foot of Washington Boulevard is the Venice Pier (2.7). Just before entering onto the pier, follow the signs right (north) to the Class I bikeway along the beach. There are residences along the beach and a small strip of grass for resting. In 0.5 mile, the path weaves past the Venice Beach Recreation Center which has a paddleboard and other courts, as well as gymnastics and weight-lifting areas. Included within is Venice's version of Muscle Beach with alike-named indoor/outdoor gym.

TRIP #1C - SOUTH BAY BIKE TRAIL: MARINA DEL REY TO PACIFIC PALISADES

The twisting bikeway passes the Venice Pavilion where there are several structures with some very interesting murals and even more interesting people (3.5). In addition to the sidewalk entertainers and preachers, this is also the home of the Kamikaze skater! In 0.1 mile, there is a palm-tree-lined area and several outdoor cafés at the sand's edge, then a quarter mile of flea markets and mobile salesrooms in the form of hawkers on foot. In a short distance, the path crosses a more traditional set of store fronts (4.1-4.3), then cruises a series of enclosed picnic shelters.

Santa Monica. The path bends toward the ocean; there is an option to stay on the path or cruise a large parking area in what is now Santa Monica Beach (4.7). There is a great view of Santa Monica Bay and the Santa Monica Mountains here. The route passes a large volleyball area and continues to a series of beachfront commercial stores (5.4).

Next there is a biker/pedestrian trail split with the bikeway nearer the beach. The route passes a gymnastics and general workout area (5.6), then reaches and passes beneath the Santa Monica Pier (5.8). The pier boardwalk itself can be reached by turning off the bikepath just north of the pier on a small boardwalk. However, our route continues north past another beach area with the palisades of the city of Santa Monica in the background. The path crosses under a walkway which passes over Pacific Coast Highway (PCH) (6.1), then cruises by a group of isolated homes/rentals. In another half mile of beach cruising, the bikepath passes a restroom just south of the California Incline on PCH (6.6) and reaches the northernmost path section (opened in 1989). Bike past the Jonathan Club below the palisades until reaching the Beach Club and Will Rogers State Beach boundary (7.5).

Pacific Palisades. Pedal past the Entrada Drive entry, cross on a bridge over a small wash, and cruise past the area lifeguard headquarters. Continue alongside a narrower beach before reaching Temescal Canyon Road and the end of the separated bikeway (8.9). Bikers are routed to the parking lot. In 0.4 mile, this grand tour comes to an abrupt halt at the Bel-Air Bay Club.

CONNECTING TRIPS: 1) Continuation with the South Bay Bike Trail to Manhattan Beach (Trip #1B) - bike south from the trip origin; 2) connection with the Santa Monica Loop (Trip #2) - from the Jonathan Club area, follow an asphalt path to PCH; pedal up steep and busy California Incline to Ocean Avenue.

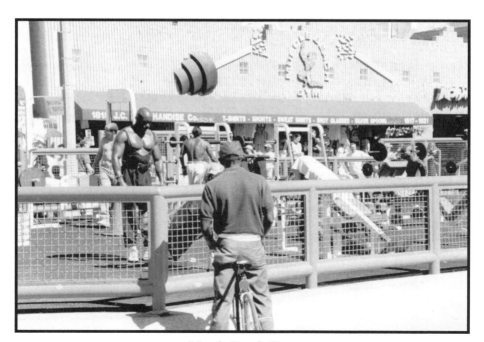

Muscle Beach Gym

TRIP #2 - SANTA MONICA LOOP

GENERAL LOCATION: Santa Monica

LEVEL OF DIFFICULTY: Loop - moderate (double loop)
Distance - 6.4 miles (single loop);
11.9 miles (double loop)
Elevation gain - single short steep grade (double loop)

HIGHLIGHTS: This is a very pleasant and scenic trip which takes in the pretty residential neighborhood along San Vicente Boulevard, Palisades Park on the bluffs above Santa Monica State Beach, Santa Monica Pier, and the beach itself. This is one of the premier trips within the "big city." The trip can be divided into two loops, the 6.4-mile loop up and back along San Vicente Boulevard and the 5.5-mile Palisades Park-Santa Monica State Beach loop. Take one or both loops and take advantage of the well-designed Class I and Class II bike trails that exist for almost the entire trip.

TRAILHEAD: There is free public parking on San Vicente Boulevard or any paralleling street above Ocean Avenue. Observe the signs before parking to ensure concurrence with the law. Another option is to "feed the meter" at Palisades Park where there is a five-hour limit. Take the Santa Monica Freeway exit at Fourth Street, drive north about 1.25 miles to San Vicente Boulevard, and turn left (toward the beach). Continue about a quarter mile and park on San Vicente Boulevard near Ocean Avenue.

   Bring a light water supply. There are commercial shops in the Brentwood Country Mart complex and public facilities at Palisades Park and on Santa Monica Pier.

TRIP DESCRIPTION: **San Vicente Boulevard Loop.** Start northeast along the tree-lined, divided San Vicente Boulevard. The entire route is a well-marked Class II bikeway. The broad grassy center strip is normally filled with joggers. Continue through this beautiful, elegant, and well-kept residential area and pass the Brentwood Country Mart, a great place to stop for exotic snacks or interesting meals (2.0). A short distance later, the route travels alongside the exclusive Brentwood Country Club (2.7) and continues past Bundy Drive to its terminus at Montana Avenue (3.2).

   Turn around and return to 26th Street (4.4). Bikers can return via San Vicente Boulevard from this junction or take one of the many lovely residential alternate paralleling routes to the left (southeast). The entire area is lightly traveled with good roads. The recommended alternate is to take Georgina Avenue (one block from San Vicente on 26th) and follow its zig-zag route back to Ocean Avenue (6.4). The upper portion of Georgina Avenue is excellent Class X which turns into Class III near 17th Street.

   Palisades Park-Beach Loop: Ocean Avenue. Turn right (northwest) on Ocean Avenue, proceed up one block, and take in the view from Inspiration Point. Turn around and head southeast on Ocean Avenue along lovely palm-lined Palisades Park. There are many scenic views along the 1.5-mile park, particularly impressive because the park is high on the bluffs overlooking Santa Monica Bay. Bikers should walk their bikes into the park at some point and look "over the edge" from the restraining wall. One of the most beautiful sections of the park is 0.3 mile from the start at Palisades Avenue (6.8).

1 - INSPIRATION POINT
2 - PALISADES PARK
3 - BRENTWOOD COUNTRY MART
4 - SANTA MONICA PIER

TRIP #2 - SANTA MONICA LOOP

At 0.9 mile from Inspiration Point (7.4), the route passes the California Avenue/ California Incline turnoff to the beach. Our tour follows Ocean Avenue past Santa Monica Boulevard (7.7) and Colorado Avenue and the auto entrance to Newcomb Pier (8.0). Palisades Park ends here. The route continues under the Santa Monica Freeway to Pico Boulevard (8.4). At Pico Boulevard, it turns to the right and diagonally onto Barnard Way.

Palisades Park-Beach Loop: The Promenade. Barnard Way descends to the beach and parallels the South Bay Bike Trail (Trip #1C). Just at the curve where Barnard Way turns towards Neilson Way and ends (9.2), turn toward the beach and link up with the South Bay Bike Trail. Pedal northward along the strand and pass under the Santa Monica Pier.

To visit the pier, turn right on the road which skirts the parking lot, then walk up the concrete steps which lead to the pier. After visiting the pier, return via the steps. Turn right (south) along Appian Way and continue two blocks to Seaside Terrace (10.4). A short testy climb up Seaside Terrace returns cyclists to Ocean Avenue. Continue across Ocean Avenue to the northbound Class II bike route and return to the parking area at San Vicente Boulevard (11.9).

Another option when leaving the pier is to continue north on the South Bay Bike Trail to the Jonathan Club, follow the asphalt path to Pacific Coast Highway (PCH), cross it, and bike up California Avenue/California Incline to Ocean Avenue. There are exposed stretches along both PCH and California Incline which make this a less preferred route.

CONNECTING TRIPS: 1) Connection with the South Bay Bike Trail (Trip #1C) - as described in the trip text above; 2) connection with the Westwood Tour (Trip #3) - from the San Vicente Boulevard/Montana Avenue intersection, follow Montana Avenue one-half mile southwest to Centinela Avenue, turn right (southeast), and continue about one-half mile to the trailhead at Texas Avenue.

Palisades Park with Santa Monica Pier backdrop

TRIP #3 - WESTWOOD TOUR

<u>GENERAL LOCATION</u>: Westwood

<u>LEVEL OF DIFFICULTY</u>: Loop Option 1 or 2 - moderate
Distance - 6.7 miles (Option 1); 7.5 miles (Option 2)
Elevation gain - periodic moderate grades

<u>HIGHLIGHTS</u>: This trip through Westwood and surrounding areas visits some pleas-
ant residential territory and skirts the edge of Westwood Village and the UCLA campus. The best part of the tour might be a free-wheeling ride through the UCLA campus
and surrounding residential areas, which is left as an exercise for the student. Although
this is a trip through exceptionally scenic surroundings, there are many roadway intersections, much traffic, and an abundance of borderline Class III bike routes. A portion
of the route is on a busy Class X roadway.

<u>TRAILHEAD</u>: The trip starts in the Sawtelle area of the city of Los Angeles, at the
beginning of the bike trail at Centinela Avenue and Texas Avenue. There are Class III
bikepaths throughout the area. This starting point was selected because it leads directly
into the Westwood area.

Exit the San Diego Freeway at Santa Monica Boulevard, turn west, and proceed
about 1.25 miles to Centinela Avenue. Turn right (north) and travel a quarter mile to
Texas Avenue. Park in the residential area nearby; observe the parking signs and do not
block driveways.

<u>TRIP DESCRIPTION</u>: **Trip Origin to UCLA.** Head northwest on the Class III bike
route past Bundy Drive (0.3) and turn right (south) at Westgate Avenue at University
High School (0.6). Head downhill and continue another 0.2 mile to Ohio Avenue. Turn
left on Ohio Avenue and continue on a moderate upgrade through pleasant residential
areas. At Sawtelle Boulevard (1.4), the route turns into a Class II bikepath. In another
0.1 mile, the route passes under the San Diego Freeway, then continues to Sepulveda
Boulevard (1.7).

Cross to the east side of Sepulveda Boulevard. In about 100-200 yards, turn right
at a walkway/bikeway entry and follow the signed Class I bikeway into Westwood
Park. This well-shaded park has water, restrooms, and tennis and basketball courts, as
well as grassy playground areas. Follow the path on the west side of Veteran Avenue
(2.0) and continue north to Wilshire Boulevard (2.4).

Cross to the northeast corner of the intersection and continue on the UCLA bike
route through the parking area. The path parallels Gayley Avenue and fuses with a
small road behind the buildings along Gayley Avenue. This is the exotic "back side" of
Westwood Village!

Turn right at Weyburn Avenue, then in 100-200 feet, turn left onto Class II Gayley
Avenue (2.6). Continue on a mild grade to Le Conte Avenue (2.8). One option is to
continue up Gayley Avenue and explore Fraternity Row and the pleasant (but hilly)
residential areas. However for this reference tour, turn right on Le Conte Avenue and
continue 0.1 mile on a Class X roadway to Westwood Boulevard. A left turn here (north)

TRIP #3 - WESTWOOD TOUR

would take cyclists into the UCLA campus and many riding areas. However, the described trip continues on to Tiverton Avenue (3.1) and a choice of two continuation options.

Loop Option 1 - Westwood Boulevard. If your desire is to see a part of the community of Westwood, this is your tour. Continue downhill on the Class III bike route on Tiverton Avenue past an automobile roadblock and follow the zig-zag path across Lindbrook Drive (3.3). The street is now named Glendon Avenue. Cross Wilshire Boulevard onto a short Class II stretch and continue another 0.1 mile to Wellworth Avenue. Turn right (west) and continue a short distance to make a left turn onto Westwood Boulevard (3.5). Take this Class III route across Santa Monica Boulevard to "little" Santa Monica Boulevard just beyond the intersection (this less traveled Class X roadway parallels the main boulevard). Turn right (west) on "little" Santa Monica Boulevard and continue another 0.5 mile to Sepulveda Boulevard (4.7). Turn right (north) on Sepulveda Boulevard and continue 0.2 mile to Ohio Avenue. From this intersection, retrace the original route back to Texas Avenue and Centinela Avenue (6.7).

Loop Option 2 - Westholme Avenue. This option provides a Class X route along Sorority Row and a pleasant Class III ride through some lovely outlying residential areas. Continue on Le Conte Avenue past Tiverton Avenue and turn left in another 0.1 mile at Hilgard Avenue (3.2). This route heads up a testy grade along Sorority Row, then flattens out and meets Westholme Avenue (3.6).

Turn right (south) and bike downhill along a pleasant tree-lined residential street which continues across Wilshire Boulevard (4.3) and meets Santa Monica Boulevard in another 0.5 mile. Cross Santa Monica Boulevard and turn right just after the intersection onto "little" Santa Monica Boulevard. Pedal another 0.5 mile on the Class X route to Westwood Boulevard and continue on the route as described for "Loop Option 1" above. The total trip length is 7.5 miles.

CONNECTING TRIPS: Connection with the Santa Monica Loop (Trip #2) - continue 0.5 mile northwest on Centinela Avenue, turn right (northeast) on Montana Avenue, and follow Montana Avenue 0.5 mile to its intersection with San Vicente Boulevard.

The Bruin Bear on the UCLA campus

TRIP #4 - BALLONA CREEK BIKEWAY

GENERAL LOCATION: Marina Del Rey, Culver City

LEVEL OF DIFFICULTY: One way - easy; up and back - moderate
                                       Distance - 6.6 miles (one way)
                                       Elevation gain - essentially flat

HIGHLIGHTS: This is one of many 100 percent Class I river and creek trails. The route starts from Marina Del Rey along a segment of the South Bay Bike Trail (Trip #1B) and continues northeast along Ballona Creek to its termination at National Boulevard and nearby Kronenthal Park. The route is lightly used, generally by folks who are adding extra miles to the South Bay Bike Trail and who enjoy the rapid-fire ups and downs at the street underpasses (or who are lost!). There is little scenery along the route and there are long stretches of wall-to-wall cement landscape. Perhaps the highlights of the route may be the side trips to three very pleasant parks, including Culver City Park with its excellent scenic vista.

TRAILHEAD: Follow the Marina Freeway to its terminus and continue west to Lincoln Boulevard. Turn left (south) on Lincoln Boulevard and continue about one-half mile to Fiji Way. Take Fiji Way to the parking area at Fisherman's Village or use the overflow parking lot between the village and Lincoln Boulevard. Kronenthal Park is tricky to reach by car. To start this trip from Kronenthal Park, turn southeast from Washington Boulevard onto McManus Avenue and continue to the parking lot near that street's end.

Bring a filled water bottle. Water is available with a short diversion to Lindberg Park or at the Kronenthal Park terminus. Be wary and also bring a bike partner, as there have been reports of harassment and assault on some isolated creek stretches.

TRIP DESCRIPTION: **Ballona Creek and Trip Diversions.** Head south to the turnaround loop at the end of Fiji Way (0.3). Cross the street and travel alongside the condominiums, passing through a gate at Ballona Creek (0.4). Take a hard left and head north along the cemented Ballona Creek channel. The route passes under Culver Boulevard (1.2), Lincoln Boulevard (1.3), and passes a small channel split (1.7). There are more ups and downs at the Marina Expressway (1.8), Centinela Avenue (2.5), and Inglewood Boulevard (2.8).

After passing another small channel split, the route passes alongside pleasant little Culver/Slauson Park (3.3). Beyond this point are the roller coaster rides below the San Diego Freeway (3.4), Sawtelle Boulevard (3.6), Sepulveda Boulevard (3.8), and Overland Avenue (4.4). An option is to cross Ballona Creek, using the small footbridge at the Culver City Junior/Senior High School, just before Overland Avenue. After crossing the creek, turn right (south) and cruise one block to shady Lindberg Park for water and a rest break.

However, the reference route continues along Ballona Creek and passes under Duquesne Avenue 0.9 mile further up the path. Another highly recommended option is

TRIP #4 - BALLONA CREEK BIKEWAY

to take Duquesne Avenue east across Jefferson Boulevard and proceed uphill to Culver City Park about one mile from the creek exit point. At the top of the route, stop and enjoy one of the most spectacular, unobstructed views of the greater Los Angeles Basin available in the South Bay area. Note that this "diversion" has some steep uphill along an unshaded route and adds two miles to the overall trip.

Kronenthal Park. Again, the reference route continues northward to Higuera Street (6.1) and ends at National Boulevard (6.5), where a chain partially blocks the path. Follow the paved switchback up to the opening in the fence which leads directly into Kronenthal Park. There are restrooms, water, playing fields, and picnic facilities in this pleasant, grassy, shaded park. If the gate to the park is locked, ride west a short distance on National Boulevard to a short stairway entry (a short bike carry is required to enter from this direction).

CONNECTING TRIPS: Connection with the South Bay Bike Trail (Trip #1) - return to the gate at (0.4) in the trip description; continuing on the route back toward Fisherman's Village leads to the northern segment of the South Bay Bike Trail (Trip #1C); following Ballona Creek to the beach leads to the middle segment (Trip #1B).

TRIP #5 - OLD SEPULVEDA HILL CLIMB

GENERAL LOCATION: Westwood, Encino

LEVEL OF DIFFICULTY: One way - strenuous; up and back -
                        strenuous to very strenuous
               Distance - 7.3 miles (one way)
               Elevation gain - long steep grades

HIGHLIGHTS: This weekend or non-rush-hour trip follows the old Sepulveda Boulevard route from the Los Angeles Basin to the San Fernando Valley via Sepulveda Pass. The hill climb to the pass is a gut-buster on what varies between a Class II and Class X bikeway, depending on road width. In a few places, there is essentially no marked bike lane. There are excellent views into both valleys, although the uphill is tough enough to force bikers into a head-down, tail-up posture, and some of the downhill will demand full attention. This trip is basically a workout! Don't take the downhill over the other side of the pass until you have thought it over carefully; the return uphill is equally rugged.

TRAILHEAD: From the San Diego Freeway, take the Montana Avenue exit in the Bel-Air/Westwood area. Park along Sepulveda Boulevard near Montana Avenue just east of the San Diego Freeway. Parking duration is restricted during weekdays.
     Bring plenty of water. This is a hot, tiring, exposed trip with no water stops.

TRIP DESCRIPTION: **The Upgrade.** The route starts along a residence-lined section of Sepulveda Boulevard and heads north, passing under Sunset Boulevard (0.4), then crossing Ovada Place/Church Lane (0.6) and Moraga Drive (0.7). There is a beautiful, live floral display in the center section of that divided street, the last of such lush beauty for a long while. There is also a gas station at the intersection. The route heads steadily uphill, and views into the scrub-lined canyon open up almost immediately. At (1.5), there is a steep uphill for about one-quarter mile, followed by the Getty Center Drive intersection (1.9). The magnificent building complex at the top of that road is the Getty Museum. In 0.2 mile, the route crosses under the San Diego Freeway and continues parallel to that thoroughfare on its west side.

TRIP #5 - OLD SEPULVEDA HILL CLIMB

For about the next mile, the route continues up a grade interspersed with limited flats. There are some sections of this part of the route where the bike lane all but disappears. Beyond about (3.2), the path heads steeply uphill; this is a good chance to stop and admire the view back into the Los Angeles Basin (that's what we call a "research stop"). The rugged upgrade continues past Mountaingate Drive (3.5) and Skirball Center Drive (4.2) and finally levels off at the tunnel which passes under Mulholland Drive (4.8).

The Downgrade. At the tunnel exit, there is a really fine view of the San Fernando Valley. (This exit is also a possible trip turnaround point.) Just beyond this exit, the road begins to twist and wind through a steep downgrade and continues almost all the way into the valley. On the way down, this residentially surrounded route passes numerous streets, including Royal Hills Drive (5.3), Valley Meadow Road (6.0), Royal Oak Road (6.3), High Knoll Road (6.7), and Sherman Oaks Avenue (6.9). Turn left at Sherman Oaks Avenue and take a break at the traffic circle about half a mile further down the road (7.3).

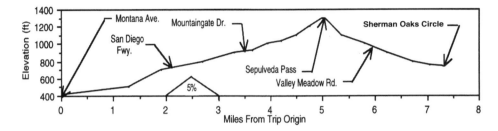

CONNECTING TRIPS: 1) Connection with the Westwood Tour (Trip #3) - at the trip origin, follow Montana Avenue east to Gayley Avenue; 2) connection with the Mulholland Drive route (Trip #37) - exit at Skirball Center Drive, pass over the freeway to the east side, and continue north to the Mulholland Drive bridge back across the freeway (west segment) or continue north beyond the bridge (east segment).

TRIPS #6A-#6D - PALOS VERDES PENINSULA LOOP

The strenuous to very strenuous Palos Verdes Loop Trip (23.2 miles, periodic steep grades) is broken up into individual Palos Verdes (P.V.) segments. The general area map is provided on the facing page. Also shown is a strenuous to very strenuous Hawthorne Boulevard option as well as a strenuous option that replaces the Palos Verdes Drive East segment with Western Avenue. Most of the routes are Class X with the exception of a major segment of Palos Verdes Drive North and some portions of Palos Verdes Drive West:

- Trip #6A explores a beautiful residential stretch through rolling hills. It starts near the Palos Verdes Reservoir and ends at pleasant Malaga Cove Plaza.
- Trip #6B follows the western Peninsula shoreline above the bluffs, starting at Malaga Cove Plaza and ending at scenic San Vicente County Park.
- Trip #6C leaves San Vicente County Park, traverses the bluffs above the southern beaches, wiggles its way through the Portuguese Bend landslide area, and terminates near the Palos Verdes Drive East junction.
- Trip #6D starts at the junction of Palos Verdes Drive East, winds its way up a steep set of switchbacks, and traverses the scenic peninsula "high country," letting out at the Palos Verdes Reservoir.

- The Hawthorne Boulevard segment is more difficult than Palos Verdes Drive East, with the steepest grade encountered just below Dupre Drive. The route is provided for variety; use of this segment also provides the option for a shorter Palos Verdes Peninsula trip (11 miles). This option features potential rest stops at Golden Cove Shopping Center, Rancho Palos Verdes Park, and Peninsula Center (south to north).
- The Western Avenue route provides the option to circumvent the steep, winding Palos Verdes Drive East trip segment. The total route mileage is increased slightly to 26 miles. The route is through rolling hills on a busy thoroughfare. Potential rest stops are the 25th Avenue Shopping Center, Peck Park, and the Park Western Plaza (shopping center) on Park Western Drive.

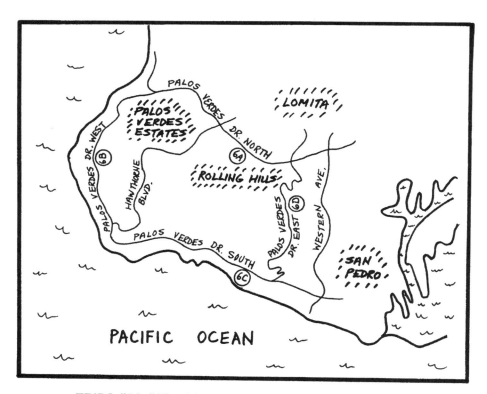

TRIPS #6A-#6D - PALOS VERDES PENINSULA LOOP

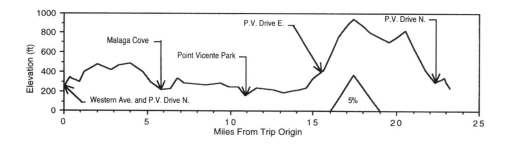

TRIP #6A - PALOS VERDES PENINSULA: PALOS VERDES DRIVE NORTH

GENERAL LOCATION: Rolling Hills Estates, Rolling Hills, Palos Verdes

LEVEL OF DIFFICULTY: One way - moderate; up and back -
                                moderate to strenuous
                                Distance - 5.8 miles (one way)
                                Elevation gain - frequent moderate grades

HIGHLIGHTS: This is a pleasant but hard-working trip through the rolling hills along the tree-lined northern segment of Palos Verdes Drive. The trip starts at Western Avenue, passes the Palos Verdes Reservoir, continues on rolling hills through several rural, wooded peninsula communities, and ends on a long downhill run to Malaga Cove Plaza. More than two-thirds of the trip is on a Class I bikeway (with a faster, paralleling Class II alternate available) and the remainder is on a wide Class X roadway with plenty of room for bikers.

TRAILHEAD: Free parking is available along Palos Verdes Drive North, west of Western Avenue. Read the parking signs carefully for current laws. Other options: 1) ask permission to park in one of the real estate office parking lots at the Palos Verdes Drive East intersection; 2) start the trip from Harbor Regional Park (see Trip #13), although this additional segment adds significant elevation to the trip; or 3) do the trip in reverse and use the parking in Malaga Cove Plaza or on nearby streets.

    Bring a moderate water supply. There is water along the way at the Rolling Hills Road Plaza and the Malaga Cove Plaza.

TRIP DESCRIPTION: **Rolling Hills.** The two-way Class I bike trail is on the north side of Palos Verdes Drive North. When riding the trail, keep an eye open for cars pulling out from the small side streets. (Another option is to ride the Class II path on the roadway, which is a higher-speed route.) The path immediately starts up a moderate grade and reaches a small shopping plaza at the summit (0.3). After another 0.6 mile of mostly downhill, the route crosses Palos Verdes Drive East and passes the Dapplegray Equestrian Park. For the next three miles, the route roller-coasters over small rolling hills along a lovely tree-lined path which has a paralleling horse path. At (2.0), the route crosses Rolling Hills Road where bikers may use a pleasant rest area which has benches and an available water faucet. In succession, the up-and-down path then crosses Crenshaw Boulevard (2.8), Hawthorne Boulevard (3.3), and the end of the Class I path at Via Campesina (4.0).

    Palos Verdes Estates. The biking in this area is Class X, but with plenty of room for bikers. The street is heavily tree-lined with a lovely center strip which is frequented by walkers, joggers, and horseback riders. The route begins a moderate downgrade of about one mile, and then a sharp downgrade (5.0). At (5.2), the route reaches the three-point intersection of Palos Verdes Drive North, Palos Verdes Boulevard, and Palos Verdes Drive West. Bikers should stay to the left and take Palos Verdes

TRIP #6A - PALOS VERDES PENINSULA:
PALOS VERDES DRIVE NORTH

Drive West into the Malaga Cove Plaza (5.8). There is a water fountain in the grassy square in the plaza, a great place for a break. The plaza also has a small market and delightful outdoor café.

CONNECTING TRIPS: 1) Continuation with the bike route along Palos Verdes Drive West (Trip #6B) - bike west from the plaza; 2) connection with the South Bay Bike Trail (Trip #1) - return to the three-point intersection just above Malaga Cove Plaza and turn left (north) onto Palos Verdes Boulevard; turn left (toward the beach) on Calle Miramar, veer left on Via Riviera, and continue about 0.1 mile to the beach parking lot; 3) connection with the Harbor Regional Park bike ride (Trip #13) - continue this trip east on Palos Verdes Drive North across Western Avenue to Anaheim Street and take the bikepath under the highway.

TRIP #6B - PALOS VERDES PENINSULA: PALOS VERDES DRIVE WEST

GENERAL LOCATION: Palos Verdes Estates, Rancho Palos Verdes

LEVEL OF DIFFICULTY: One way - moderate; up and back - moderate
Distance - 5.1 miles (one way)
Elevation gain - periodic moderate grades

HIGHLIGHTS: This highly scenic route leaves Malaga Cove Plaza and follows a moderately hilly route along Palos Verdes Drive West, ending at Point Vicente County Park. Along the way, the route passes a spectacular scenic overlook of the local coastline and Santa Monica Bay. Part of the trip is along a pleasant divided highway in Palos Verdes Estates. There is also a nice side trip which explores the Lunada Bay area. Point Vicente Park sports a lighthouse and small museum, and serves as a whale watch center.

Most of the trip is on a Class X bike route (i.e., on open roadway). The initial half mile is narrow, but the road widens beyond.

TRAILHEAD: There is free parking in the Malaga Cove Plaza on Sunday or on nearby streets on other days of the week. From the South Bay area, take Palos Verdes Boulevard south and stay to the right after passing the intersection with Palos Verdes Drive North. This road fuses into Palos Verdes Drive West. Turn left, in a couple of hundred yards, into the plaza. Another option is to do the trip in reverse. Park at the periphery of the Golden Cove Shopping Center on Hawthorne Boulevard or at Point Vicente Park. To reach this area, continue 4.7 miles and 5.1 miles, respectively, from Malaga Cove Plaza on Palos Verdes Drive West.

Bring a moderate water supply. There are public water fountains at the trip origin and terminus.

TRIP DESCRIPTION: **Malaga Cove - Lunada Bay.** The route leaves Malaga Cove Plaza and proceeds about 1.0 mile on a steady upgrade to a spectacular overlook of Malaga Cove, Santa Monica Bay, and the beaches up to and beyond Santa Monica. A little further, there is a turnoff to the right at Paseo Del Mar (1.1). This leads to a nice

TRIP #6B - PALOS VERDES PENINSULA: PALOS VERDES DRIVE WEST

side trip into the charming residential area around Lunada Bay. The reference trip remains on Palos Verdes Drive West, along a separated roadway with a foot and horse path in the center section of the road. Continue on a relatively flat roadway, passing a small shopping center at Yarmouth Road (2.7). There are scattered views out to the ocean until the view completely opens up at about (3.5).

    Golden Cove - Point Vicente. Shortly afterward, the route passes the Golden Cove Shopping Center at Hawthorne Boulevard (4.7), which has a homey little delicatessen hidden within. In another 0.4 mile of moderate downhill, the route intersects a small sharp turnoff towards the ocean. Take this signed roadway a short distance to the parking/rest area at Point Vicente County Park (5.1). There are restrooms and water here. Stop and enjoy an excellent ocean view, a museum, and the Point Vicente Lighthouse. This is also a great picnic spot.

CONNECTING TRIPS: 1) Continuation of the Palos Verdes Drive North trip (Trip #6A) - ride east from Malaga Cove Plaza; 2) continuation of the Palos Verdes Drive South trip (Trip #6C) - ride east from Point Vicente Park; 3) connection with the Hawthorne Boulevard (strenuous) alternate route over the Palos Verdes Hills ridge (Trip #6D) - turn north at Hawthorne Boulevard.

TRIP #6C - PALOS VERDES PENINSULA:
PALOS VERDES DRIVE SOUTH

GENERAL LOCATION: Rancho Palos Verdes

LEVEL OF DIFFICULTY: One way - moderate; up and back - moderate
Distance - 5.7 miles (one way)
Elevation gain - periodic moderate grades

HIGHLIGHTS: This highly scenic route leaves Point Vicente County Park, travels along rolling hills past the old Marineland turnoff, passes alongside the lovely Wayfarer's Chapel, and winds its way along the bumpy road through Portuguese Bend. The route continues up a long scenic grade, passes the junction with Palos Verdes Drive East, and continues to 25th Street overlooking Palos Verdes Shoreline Park. There are numerous grand views of the coastline, Pacific Ocean, and Catalina Island along the way.

This is not a trip for children or for inexperienced or nervous bikers. Though an excellent trip, it is mostly on Class X roadway with a very narrow, hilly, and bumpy stretch through the Portuguese Bend slide area. There are portions of the 0.5-1.0 mile Portuguese Bend slide area where automobiles and bikers literally share the roadway. (Note that the road was improved significantly in the late 1980s, although it still has its uplifted patches.)

TRAILHEAD: There is parking at Point Vicente County Park, as described in Trip #6B. Another option is to park along 25th Street in San Pedro, roughly half a mile east of the Palos Verdes Drive East intersection, and do the trip in reverse. Read the parking signs to ensure compliance with the latest laws. To reach the 25th Street parking area, take Western Avenue south to within about half a mile of the ocean and turn right (west) on 25th Street. Continue about 0.75 mile to reach the parking area.

Bring a moderate water supply. There are restrooms and water at Point Vicente County Park. The next facilities are available on a "beg and borrow" basis in the shopping area near 25th Street and Western Avenue, about 0.75 mile from parking on 25th Street.

TRIP #6C - PALOS VERDES PENINSULA: PALOS VERDES DRIVE SOUTH

TRIP DESCRIPTION: Point Vicente - Old Marineland Site. From the Point Vicente County Park parking area, turn right onto Palos Verdes Drive South and begin the journey through the rolling hills. In 0.8 mile, the route passes the old Marineland turnoff on Long Point. (Thanks to some very unpopular corporate manipulations,

Point Vicente County Park

Marineland is now ancient history.) There are views of the ocean and Catalina Island along this stretch, and the scenery gets even better later on. Another mile down the road is Frank Lloyd Wright's stunning glass church, the Wayfarer's Chapel.

Portuguese Bend. In 0.5 mile (2.3), the road enters the Portuguese Bend land-slide area. The road is bumpy and very narrow, with little or no shoulder. The ride is also very hilly and requires the biker's complete attention between avoiding the largest bumps and the accompanying automobiles. Stop or slow down and enjoy the lovely views into Portuguese Bend and the surrounding hills, as well as of the cliffs and beaches on the opposite side of the road. A short bicycle tour of the residential portion of Portu-guese Bend is, in itself, a real experience. The route is on Narcissa Drive.

Palos Verdes Drive South - 25th Street. Once out of the slide area, the route returns to an improved and roomy Class X roadway and, at (3.7), begins a gradual steady ascent. There are more sweeping vistas that take in the coastline and Catalina. Near the top of the grade is the intersection with Palos Verdes Drive East (4.7), the most strenuous of the four Palos Verdes Drive routes. There is a glorious unbroken ocean view in this area. Bike on Palos Verdes Drive South until it becomes 25th Street and the route transitions to Class II (5.2). A continuation on the bikepath leads past (above) undeveloped Shoreline Park (5.7) and the turnaround point. A option is to continue on 25th Street through residential areas to Western Avenue (6.4).

CONTINUING TRIPS: 1) Continuation of the Palos Verdes Drive West ride (Trip #6B) and Palos Verdes Drive East ride (Trip #6D) - from the trip origin or terminus, respectively, continue on the Palos Verdes Drive loop; 2) connection with the San Pe-dro Beaches Tour (Trip #7) - continue east on 25th Street about one mile past the intersection of Palos Verdes Drive South and Palos Verdes Drive East, turn right (south) on Anchovy Avenue, and free-wheel downhill about half a mile to Paseo Del Mar.

TRIP #6D - PALOS VERDES PENINSULA: PALOS VERDES DRIVE EAST

GENERAL LOCATION: Rancho Palos Verdes, Miraleste, Rolling Hills Estates

LEVEL OF DIFFICULTY: One way - strenuous; up and back - strenuous to very strenuous
Distance - 6.6 miles (one way)
Elevation gain - periodic steep grades

HIGHLIGHTS: This segment of the Palos Verdes Drive loop is a gut-buster! The uphill ride to the crest of the roadway is steep and the downhill is winding and fast. Yet for those in shape to bike this segment, it offers the finest views of the Los Angeles Harbor and the surrounding basin that can be found. On the early leg of the trip, there are clear Catalina Island views; near the terminus, there are excellent views into the city of Los Angeles and of the surrounding mountains. The route is highly scenic in itself, passing through some of the most beautiful residential areas in Los Angeles County.

TRAILHEAD: Park on 25th Street in San Pedro, roughly one-half mile east of the intersection of Palos Verdes Drive South and Palos Verdes Drive East (see description in Trip #6C). Another option is to park along Palos Verdes Drive North (as described in Trip #6A) and do the trip in reverse.

There are no public facilities along this route. Bring a filled water bottle on hot days.

The entire route is Class X. Sections of the roadway are narrow and, when combined with the high-speed downhill stretches, are dangerous. It should be noted that in spite of these conditions, this roadway is well used by experienced bikers.

TRIP DESCRIPTION: **The Switchbacks.** From the parking area on 25th Street, continue west 0.5 mile and make a sharp right turn up Palos Verdes Drive East. The road starts steeply upward immediately and proceeds through a series of three challenging switchbacks to the crest near Marymount College. In this stretch, the biker pumps through an elevation gain of 600 feet in 1.8 miles, roughly an 11 percent average grade! There are great views of Catalina Island, San Pedro's South Shores community, and Long Point (the site of old Marineland) along this stretch of the roadway (and an excuse for a rest break along one of the turnouts).

The Second Crest. The route continues through roughly a mile of moderate downhill and then becomes a fast, winding, free-wheeling descent leading to the intersection with Miraleste Drive (3.9). There are fantastic views of the harbor area in this stretch of the route. Near this intersection, there is a gas station and a small strategically placed delicatessen. The road winds uphill again through some extremely pleasant, wooded residential areas, and crests at Rockinghorse Road (4.9).

The Mad Downhill. Now begins a narrow, winding downhill section. Hug the shoulder and watch for automobiles. This dangerous route segment lasts for about 1.5

TRIP #6D - PALOS VERDES PENINSULA: PALOS VERDES DRIVE EAST

miles. At Conestoga Drive (6.1), the route diverts over to a Class II bikepath (a little late!) and continues on the downgrade past the Palos Verdes Reservoir to Palos Verdes Drive North (6.6). Just above Conestoga Drive, there is a premier view across the Los Angeles Basin into the city of Los Angeles and into the San Gabriel Mountains and San Bernardino Mountains. Cross Palos Verdes Drive North and turn right (east) or onto Class I bikeway to your parked shuttle vehicle. Otherwise stand by for a rugged return trip.

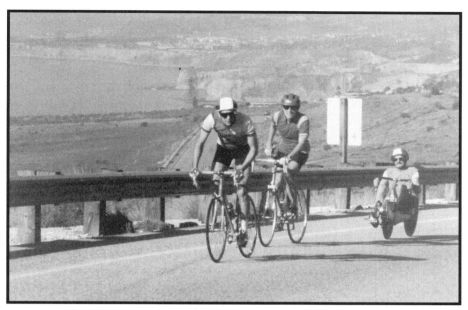

Palos Verdes Drive East switchbacks above 25th Street

CONNECTING TRIPS: 1) Continuation of the Palos Verdes Drive North pedal (Trip #6A) and the Palos Verdes Drive South tour (Trip #6C) - from the trip terminus or the trip origin, respectively, continue on the Palos Verdes Drive loop; 2) connection with the San Pedro Beaches Tour (Trip #7) - see directions from the Trip #6C description; 3) connection with the Harbor Regional Park ride (Trip #13) - see directions from the Trip #6A writeup.

TRIP #7 - SAN PEDRO BEACHES TOUR

GENERAL LOCATION: San Pedro

LEVEL OF DIFFICULTY: One way - easy to moderate; up and back - moderate
Distance - 6.2 miles (one way)
Elevation gain - periodic moderate grades; two short
steep grades

HIGHLIGHTS: This trip starts from the 22nd Street Landing at the terminus of Trip #8. Bikers visit the Cabrillo Marina, Cabrillo Beach, Point Fermin Park, Angel's Gate Park, and Royal Palms County Beach. This is one of the most scenic trips in Los Angeles County, particularly due to the views of the rugged bluffs and coastline along Paseo Del Mar. This trip is primarily Class I or Class II, with a small stretch of Class X roadway on the lightly traveled stretch of Paseo Del Mar west of Western Avenue. There is a slightly different route provided for the return leg of this trip.

TRIP #7 - SAN PEDRO BEACHES TOUR

TRAILHEAD: Free parking is available along 22nd Street or along the periphery of the Cabrillo Marina parking lot. To reach 22nd Street, travel south on Pacific Avenue and follow the numbered streets (numbers increase in the southbound direction). Turn left (east) and find a parking spot within the next mile or so, along 22nd Street; check parking signs to ensure compliance with current laws. Another option is to park along the west section of Paseo Del Mar and do the trip in reverse.

Water and restroom facilities are available at each of the beaches and parks mentioned, except for Angel's Gate Park, which has only a water fountain.

TRIP DESCRIPTION: **Cabrillo Marina and Cabrillo Beach.** About a quarter mile east of Pacific Avenue, on 22nd Street, turn south onto Via Cabrillo Marina. Travel about 0.2 mile and turn into a large parking loop with water and private restrooms. From this area, there is a view of the Cabrillo Marina/hotel complex and a view across the bay to the Cabrillo Beach area. Return to the main road and check out the benches up on the bluff; there is a steep bikeway/walkway up to that overlook for the adventurous.

Continue down Via Cabrillo Marina a few hundred feet, veer right, and use the walkway around the roadway gate which separates the marina from Cabrillo Beach. The roadway name becomes Shoshonean Road. Bike around a second gate, pass a boat launch area a few hundred yards further, and enter the bikepath along the beach at (0.4) mile. In the background is the Cabrillo Beach Marina Museum. In another 0.3 mile, follow the path and roadway out towards the Cabrillo Beach jetty. Along this jetty, there are nice views of Cabrillo Beach to the left and the open ocean and Catalina Island to the right. In 0.3 mile, there is a large fence with an ever-reopened hole in it. Through these portals pass the "crazies" who (illegally) fish directly on top of the breakwater. Don't follow, just look!

The path jogs to the left and enters Cabrillo Pier. Continue another 0.2 mile to the end of the pier. (This may mean walking your bike if the pier is heavily crowded with fishermen.) There is a fine view of the ships in the harbor and the opening in the harbor breakwater known as Angel's Gate.

There are also restrooms and water on the pier. Return back to the end of the jetty, turn left, and take Oliver Vickery Circle Way through the Cabrillo Beach entrance (1.8). Turn right on Stephen M. White Drive and, in 0.1 mile of testy upgrade, turn left (south) onto Class II Pacific Avenue.

Point Fermin. Continue another 0.1 mile on a testy upgrade to the top of the hill and then 0.2 mile to the end of Pacific Avenue at scenic Point Fermin parking area and overlook. There is a fine Catalina Island view from here and frequently a nice view of one of the entering or departing ships. Follow Shepard Street west on the Class II bikepath and, in another 0.5 mile (2.6), turn left on Gaffey Street to Point Fermin Park. There are park benches and barbecue areas. Ride through this lovely treed park which sits on a bluff overlooking the Pacific Ocean; one of the best routes is along the walled periphery of the park. If time permits, stop over at Walker's Burgers across from the park; this is one of the favorite biker stops (chopper bikers, that is). Return to Gaffey Street and head north across Shepard Street.

Angel's Gate Park. Pedal on Gaffey Street and head up a very steep hill; chances are, unless you're in very excellent shape, this will be an opportunity to walk your bike about 0.1 mile to 37th Street. Turn left (west) into Angel's Gate Park and enjoy a spectacular unobstructed view of the south-facing coastline. You can walk your bike up to the temple on the knoll to look over the Bicentennial Korean Friendship Bell. Just north of the bell is the Fort MacArthur Military Museum. Exit the park and take in the fine view (down 37th Street) of Angel's Gate. For the hearty souls, one of the best Los Angeles Harbor views is just a little further up Gaffey Street at small Lookout Point Park. The park has pay-for-view telescopes. Return downhill to the intersection of Gaffey Street and Shepard Street and turn right (3.4) on Shepard Street.

Bicentennial Korean Friendship Bell

Paseo Del Mar and Royal Palms County Beach. Cycle on Shepard Street on the Class II bikeway; in a short distance, the street becomes Paseo Del Mar. There are spectacular views of the bluffs and cliffs, the general southern coastline, and the ocean for the next 0.3 mile. At (3.9), there is a grassy rest area with a restroom and water on the ocean side of Paseo Del Mar. This is a pleasant tree-lined section of road. In another 0.6 mile, there is another impressive view/overlook of the general coastline.

At (5.0), there is a small park and restroom followed by the Kay Fiorentino Drive turnoff, both to the seaward side of Paseo Del Mar. The road leads about 0.2 mile very steeply downhill to Royal Palms County Beach. It is work walking your bike both down and back uphill just to see this area close up. There is a small beach area to the right (west) and there are some excellent tidepools and natural reefs to the left. (Don't go out into this area near high tide!) Return to Paseo Del Mar and enjoy another fine coastline view about 0.2 mile down the road. At Western Avenue, the bikepath ends. Continue another 0.6 mile along Paseo Del Mar through a quiet and pretty residential section to a locked gate (6.2) near Anchovy Avenue.

A convenient alternate method of return is to continue back on Paseo Del Mar/ Shepard Street to Pacific Avenue, turn left (north), and take this Class II route back to 22nd Street. This is a mild return leg which passes along the west (entry) side of the lower reservation of Fort MacArthur Military Reservation.

CONNECTING TRIPS: 1) Connection with the Palos Verdes Drive South ride (Trip #6C) - near the trip terminus, turn north on Anchovy Avenue, bike up a very steep grade for 0.5 mile to 25th Street, turn left, and continue to Palos Verdes Drive South; 2) continuation with the Los Angeles Harbor: Main Channel tour (Trip #8) - from the starting point, head east on 22nd Street (toward the harbor).

TRIPS #8-#12 - LOS ANGELES AND LONG BEACH HARBORS

The five trips, #8, #9, #10, #11, and #12, are connecting tours which explore the Los Angeles Harbor and Long Beach Harbor. Note that trips #9 through #11, in particular, require that you develop the skills to bike safely across railroad tracks. Note also that, since 9/11, many of the docking facilities are off-limits to non-authorized personnel. The general area map for these excursions is provided below:

- Trip #8 explores the scenic Main Channel of Los Angeles Harbor and includes several sightseeing attractions, such as Ports O' Call Village.
- Trip #9 visits the East Basin and West Basin of the Los Angeles Harbor, which have loading docks and yacht basins.
- Trip #10 tours the Long Beach Harbor, Cerritos Channel, and Back Channel. This is the "working man's" look at some of the most remote parts of the harbor area.
- Trip #11 explores the Southeast Basin of the Long Beach Harbor. The route has several scenic highlights, including the *Queen Mary* and Mary's Gate Village.
- Trip #12 visits Terminal Island; this includes visits to the aromatic Fish Harbor and the drydocks near Reservation Point.

TRIPS #8-#12 - LOS ANGELES AND LONG BEACH HARBORS

TRIP #8 - LOS ANGELES HARBOR: MAIN CHANNEL

<u>GENERAL LOCATION</u>: San Pedro

<u>LEVEL OF DIFFICULTY</u>: Up and back - easy
                              Distance - 6.2 miles (one way)
                              Elevation gain - essentially flat

<u>HIGHLIGHTS</u>: This harbor trip is on the west side of the main channel of the Los Angeles Harbor. The route passes the Los Angeles World Cruise Center, the large passenger ship terminal visited by such ships as the *Queen Mary II*, the *Elation*, and the "Love Boat." In addition, the trip includes the Los Angeles Maritime Museum, Ports O' Call Village, and 22nd Street Landing. There are several particularly scenic spots on the tour, including the point at the end of Admiral Higbee Way. This is probably the best view point along the Los Angeles Harbor Main Channel.

Most of the trip is on Class X roadway. However, much of the ride is through parking lots, along wide sidewalks, or in areas where motor vehicle traffic is very light. This is an "any-day-of-the-week" trip; however, the best time to travel along Signal Street and Miner Street in the dock area is probably the weekend, when traffic is lightest.

<u>TRAILHEAD</u>: Free parking is available at the Los Angeles "Park and Ride" area on Channel Street directly below the Harbor Freeway in San Pedro. From the Harbor Freeway southbound, take the Channel Street off-ramp to Gaffey Street. Turn right (north) and, in one block, turn right on Channel Street, then left into the parking area. From central San Pedro, take Gaffey Street north to Channel Street, as above. From Pacific Avenue northbound, take a left at Channel Street and turn right into the parking area. Another free parking option is at the periphery of Ports O' Call Village. In the latter case, the full round trip can be exercised with a modified itinerary.

Bring water for the first part of the trip, although water and restrooms are available at Ports O' Call in the middle section. There are several restaurants to stop at, should hunger or thirst strike along the way.

<u>TRIP DESCRIPTION</u>: **Upper Main Channel.** From the "Park and Ride" area, exit to the left (east, toward the harbor) on Channel Street and, in about 100 feet, turn right on Pacific Avenue. At (0.2), turn left on Front Street and pedal 0.2 mile past the old Todd Shipyard. At one time it was home to drydocks and a myriad of cranes and ship repair equipment. This street fuses into Harbor Boulevard and, in 0.8 mile, reaches Swinford Street.

Turn left and cruise on Swinford Street into a small parking area with a close-up view of the U.S. World Cruise Center (to the right) and, most likely, a large cruise ship. Continue east and cycle through the pay parking gate (don't pay) and pass by the U.S.S. *Lane Victory*, a refurbished World War II merchant ship and scenic attraction. (This operational vessel replaced the *Spirit of Los Angeles* and the venerable S.S. *Princess Louise*, where we were married!)

Continue to the Banquet Pavilion, Catalina Island boat terminal and helicopter pads and enjoy a neck-breaking view of the Vincent Thomas Bridge from below.

START HERE

HARBOR FWY.

JOHN S. GIBSON BLVD.

CHANNEL ST.

1 (FORMER SITE)

FRONT ST.

VINCENT THOMAS BRIDGE

SWINFORD ST.

2

3

1- TODD SHIPYARDS
2- U.S.S. LANE VICTORY
3- L.A. WORLD CRUISE CENTER
4- L.A. MARITIME MUSEUM
5- PORTS O' CALL
6- LOOKOUT POINT
7- 22ND ST. LANDING

TERMINAL ISLAND

6TH ST.

HARBOR BLVD.

4

MAIN CHANNEL

SAMPSON WAY

5

NAGOYA WAY

SAN PEDRO

MESA ST.

CRESCENT AVE.

SAMPSON WY.

LOS ANGELES

HARBOR

22ND ST.

25TH ST.

7

SIGNAL ST.

MINER ST.

ADM. HIGBEE WAY

6

GAFFEY ST.

PACIFIC AVE.

N

0   ½   1
MILE

TRIP #8 - LOS ANGELES HARBOR: MAIN CHANNEL

Return to Harbor Boulevard (1.0) and turn left onto the sidewalk along the street. Bike beside the harbor cranes and cargo containers for 0.9 mile and turn left at Sixth Street.
  Los Angeles Maritime Museum and Ports O' Call Village. Just beyond the turnoff is the Los Angeles Maritime Museum with a fine display of nautical artifacts, historical Los Angeles maritime goodies, and a great scale model of the *Titanic*. Turn right on Sampson Way and continue to the middle of the Ports O' Call Village parking lot (2.4). Stop and take a walking tour of this interesting village. Shop, have a bite to eat, or, for "hard-core" bikers, forget the rest break and continue along Nagoya Way.

In 0.1 mile at a locked gate, make a sharp right turn and return along Timm's Way. This is a great area to check out the local fishing fleet, close up. Bike 0.1 mile, passing a little outdoor café, and make a hard left, returning to Sampson Way. Continue south on Sampson Way, staying on the marked scenic route. At (3.0), there is an interesting view across the channel into a Navy drydock. Shortly, the road turns to the right (west) and passes the landmark Canetti's Seafood Grotto (great fish dishes); the street name is now 22nd Street.

The "Piers" and Twenty-Second Street Landing. In a few hundred feet, turn left on Signal Street. Cruise down the road until it jogs to the left and becomes Admiral Higbee Way. At (3.6), the road ends at the tiny parklike area at the end of the landfill pier. There is a great view across the main channel into Reservation Point and to outer Los Angeles Harbor, and this is a pleasant place to stop for a breather.

Return to 22nd Street (4.2), make a left turn, and continue for about 0.1 mile. Turn left at Miner Street and head down another landfill pier. There is nearly continuous marina and a string of pleasure boats to the right. At (4.7), the route passes a yacht and marine supply store. At (5.1), at a parking lot near the pier's end, check out the San Pedro Boat Works or gaze in awe at the mammoth coal conveyer on the east side. Return to 22nd Street, turn left, and pedal to the 22nd Street Landing for a close-up look at the local fishing fleet (6.2). This is a great place to buy fresh fish before heading back to the car and home.

CONNECTING TRIPS: 1) Connection with the bike route to San Pedro Beaches Tour (Trip #7) - continue west on 22nd Street 0.7 mile past the 22nd Street Landing and turn left on Via Cabrillo Marina to the Cabrillo Marina; 2) connection with the bike route to Los Angeles Harbor/East and West Basins (Trip #9) - after returning almost to the "Park and Ride" area on Pacific Avenue, continue past Channel Street on Pacific Avenue as it transitions into John S. Gibson Boulevard.

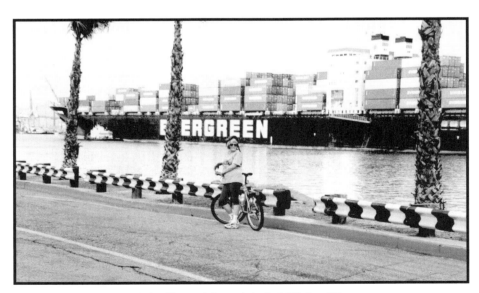

Main Channel from Admiral Higbee Way

TRIP #9 - LOS ANGELES HARBOR: EAST AND WEST BASINS

<u>GENERAL LOCATION</u>: San Pedro, Wilmington, Los Angeles Harbor

<u>LEVEL OF DIFFICULTY</u>: One way - easy; up and back - easy to moderate
Distance - 9.6 miles (one way)
Elevation gain - essentially flat

<u>HIGHLIGHTS</u>: At its best, this is a free-form bike trip with no set route. However, a reference route is provided which allows a chance to visit the Los Angeles Harbor, first hand and close up. This is one of three trips (also see Trips #10 and #11) that tour the harbor area west of the Los Angeles River. Most of the suggested route is Class X, but generally on small streets with limited traffic on weekends. The tour passes near several freighter loading docks and the classic old Matson Terminal, and terminates at the East Basin Yacht Center (anchorage).

<u>TRAILHEAD</u>: Free public automobile parking is available at the Los Angeles "Park and Ride" area located on Channel Street directly below the Harbor Freeway in San Pedro. From the Harbor Freeway southbound, take the Channel Street off-ramp to Gaffey Street. Turn right (north) and, in one block, turn right again on Channel Street, then left into the parking area. From central San Pedro, take Gaffey Street north to Channel Street, as above. From Pacific Avenue northbound, take a left at Channel Street and turn right into the parking area.

Bring a full water supply. There are gas stations near the trailhead and cafés at the end of the trip, but no water stops in the middle segment.

<u>TRIP DESCRIPTION</u>: **West Basin.** From the "Park and Ride" area, exit to the left (east, toward the harbor) on Channel Street. Turn left at the road's end (in a few hundred feet) onto John S. Gibson Boulevard (note that the street is named Pacific Avenue to the right). Ride onto the Class I bikepath along the harbor. At about one mile, there are excellent views, from behind the restraining fence, of ships unloading containerized cargo. At Figueroa Street (1.3), the road name becomes Harry Bridges Boulevard and the marked bike route ends.

Pedal another 0.6 mile and make a right turn on Neptune Avenue. The road passes an electrical generating plant and reaches Water Street. Turn left, then turn right in a short distance at Fries Avenue (2.5). The first turn to the right is Pier "A" Street where bikers parallel the railroad tracks and head directly toward the massive Vincent Thomas Bridge. Pier "A" Place is effectively at road's end where there is a closer look at the bridge, as well as views of the Los Angeles World Cruise Center (3.3).

Return on Pier "A" Street and turn right on Fries Avenue. Turn right again on La Paloma Avenue (4.4) and take the "loop" tour of Mormon Island (La Paloma Avenue to Falcon Street to San Clemente Avenue and back to Fries Avenue). San Clemente Avenue runs right alongside some busy berths and provides ship viewing up close, while Falcon Street leads through a liquid bulk terminal.

TRIP #9 - LOS ANGELES HARBOR: EAST AND WEST BASINS

Turn right from Fries Avenue onto Water Street (5.4) and bike across Avalon Boulevard, where the road name is now Nissan Way. True to form, there is an auto storage area near road's end, together with a restricted entry gate leading to a fire station. Return to Avalon Boulevard (6.1), turn right, and veer to the right again at Broad Avenue, biking to Harry Bridges Boulevard (6.5).

Turn right and follow the road as it bends northeast and becomes Alameda Street. In this bleak territory to the right are wide expanses of auto storage and the upper East Basin boat docks. The route turns right on Anaheim Street (7.6). Bike on this poor-quality, well-traveled road and make a right turn (south) on Henry Ford Avenue in 0.1 mile.

East Basin. Follow Henry Ford Avenue and pass over a small marina via a bridge. Stay on this road (do not turn onto the bridge route to the left, as bikers are not permitted) and pedal down to the end at the "retired" Henry Ford Bridge (8.7). Turn right and bike on Anchorage Road along the Cerritos Channel; pick your own "dream" yacht or stop and watch some hard work being done on others.

Continue past Shore Road (at the Holiday Harbor sign) (9.1) and take in the additional boat works and boats. Bike to a large free parking lot near the East Basin Yacht Center and turn toward the right on Peninsula Road. Here is an outstanding view of the container ship terminals and scrap iron "mountains" across the channel. At (9.6), the route ends at a locked gate (walking access only) at the edge of another part of the marina. This is a good spot to take a break at one of the local cafés.

CONNECTING TRIPS: 1) Continuation with the bike route to Long Beach Harbor: Cerritos and Back Channels (Trip #10) - at the trip terminus, return to Henry Ford Avenue and continue to Anaheim Street, then turn right; 2) connection with the bike route along the Los Angeles Harbor: Main Channel (Trip #8) - at the trip origin, leave the "Park and Ride" area, turn right on Pacific Avenue (street name is John S. Gibson Boulevard across the intersection); 3) connection with the bike route at Harbor Regional Park (Trip #13) - turn left from John S. Gibson Boulevard onto the Figueroa Street bikepath (1.3), continue north on Figueroa Street, take the "L" Street tunnel below the Harbor Freeway, and continue on "L" Street to the park.

TRIP #10 - LONG BEACH HARBOR: CERRITOS AND BACK CHANNELS

GENERAL LOCATION: Long Beach Harbor, Long Beach

LEVEL OF DIFFICULTY: One way - moderate; up and back - moderate
Distance - 13.1 miles (one way)
Elevation gain - essentially flat

HIGHLIGHTS: There is a multitude of ways to bike the harbor. This sample route provides a "working-man's tour" of Long Beach Harbor. This is one of three trips (see also Trips #9 and #11) that tour the harbor area west of the Los Angeles River. It can serve as the middle link between the other two trips, for the truly hearty (nearly 30 miles one way for the suggested routes). Most of the reference tour is Class X, but generally on small streets with limited traffic on weekends. This link of the three harbor trips is probably the least exciting in terms of scenery and landmarks, but has the true harbor flavor for harbor lovers. The tour passes near several freighter docks, provides a spectacular view, from below, of the Gerald Desmond Bridge, and ends at the tourist-friendly Sports Fishing Landing.

TRAILHEAD: Free parking is available at the East Basin Yacht Center at the terminus of Trip #9. Another option is to start from the large parking area near the Long Beach

TRIP #10 - LONG BEACH HARBOR: CERRITOS AND BACK CHANNELS

Pilot Station (Trip #11) and do this trip in reverse. Another option, less attractive, is to park along Ninth Street between Santa Fe Avenue and Pico Avenue in Wilmington. The parking locations are described as part of the trip route. In all cases, read the parking signs for latest parking rules.

Bikers should come prepared with a couple of filled water bottles or plan to "beg or borrow" at the commercial establishments along the way. There are cafés at both start and end points, as well as eateries on Henry Ford Avenue and Ninth Street along the way in the middle segment.

TRIP DESCRIPTION: Cerritos Channel Area. Start at the East Basin Yacht Center along Anchorage Road and turn left at the road terminus onto Henry Ford Avenue. At (1.7), turn right on Anaheim Street and continue on a bridge over the Dominguez Channel (2.0). The route passes under the Terminal Island Freeway (2.8) and, in another 0.1 mile, there is an option to get off Anaheim Street at Paul Jones Avenue and continue on Pier "B" Street. For bikers willing to stay with a relatively unattractive but classic harbor route, continue on Anaheim Street to Ninth Street (3.1). Veer right (southeast). The route soon passes a grill and pub on the right. At (3.9), the street ends and leaves the run-down industrial area. The intersecting street is Pico Avenue to the left and Pier "B" Street to the right.

Turn right and head into biker territory with its light traffic. Just beyond, the tour passes a mountain of large tires suited for construction machinery. At (4.8), the route meets Paul Jones Avenue. At (5.3), the road splits, with our route following Pier "B" Street to the right. Bike to the end of the road across from Hanjin Container Terminal (6.9) and turn left on Pier "A" Way, completing a small loop by turning left again on Carrack Avenue. There is a superb over-the-shoulder view of the Gerald Desmond Bridge here. Return about 0.4 mile and turn right on Pier "B" Street.

In 0.5 mile (7.9), turn right on Edison Avenue. Cruise about 0.4 mile for another great view of the channel, as well as a mammoth gypsum storage dome, then return to Pier "B" Street. Turn right and, at (8.9), return to Pico Avenue.

Turn right and, almost immediately, pass the freeway ramps, bike beneath an overpass, and then turn right at Pier "C" Street. At the gate, make a U-turn onto the one-way street going in the opposite direction, then jog over to a small paralleling road which reverses your direction again. This small road leads to a parking area sitting next to several massive cranes.

Cerritos Channel container terminal

Return almost to Pico Avenue (10.1) and turn right into the Queen's Wharf parking area. The wharf has a coffee shop, the venerable Queen's Wharf Restaurant, and a well-stocked fresh fish market. Behind the market is the Sports Fishing Landing, the starting point for many "part-time" fisherman's trips.

Back Channel Area. Cycle 0.3 mile on Pico Avenue and turn right on Pier "D" Street. Continue about 0.6 mile to the gate at the fire boat station (11.3) and turn left on Pier "D" Avenue. This route travels directly under the middle of the Gerald Desmond Bridge and along the Back Channel; the spectacular view of the bridge is a guaranteed "neck breaker." At (11.5), the road swings left before reaching a locked gate and then continues about 0.1 mile to another closed gate. Barring the ship traffic, this seems like the end of the world!

Return the same way and turn left at Pico Avenue (12.8). All that remains is to backtrack 0.3 mile to the Sports Fishing Landing.

CONNECTING TRIPS: 1) Continuation of the Los Angeles Harbor: East and West Basins route (Trip #9) - from the East Basin Yacht Center, return to Henry Ford Avenue, turn left, pedal to Anaheim Street, and turn left; 2) linkage with the Long Beach Harbor: Southeast Basin route (Trip #11) - bike south on Pico Avenue from the trip terminus at the Sports Fishing Landing.

TRIP #11 - LONG BEACH HARBOR: SOUTHEAST BASIN

GENERAL LOCATION: Long Beach Harbor, Long Beach

LEVEL OF DIFFICULTY: One way - easy; up and back - easy to moderate
Distance - 8.4 miles (one way)
Elevation gain - essentially flat

HIGHLIGHTS: This free-form trip has no set route; however, the reference route provides a chance to see the harbor area at its best. Of the three trips visiting the Los Angeles Harbor/Long Beach Harbor areas (Trips #9 and #10), this is definitely the most scenic and landmark-filled.

This trip can serve as the end link of Trips #9 and #10 (over 30 miles one way for the suggested route) or can be taken alone. Most of the suggested route is Class X, but generally on small streets with limited traffic on weekends. The trip starts in a super-tanker berthing area, includes the Long Beach Pilot Station and harbor views, visits the *Queen Mary*, and ends at the end of Harbor Scenic Drive with views of San Pedro Bay.

TRAILHEAD: Free parking is available at several places along the suggested route, allowing bikers to choose their own starting point and free-form route. Parking is available in the Port of Long Beach Administration Building parking lots (Sunday only), in either of two large scenic parking areas off Pier "F" Avenue near the Long Beach Pilot Station, or at the equally scenic parking area at the end of Harbor Scenic Drive.

TRIP #11 - LONG BEACH HARBOR: SOUTHEAST BASIN

Another option is to park at Shoreline Park in Long Beach (Trip #14) and cross Queensway Bridge to the Southeast Basin.

Bikers should come stocked with a filled water bottle or plan once again to "beg or borrow" along the way. There is a café near the starting point and there are public facilities at the Queen Mary shopping village area.

TRIP DESCRIPTION: **Pico Avenue and Pier "F" Avenue.** Our route starts from the Sports Fishing Landing, as described in Trip #10. Bike south on Pico Avenue past Pier "D" Street and Broadway, then duck under the Gerald Desmond Bridge ramps. Pass Pier "E" Street (0.6) and cycle onto a bridge with interesting harbor views and a great shot of the city of Long Beach Skyline. A downhill leads to Harbor Plaza and a right turn (1.3). A short climb and a veer to the left place bikers on Pier "F" Avenue heading south. The road passes a large coal storage facility, bends right, and cruises by a house-size mound of sea salt.

Turn right into a large parking area and check out the now-closed Long Beach Naval Station which still houses a few U.S. Navy ships in its harbor. Returning to Pier "F" Avenue, bike to the end into a large parking lot with a harbor fire station on one edge (2.5). From this lookout point, check out the busy channel leading to the outer harbor and the old Long Beach Naval Station Mole. With any luck, the Boeing consortium sea-going space launch platform and launch control ship will be in port and berthed there.

Pier "F" Avenue bends to the left just beyond and passes alongside several terminals before reaching a closed gate near pier's end (3.1). There are views of the outer breakwater, the Queen's Gate breakwater entrance, and the old naval station site, and there is a long-distance look at San Pedro Hill.

Port of Long Beach Administration Building. Return to Pico Avenue and turn right. The street, now named Pier "G" Avenue, continues to a locked gate near two large storage elevators (5.4). Return on the Pier "G" Avenue northbound loop (one-way traffic) and turn right at Harbor Plaza (6.2). In 0.2 mile, the road angles to the right. A left turn at the next junction leads to Queensway Bridge, but the reference route stays to the right and passes the Port of Long Beach Administration Building (6.4). Stop and take a close look at the historical murals painted on the face of this building.

H.M.S. *Queen Mary*. Harbor Plaza bears left and ends at Harbor Scenic Drive (6.8). Turn left, cross Harbor Scenic Drive, and ride under the freeway overpass. Turn right on Queens Highway North and revel in the glory of the Queen Mary, the dome that previously housed the Hughes Flying Boat Exhibit Center ("Spruce Goose"), and Mary's Gate Village. The village is a nice place for a rest and replenishment stop and has sturdy racks for locking bikes.

Harbor Scenic Drive. Pedal back on Queens Highway North and Windsor Way until the latter fuses with Harbor Scenic Drive (7.5). Stay right and duck beneath an overpass, then bike along a 0.6-mile string of public parking sites beside the road's eastern edge. There are excellent views of the Long Beach Outer Harbor, Long Beach city skyline, cruising yachts, and (with a little luck) maybe even a supertanker. The ride on the roadway ends at a private entry gate (8.4). Continue back north to the open public parking area and have a few laughs with the individuals and families who are fishing at land's end. There is a simply unique view of the outer harbor from this area.

CONNECTING TRIPS: 1) Continuation with the Long Beach Harbor: Cerritos and Back Channels route (Trip #10) - at the trip origin at the Sports Fishing Landing, continue north on Pico Avenue; 2) connection with the Long Beach Shoreline Park tour (Trip #14) - at (4.5) on Harbor Plaza, turn left (northeast) on Queensway and continue over Queensway Bridge (there is a Class I path on the south side of the bridge); exit right at the "Convention Center/Shoreline Area" turnoff and right again at Pine Avenue; parking is available around the Shoreline Park lagoons, in the Shoreline Marina Village parking lot, or on the side streets of Shoreline Drive.

TRIP #12 - TERMINAL ISLAND TOUR

GENERAL LOCATION: Terminal Island

LEVEL OF DIFFICULTY: Loop - easy
Distance - 6.0 miles (loop);
  12.8 miles with excursion trip
Elevation gain - essentially flat

HIGHLIGHTS: This is a touring trip around an island that is little known to most bikers (or anybody else for that matter). The tour offers some great vistas across the Los Angeles Harbor Main Channel, a visit to the home of the long-departed tuna fleet at Fish Harbor, and a spectacular close-up of drydocked ships. This is one of those trips for bikers who have a special liking for the harbor environment or who just flat out like to explore out-of-the way territory. The entire route is Class X, but on wide roadways with very little traffic on weekends.

TRAILHEAD: On weekends, free parking is readily available throughout the island. (During the week, the streets are overrun with truck and auto traffic.) This journey starts from Ferry Street across from the Federal Building where there is parking in the shade of a few eucalyptus trees. From San Pedro, cross the Vincent Thomas Bridge and exit to the right, just beyond the toll gate ("free" direction). Follow the road through a hairpin turn and continue to the road's end at Ferry Street. Cross Ferry Street and find parking.

From the Long Beach area, cross the Gerald Desmond Bridge and continue on Ocean Boulevard which eventually changes its name to Seaside Avenue. Just before passing under the Vincent Thomas Bridge, turn left on Ferry Street and proceed under the bridge to parking across from the Federal Building. From Wilmington, take the Terminal Island Freeway across the Commodore Schuyler F. Heim Bridge to the road's terminus at Ocean Boulevard. Turn right and continue on Ocean Boulevard/Seaside Avenue as just described.

The single walking access to the island is over the Gerald Desmond Bridge. The views from the bridge are breathtaking! However, the access is steep, on a small raised walkway (it is nearly impossible to walk a bike on the walkway), and right next to fast-moving traffic. Truck your bike over on a car bike rack unless you enjoy cheap thrills!

Bring water and munchies, and make a pit-stop before you start. There are only two small cafés and a mini-market, but no gas stations, on the island.

TRIP DESCRIPTION: Earle Street. Head north on Ferry Street and pass under the Vincent Thomas Bridge. At Seaside Avenue, turn left and pedal back under the bridge. From this area, there is an excellent view across the channel to the Los Angeles World Cruise Center and the U.S.S. *Lane Victory*, and a "neck breaker" view from below the Vincent Thomas Bridge. The street name changes to Earle Street and continues another 1.1 miles past massive coal conveyers as well as large lots of cargo containers and new

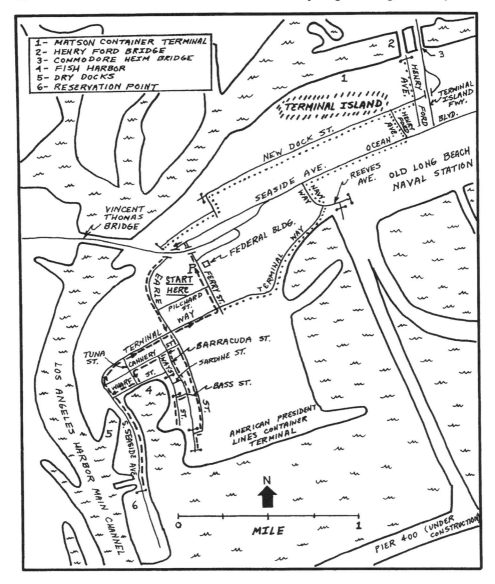

TRIP #12 - TERMINAL ISLAND TOUR

cars. At the end of Earle Street, jog right and work toward harborside at a tugboat docking area.

Fish Harbor. Backtrack along the same route and turn left (west) on Cannery Street (2.1). In a short distance, turn left and follow Barracuda Street south to a terminus at a pet food processing plant. Turn right on Sardine Street and left at road's end onto Ways Street. A short spur leads to street's end at Fish Harbor. At this pleasant point (pleasant view, unpleasant odor), there is a view down the docks which berthed a massive tuna fleet 20-25 years ago.

Return along Ways Street and turn left on Cannery Street. The area here almost has the appearance and desolation to remind one of a long-deserted razed town (at least on weekends). Turn left (south) on Tuna Street (3.3) and pass the local mini-mart. The street terminates at Wharf Street at a classic Fish Harbor viewpoint. Turn right and continue to South Seaside Avenue (3.6).

Drydocks/Federal Prison. The tour reaches a nice viewpoint in 0.2 mile, which provides a view of outer Fish Harbor as well as the ships at anchor in outer Los Angeles Harbor. The road veers right and passes a small rustic café (3.9). In a short distance, there are two massive drydocks; if the drydocks are occupied, the close-up, bow-on look at these mammoth ships is nothing but impressive! The path terminates at the Federal Prison at the visitors' parking area (4.1). (Don't venture in and take notes, as we found out when a guard in the tower above used a bullhorn to ask that we leave!)

Terminal Way Return Route. Retrace the original route and continue on South Seaside Avenue past Wharf Street. South Seaside Avenue bends right (east) and fuses into Terminal Way (4.7). In 0.2 mile, the bike route meets Earle Street; here a biker can take a well-deserved food and drink break at "salty" Joe Biff's Bar and Grill and shoot some pool, too. Continue on Terminal Way to Ferry Street and turn left (north). The route passes Pilchard Street (5.8) and returns to the Federal Building at 6.0 miles from the trip start.

Trip Excursion. At Ferry Street and Terminal Way (at 5.3 miles in the description above), cycle east on the latter street. The road veers right and enters an elevated area with a nifty vista of the Long Beach city skyline. The route passes a multi-domed sanitation facility and a gigantic container storage area, then cruises the periphery of a massive coal/petroleum coke facility. Continue to Navy Way and turn left (north), then go 0.1 mile to the road's end at Seaside Avenue and turn right (east).

Bike on busy Seaside Avenue/Ocean Boulevard and turn left at Henry Ford Avenue. A right turn at the next intersection (New Dock Street to the left) leads to a close-up look of the long-retired Henry Ford Drawbridge at the end of Henry Ford Avenue (7.7). Return to New Dock Street and cycle 1.5 miles past a series of shipping terminals and into a massive truck/container/railroad car staging and storage area.

Backtrack to Henry Ford Avenue and Ocean Boulevard (11.0). Turn right and bike with the heavy traffic, following Seaside Avenue to the right at the Vincent Thomas Bridge entry junction (12.2). Pedal another 0.5 mile to Ferry Street, turn left, and pass under the bridge. Continue a short distance to the trip origin (12.8).

CONNECTING TRIPS: Review the warnings in the "Trailhead" section before attempting the Gerald Desmond Bridge connector. 1) Connection with the Long Beach Shoreline Park route (Trip #14) - continue over the Gerald Desmond Bridge and the bridge over the Los Angeles River; turn right on Shoreline Drive and turn right again at Golden Shore Boulevard; 2) connection with the southern segment of the Lario Trail (Trip #32B) - continue as above except turn right into the first public parking area on Shoreline Drive.

TRIP #13 - HARBOR REGIONAL PARK

<u>**GENERAL LOCATION**</u>: Harbor City

<u>**LEVEL OF DIFFICULTY**</u>: Loop - easy
                        Distance - 4.5 miles (loop); 5.5 miles (with
                            campus excursion)
                        Elevation gain - essentially flat

<u>**HIGHLIGHTS**</u>: This is a short trip that explores Harbor Regional Park. More specifically, it visits Harbor Lake and its highly accessible west side, as well as its less visited east side. The trip provides a good look at the lake and the marshy wildlife preserve that surrounds it. In addition, there is a side excursion through the Los Angeles Harbor College campus. The segment along the lake is Class I. The route along Pacific Coast Highway (PCH) and Figueroa Place is on Class X roadway; however, there is plenty of room for bikers. The route through the ride mixes travel on roads with light traffic and combination bikeways/walkways.

<u>**TRAILHEAD**</u>: Free parking is available at the park. From the Harbor Freeway, exit at Anaheim Street and head west about one mile. Turn right into the park at the Harbor Regional Park sign. From Anaheim Street, Palos Verdes Drive North, or Gaffey Street (these streets intersect near the park), take Vermont Avenue north at the intersection. In about 0.3 mile, turn right into the park at the park sign. Note that there is a separate bike/walk access to the park. Just east of Gaffey Street at the intersection is a path which travels under Anaheim Street and enters at an undeveloped area near the southwest end of the park.

    Bring a light water supply. Water and restroom facilities are available at the park and college.

<u>**TRIP DESCRIPTION**</u>: **The Overlook.** The bikepath follows the edge of the lake, with spokes radiating out from this path to the individual parking areas. From the southernmost parking lot, head toward the Anaheim Street entrance and take a paved turnoff to the small roofed overlook above the south edge of the lake (0.1). There is a water fountain at this dandy spot.

    Harbor Lake, West and North Sides. Head back to the parking lot and then follow the path which leads to the main bike trail/walkway along the lake. At (0.3), cruise by an observation area with a couple of sheds and a porta-potty. At (0.5), pass a point which juts out into the lake; this is "duck city" with every type of duck you can imagine. There are usually plenty of fishermen along the lake in harmony with the ducks. At (0.6), pass a second lake finger and restroom just beyond. Continue around to the north end of the lake to the end of the trail (1.1). Head toward the northern parking lot and follow it parallel to PCH for about 0.1 mile. At the end of the parking lot, join PCH and ride along the Harbor Lake drainage (1.3). At (1.8), turn right (south) on Figueroa Place and continue 0.4 mile to "L" Street. Next is a right on "L" Street onto the Los Angeles Harbor College campus.

TRIP #13 - HARBOR REGIONAL PARK

Westside lakeshore in Harbor Regional Park

Harbor College Campus and East Side. Ride 0.2 mile on "L" Street until it jogs to the left along a fence. The Class I path zigs left in a short distance. A diversion trip through the campus (described later) is straight ahead, while the reference route follows the road right (south) to an auto blockade near the head of the driving range. The Class II path heads south to the lake proper and then bends southeast (2.7).

The South Side Return. The path skirts the lake, passing alongside the campus' outer reaches before reaching its easternmost point (3.5). What remains is a one-mile traverse next to the undeveloped south side of the lake. This segment includes a pass directly below the scenic overlook and a return to the start point (4.5).

Additional Campus Excursion. At the diversion junction mentioned above, cycle south next to the athletic fields. Cycle along the parking area and enjoy the view into the southeast corner of the preserve. The roadway continues along the marsh and, in about 0.3 mile, returns to Figueroa Place. A left turn onto that street leads back to "L" Street and the college entrance, then back to the diversion junction. The diversion route is about one mile. Note that bikers can make an interesting route completely off the roads by just wandering throughout the campus.

CONNECTING TRIPS: 1) Connection with the northern section of Palos Verdes Peninsula Loop (Trip #6A) - take the bike underpass to Gaffey Street; continue along the south side of Palos Verdes Drive North for 0.8 mile; at Western Avenue, cross the street to the west side; 2) connection with the Los Angeles Harbor: East and West Basins tour (Trip #9) - take "L" Street under the Harbor Freeway and, in 0.1 mile, turn right (south) on Figueroa Street; bike about one mile to link up with Trip #9 on Harry Bridges Boulevard.

TRIP #14 - LONG BEACH SHORELINE PARK

GENERAL LOCATION: Long Beach

LEVEL OF DIFFICULTY: Loop - easy
Distance - 7.6 miles; 9.0 miles with excursion trip
Elevation gain - essentially flat

HIGHLIGHTS: This is one of the prime candidates for an easy-going family trip. Almost the entire trip is on an excellent, well-marked Class I bike route and resides within the Shoreline Park/Long Beach Marina area away from heavy traffic. The scenery is great and there are plenty of recreation spots along the way, including playgrounds, barbecue and picnic facilities, and fishing platforms. The trip is of modest length but provides a wide variety of interesting biking territory, including activity-filled Rainbow Harbor, the Long Beach Aquarium, views of water skiers in Queensway Bay, the Catalina Island cruise ships at Queensway Landing, the yacht-filled downtown Long Beach Marina, and terrific views of the *Queen Mary*. Bike traffic is light and the bike lanes are large; however, the Shoreline Park and Marina Green Park areas have heavy competing foot traffic on pleasant days, particularly weekends.

An option exists to add a small segment to the trip. This involves crossing Shoreline Drive and traveling the bikepath along the Hyatt Regency/Rainbow Lagoon Park and into the Long Beach Convention Center area.

TRAILHEAD: From Ocean Boulevard in Long Beach, turn south (toward the harbor) on Pine Avenue and continue to its terminus at South Pine Avenue Circle. There is limited, time-restricted parking here. From the Long Beach Freeway, head south and take the *Downtown Long Beach* exit. Use the turnoff to *Convention Center/Catalina Island* and drive along Shoreline Drive past the *Golden Shore* exit. Turn right on South Pine Avenue Circle, which is the southward extension of Pine Avenue.

There is also pay parking at the parking structure north of the aquarium, as well as at the area east of Shoreline Village. (The easternmost parking lot is free.) For busy days, pay parking is available between Ocean Boulevard and Shoreline Drive. An option is to park for free along the north-south streets above Ocean Boulevard, then bike to the trailhead. Check parking signs carefully if the latter option is used.

Plenty of water and public restroom facilities are available along the route. Shoreline Village offers many options to "eat, drink, and be merry."

TRIP DESCRIPTION: **Rainbow Harbor and Los Angeles River Channel.**
From the parking area, bike to the harbor edge and take the bike/walk path west (towards Queensway Bridge). Near the west end of the harbor, veer left and pass alongside the Long Beach Aquarium of the Pacific. Pass the Pierpoint Landing (with a bait/tackle/snack/drink shop) and continue on this path to the Los Angeles River channel. Take a hard right turn (north), staying along the channel. Note the steps leading to the south side of the Queensway Bridge, just before passing underneath (0.4). There is a Class I path on the bridge's south lane. Follow the path around the entire Queensway Landing rim and admire both the small lighthouse and Catalina cruisers (1.1).

TRIP #14 - LONG BEACH SHORELINE PARK

Return from the rim to the main bikepath, turn right, and backtrack about 100 yards. Bike up the east ramp of the Catalina Landing Building to the second-story walking plaza. Leave the building via the west ramp and pass in front of the CSU Chancellor's Offices, then turn left (south) along the Golden Shore Reserve and bike to its terminus (1.5). Backtrack and turn left (west), following the path as it makes a sharp turn to the left and travels alongside a recreation vehicle parking area. In 0.1 mile, reach the Los Angeles River and the marked entry to the Lario Trail (1.9). This is a great spot to watch water skiers and jet skiers.

Return to the Queensway Landing. Just before passing under the Queensway Bridge, note the steps to the left; this is a route up to the bridge's southbound lanes. Pedal along the river to a three-way junction (2.6). A hard left leads to Aquarium Way. This trip continues back to the Pierpoint Landing area and hugs the river, heading to an excellent vantage point at the entrance to Rainbow Harbor (2.9). Along the way are alternate paths that criss-cross the grassy knolls to the left. There are benches, playgrounds, restrooms, and vista points scattered among the knolls. Next, follow the path as it curves and reverses direction, now following along the Rainbow Harbor edge. The harbor and Long Beach city views are gorgeous! The loop is completed near the Pierpoint Landing area (3.1).

Long Beach Marina. Return to the original parking area and turn east along the harbor's edge. Follow the bike/walk path for about 0.1 mile. The bikeway crosses under a concrete walkway (3.4). Stop and climb the overhead walkway which provides views of the harbor, channel, marina, and the convention center area.

Turn right (east), paralleling Shoreline Drive, and bike to Shoreline Village Drive, the entry road to Shoreline Village. Turn right and soon cross the access to the village pay parking area. The southbound route then crosses a street which is along the marina edge. There is a flower-bedecked vehicle turning circle here. The bike route will explore both directions at this reference junction (3.8).

First take a right turn (west) at the junction and bike along the Shoreline Village perimeter about 0.1 mile to the road's end. To the right is Parker's Lighthouse. Turn left onto the outermost bike trail along the jetty. Ride along the jetty and enjoy the vista of the pleasure craft and large commercial ships in the harbor, a spectacular view of the *Queen Mary* across the channel, and a good look at the yachts in the marina. Stop and watch from one of several observation/fishing platforms.

Ride to the end of the jetty at the Downtown Marina Office Building (Department of Parks, Recreation, and Marine Activities) (4.5). There are benches, playgrounds, restrooms, and view areas scattered among the knolls. This is a fine spot to watch the marine craft slipping by Island Grissom on their way to or from the marina. Follow the same path back to the reference junction noted above, since the inner path along the jetty is off-limits to bikers (5.3).

Pass this reference junction and pedal east along the path through the parking area to the excellent city beach (5.8). At a nearby junction, there is a small southbound asphalt road along a chain-link fence. Bypass this route and swing north, passing a restroom, then a snack shop/equipment rental shop. There is a Class I path which junctions east in this area, continuing three miles along the beach to Belmont Shore. However, the reference bikepath turns north at this point and terminates in the parking lot just beneath the historic Via Riviera Hotel (6.0).

View from Catalina Landing Building

Return 0.2 mile and turn south onto the previously bypassed small asphalt road. This road follows the jetty which forms the east end of the marina. It passes alongside the edge of one of the favorite local beach spots. The road terminates at one of the more popular fishing spots just across from Island Grissom (6.6).

Return to the reference junction and turn left (west). Follow the route back to the Pine Avenue intersection (7.5). Turn left and continue another 0.1 mile to the parking lot at the trip origin. An option at the Pine Avenue intersection is to take the short side trip below.

Long Beach Convention Center. Pedal north across Pine Avenue and take the bikepath to the right, alongside the Hyatt Regency Hotel. Soon the path travels along a lagoon. Take a short trip around the lagoon and enjoy the birds, water fountains, and the serene surroundings (do not bike across the footbridges over the lagoon, as they were not designed for bicycle travel). At (0.5), return to the lagoon loop starting point and bike on the path along Shoreline Drive until it terminates at the Long Beach Convention Center (0.7). Options here are to cruise the convention center area and then the quaint Seaside Avenue area (Class X roadway) or to return directly to the parking area at the Rainbow Harbor.

CONNECTING TRIPS: 1) Continuation with the Los Angeles River/Lario Trail (Trip #20B) - bike to the marked Lario Trail, as described above; 2) connection with the Long Beach Harbor: Southeast Basin route (Trip #11) - bike to the northwest corner of the aquarium parking structure (at Shoreline Drive across from South Chestnut Place); stay to the left and enter the separated Class I path on the Queensway Bridge; 3) connection with the Belmont Shore/Naples Tour (Trip #15) - turn east at the junction at (5.8) in the trip writeup.

TRIP #15 - BELMONT SHORE/NAPLES TOUR

GENERAL LOCATION: Long Beach

LEVEL OF DIFFICULTY: Loop - easy
                              Distance - 10.9 miles; 12.9 miles with
                                        Marine Stadium Park extension
                              Elevation gain - essentially flat

HIGHLIGHTS: This is a very pleasant trip, particularly for sightseeing, which concentrates on the beach community setting. The trip starts at the Belmont Pier, traverses a jetty to the Alamitos Bay entrance, passes onto Naples Island, and ends at Long Beach Marine Stadium. An alternate and more direct return route along the Alamitos Bay shore is also provided. The highlight of the trip is the Naples tour.

A reference route is provided, although bikers might plan for a more thorough exploration of this island community, particularly around the Rivo Alto Canal and Naples Canal. The route is a mix of Class I along the jetty, Class I and Class X throughout the Naples area, and a mix of Class II and Class X along the Marine Stadium. The only heavy traffic area is along Second Street leading into Naples.

TRAILHEAD: Free parking is available along Ocean Boulevard, or pay parking near the Belmont Pier. Other options are to alter the trip itinerary and start at other free parking locations along the route (for instance, at the end of the jetty or along Appian Way in Naples).

From Long Beach proper, take Ocean Boulevard southeast into Belmont Shore. Continue to the right on Ocean Boulevard at the Livingstone Drive junction and park along the street or in the pay parking area on the beach side of Ocean Boulevard. From Pacific Coast Highway (PCH), turn west onto Second Street (Westminster Avenue to the east) and drive 1.2 miles across two bridges. Just after the second bridge, turn left on Bay Shore Avenue and continue to its terminus with Ocean Boulevard. Turn right and park along Ocean Boulevard, or ride one mile further and park at Belmont Pier.

Bring a light water supply. Water and restrooms are available at the pier. There is plenty of water along the way and there are several opportunities for other "pit stops."

TRIP DESCRIPTION: Belmont Shore. Pedal southeast on Ocean Boulevard and pass Bay Shore Avenue (0.7). Continue about 0.1 mile and turn right (toward the ocean) on 55th Place. At the end of this pleasant little street is Seaside Walk. Follow this walkway/bikeway and enjoy the beach folk as well as the great views of outer Long Beach Harbor and the ocean. (The maximum speed limit on all walkways is 15 mph, and 5 mph when pedestrians are present.)

Ride to the path's end at 69th Place (1.7), then follow Ocean Boulevard 0.1 mile further to the end of the jetty. At this point there is parking, a lifeguard building, and a nice view of the channel and Seaport Village across the channel.

For the return trip, turn right (toward the bay) at 69th Place and pedal along Bay Shore Walk to Bay Shore Avenue (2.5). Turn right (north) and cruise along one of the

TRIP #15 - BELMONT SHORE/NAPLES TOUR

nicer, better sheltered, and more populated beaches in the territory. Ride about 0.6 mile further and turn right (west) on Second Street. Continue on this busy and rather narrow street over the bridge into beautiful Naples.

Naples. This small community consists of three islands: one large island, one small island which is nearly surrounded by the large island, and a second small island which nearly "seals off" the small central island. At the next intersection, turn right at The Toledo and pedal about 0.3 mile (3.4) to another smaller bridge. Cross onto the small central island, pass a small market, and bike to the lovely spray water fountain (and drinking fountain) in the pleasant outdoor central plaza (3.6).

Take a spin around the traffic circle and find The Colonnade; follow this little street to its terminus at the grassy mini-park along the bay and turn left (east). Follow the walkway/bikeway around the island and cross the following streets (bridge exits) in succession: Neapolitan Lane East, The Toledo (east), Ravenna Drive, The Toledo (west), and Neapolitan Lane West (4.9). (Note that the route zig-zags and appears to end at every street crossing, but continues on the opposite side of the street.) Cross over the bridge at the latter junction and take the small walkway/bikeway (Corso Di Napoli) around the smallest of the three islands. Return across the Neapolitan Lane West bridge (5.4) and backtrack across the central island bridge, returning to the main island.

Turn right immediately at Garibaldi Lane and follow a small walkway/bikeway along the Rivo Alto Canal. Bike along the small path and admire the tightly packed little community of gardens and varied architectural styles along the canal. There are small sailboats, powerboats, kayaks, and canoes in this 0.8-mile stretch of canal. The street crossings in order are at Ravenna Drive, The Toledo (east), and Neapolitan Lane West.

The path takes a sharp change of direction (6.4) and leaves the canal for a 0.7-mile open stretch along Alamitos Bay. At (6.9), the route passes a cozy little overlook park and, at (7.1), ends near the Long Beach Yacht Club. This spot is at the southern terminus of Appian Way and is one of the better spots to watch the water traffic in Alamitos Bay. Bike 0.1 mile north on Appian Way past the yacht basin (parking, water fountain, private restrooms), pass under the Second Street bridge, and reach Marine Stadium Park (7.3).

Marine Stadium Park. Marine Stadium Park has parking, a grassy lawn for resting, water and restrooms, a great beach, and a fine place to watch the sailboaters and windsurfers. Pedal north along Appian Way (Class II bikepath), pass over the small bridge, and turn right about 100 yards before Nieto Avenue. At (8.3) is the entrance to

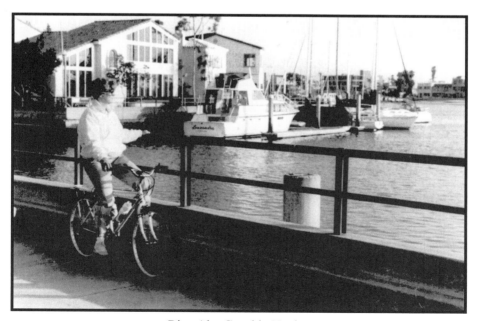

Rivo Alto Canal in Naples

the Marine Stadium parking lot (free to bikers). The stadium is a great place to watch boat races and individual powerboats performing time trials.

One option at this point is to head north to Nieto Avenue, turn right on Colorado Street, right again on Eliot Street, and bike down Marina Drive on the other side of the stadium. This route terminates at a launch ramp/view point at the Pete Archer Rowing Center and adds 2.2 miles to the total trip mileage.

Return Route. This route returns directly to Appian Way from Marine Stadium. Return south about 0.7 mile and turn right just before the bridge at Bay Shore Avenue (9.0). Cruise 0.9 mile across Second Street to Ocean Boulevard and turn right. About one mile up the road is the Belmont Pier. The total trip length is 10.9 miles.

CONNECTING TRIPS: Continuation with Long Beach Shoreline Park (Trip #14) - at the trip origin, bike toward the ocean to the Class I beachfront path and turn right (northwest); 2) connection with the trailheads for San Gabriel River Trail and Coyote Creek (Trips #20A, #24, respectively) - from Marine Stadium Park, take Appian Way south of the Second Street bridge, turn onto the marked "on-ramp" to Second Street, and turn right at the next traffic signal at Marina Drive; take Marina Drive to the parking area along the San Gabriel River (see Trip #20A instructions for further specifics).

TRIP #16 - EL DORADO PARK

GENERAL LOCATION: Long Beach

LEVEL OF DIFFICULTY: Loop - easy
                          Distance - 4.3 miles (eastside peripheral loop)
                          Elevation gain - essentially flat

HIGHLIGHTS: This is near the top of the list as a great family bike route and general outing. The entire route resides within El Dorado Regional Park East. There is something for everybody. The Class I bikepaths and routes along the park roadways are relatively uncrowded and in great condition. Cyclists can roam just the park boundaries in the two basic picnic areas (Area II north of Spring Street and Area III north of Wardlow Road) and travel 4.3 miles. The route is free-form and bikers can travel the interior park paths as well, putting in whatever mileage is suitable. There are four small lakes to cruise around, lovely stands of trees, and a variety of beautiful birds, including ducks and geese in the lakes.

In addition to the biking paths, the park has an archery range, a model boat pier, a model glider area, paddle boats, a youth camping area, and plenty of nice picnic sites with barbecue facilities. There is a Nature Center in Area I across Spring Street (near the Area II entrance) with an excellent nature hike (for a small fee). Finally, one can leave El Dorado Regional Park East and head across the San Gabriel River to the west portion of the park. This is a non-fee area with a tennis center and baseball diamond just south of Spring Street, and an additional picnic area with a small lake south of Wardlow Road. The entry to both areas is via Studebaker Road.

TRIP #16 - EL DORADO PARK

TRAILHEAD: From the San Diego Freeway, turn north on Palo Verde Avenue and drive 0.9 mile to Spring Street. Turn right (east) and continue about 0.8 mile to free parking along Spring Street just west of the bridge over the San Gabriel River. Other options are to continue over the bridge and park in the Nature Center parking area (turn south at the park entrance) or continue up Spring Street, make a U-turn, and return to the Area II park entrance to the north (right). Both the latter options have pay parking.

From the San Gabriel River Freeway, turn west on Willow Street (Katella Avenue to the east), continue about one mile to Studebaker Road, and turn right (north).

Continue about 0.3 mile to Spring Street and turn right (east). Follow the parking instructions above. For direct entry at Area II (pay parking) from the southbound San Gabriel River Freeway, take the Spring Street exit and turn right into the park entrance.

The park has plenty of water and many restroom facilities. Bring some good food to barbecue and enjoy great munchies after a "tough" bike ride.

TRIP DESCRIPTION: From the free parking area on Spring Street, ride over the bridge and turn right (south) at the Nature Center entrance (0.3). Make another sharp right and continue parallel to Spring Street (but now in the opposite direction) along the Nature Center roadway. Continue 0.2 mile to the fence along the San Gabriel River bike route. Rather than passing through that fence entry, follow the roadway as it turns to the right (north) and passes under Spring Street. The road enters Park Area II.

Park Area II. Turn to the right at (0.5) and travel along the bikepath paralleling Spring Street. At (0.7), the trail passes the archery area and, 0.1 mile later, crosses the park entry roadway and a little outlet stream from the lake to the north. The path turns north a short distance later and passes along several tree-covered grassy knolls. At (1.4), the now west-heading path crosses over the feeder stream between Areas II and III; this is near one of the prettiest picnic areas on the lake. At (1.8), the path again reaches a junction. By heading left (south), the Area II loop (2.3 miles total) can be completed; however, the reference trip heads right.

Park Area III. Cross under the Wardlow Road overpass and continue over to Area III. To the left is another access to the San Gabriel River Trail; however, this route proceeds to the right and continues along a roadway which nearly skirts the entire Area

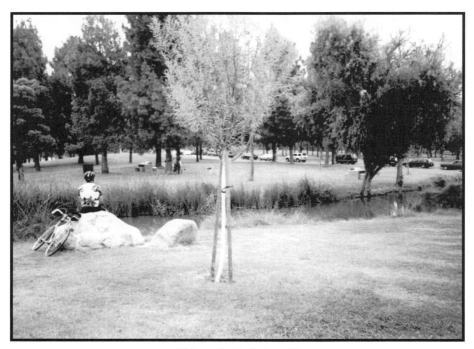

El Dorado Park Area II

III. In 0.5 mile from the Area III entry, the road passes one of the nicer picnic areas near the south end of the lake at the outlet stream. This is a great place for watching waterfowl and birds. At 0.6 mile from the Area III entry (2.4), the road turns north and, in another 0.1 mile, passes the paddle boat rental area.

Next, the road bends west (2.9) and passes alongside the northern end of the lake. At (3.2), the roadway passes a firing range (outside the park) and begins to head south along the model glider bluff. Continue south on both roadway and bikepath and close the Area III outside loop at 2.0 miles. Cross back under the Wardlow Road overpass and cycle another 0.5 mile south to the Area II trip origin.

Additional Sightseeing. This completes the 2.3-mile Area II loop and the 2.0-mile Area III loop and allows plenty of time to investigate the inner bikeways. Particular points of interest in Area III are the bridge over the isthmus, the lovely wooded area near the ranger station, the Billie Boswell Bike Path Memorial marker, and the little walkway/bikepath along the edge of the lake below the bridge.

CONNECTING TRIPS: 1) Connection with the San Gabriel River Bike Trail (Trips #20A and #20B) - use access points south of the Spring Street underpass or north of the Wardlow Road underpass, as described in the trip above; 2) connection with the Coyote Creek Trail (Trip #24) - take the San Gabriel River Bike Trail south and cross the footbridge over the river at 0.6 mile south of Spring Street, then turn left (north) onto Coyote Creek.

TRIP #17 - SANTA MONICA MOUNTAINS WORKOUT

GENERAL LOCATION: Santa Monica Mountains

LEVEL OF DIFFICULTY: Loop - very strenuous
Distance - 43.8 miles
Elevation gain - 2500 feet total elevation gain;
continuous moderate-to-sheer grades

HIGHLIGHTS: This journey is an absolute scenic masterpiece! The tour starts with a long warm-up in the see-forever coastal hills between Leo Carrillo State Beach and Malibu Canyon Road. Next is a climb on the latter road between the canyon walls carved out by Malibu Creek. A turn west on Mulholland Highway leads to a steep climb above Malibu Creek State Park, a pass-by of Strauss Ranch/Lake Enchanto and The Rock Store, a very rugged climb to the Seminole Overlook, and a crest near the Decker Road intersection. The final 10-mile Mulholland leg is a free-wheeling downhill with long-distance vistas to the Channel Islands and the valleys nestled within the Santa Monica Mountains.

TRAILHEAD: The trailhead has been selected such that the final trip segment is an extended downhill. There are options to start the trip from points closer to Santa Monica, for instance, Malibu or Zuma County Beach.

TRIP #17 - SANTA MONICA MOUNTAINS WORKOUT

From the Santa Monica Freeway terminus at Pacific Coast Highway (Highway 1) in Santa Monica, drive west 28 miles and turn right at Mulholland Highway. (If you pass Yerba Buena Road, you've gone too far.) Turn right in a short distance into the Leo Carrillo State Beach picnic/camping area (shade, water, restrooms, barbecues).

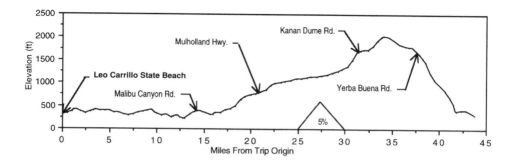

From the Ventura Freeway in the San Fernando Valley, drive west and exit south at Westlake Boulevard. Continue on what becomes Decker Road (Highway 23) to the coast. Turn right (west) and continue 2.5 miles to Mulholland Highway.

For folks going the entire loop, bring at least two filled water bottles. In the mountains, we found water at Tapia County Park, Malibu Creek State Park (requires a short diversion), The Rock Store just beyond the Peter Strauss Ranch, and at Rocky Oaks Park just beyond Kanan Road on Mulholland Highway. Perform a thorough bicycle maintenance check, including brakes, before starting this mountain tour.

TRIP DESCRIPTION: **Pacific Coast Highway (Leo Carrillo State Beach to Malibu Canyon Road).** The trip starts on the Pacific Coast Bicentennial Bike Route. (Note that a more detailed discussion of this segment is found in Trip #18B.) Most of this segment and that on Malibu Canyon Road is on a highway with a striped shoulder. The Malibu Canyon Road stripe disappears in some areas, so caution is required. Bike east on Pacific Coast Highway (PCH) and follow a half-mile steep upgrade which levels and passes Nicholas Canyon County Beach (1.2). Ride a roller-coaster downgrade-upgrade, passing Decker Road at the low point. Pass La Piedra State Beach, Encinal Canyon Road, and El Matador State Beach (3.4), and follow another roller coaster to a flat near Trancas Canyon Road (gas station) (5.4).

Continue past the entrance to Zuma County Beach (water, restrooms) (7.0) and follow a long workout upgrade past the Corral Beach turnoff. This grade crests near Heathercliff Road (gas station) (7.8). Just beyond, the road heads back downhill past Kanan Dume Road (8.1) and stair-steps its way down to Paradise Cove Road (9.0). Next is a stair-step upgrade which leads to a flat near Geoffrey's Restaurant (9.9).

Follow the continued steep roller-coaster route past Latigo Canyon Road (11.1) and then pedal on the flat to Corral Canyon Road (gas station) (11.7). Just beyond, there is a long and steep upgrade; at the crest, there is an excellent coastal view back to the north (12.8). Continue past John Tyler Drive and bike uphill to a crest at Malibu Canyon Road (13.9).

Malibu Canyon Road. Turn left and follow a mild upgrade past the elegant, well-manicured Pepperdine University Campus. Bike on a flat past Seaver Drive; there is a fine long-distance view west and south, as well as a nice look down into the Malibu Lagoon. Start a steeper upgrade and pass Harbor Vista Drive (14.8); the coastal view is even more spectacular here. Follow the winding roadway and, in another mile, bike a steady, moderate-to-steep upgrade with the Santa Monica Mountains peaks dead ahead.

In 2.6 miles from PCH, the roadway is clearly within the canyon. There is a turn-out with a great canyon overlook in this area plus a peek back to the ocean (16.8). (Note: Pull completely to the edge of the turnouts or take the chance of becoming a large automobile hood ornament!) Follow the winding downhill which hugs the mountainside; the deep canyon and surrounding mountain views in this area are noth-ing short of spectacular! At the canyon bottom is Malibu Creek. The road continues winding through the canyon between the towering peaks, then follows a workout up-grade. This grade becomes steep just before cresting near yet another turnout (Don used these turnouts for "research breaks"). Just beyond is the Malibu Canyon Road tunnel (18.0). The roadway roller-coasters northward in this area alongside the paral-leling canyon. There is a nifty open area canyon view to the north and east at about a mile north of the tunnel.

The grade lessens as the route passes Piuma Road (19.1) and Tapia County Park (camping, shade, water). The road follows another roller-coaster section of more open canyon and reaches a little valley just beyond (20.5). In 0.3 mile and 6.9 miles from PCH, there is an entry to Malibu Creek State Park and just beyond is Mulholland High-way.

Mulholland Highway: Malibu Canyon Road to Cornell Road. The re-mainder of the tour is on Mulholland Highway. The little two-lane country road heads uphill almost immediately, becoming progressively steeper and eventually transitioning into a series of switchbacks. (Don calls this "Pukeout Hill," a carryover from his long-distant first try at this tour.) There is an exceptional view from the summit down into Malibu Creek and Malibu Creek State Park (22.7). Next the road traverses a small valley on a moderate uphill and proceeds to Cornell Road (north)/Lake Vista Drive (south) (24.3).

Cornell Road to Kanan Road. The first mile is through rolling hills with a nice view across the paralleling canyon to the left (south). The roadway passes the west end of Lake Vista Drive (25.5), crosses a small meadow, and reaches Peter Strauss Ranch/Lake Enchanto (possible water, restrooms) and Troutdale Drive (26.5). Next the road stair-steps upward past Sierra Creek Road and, in a half mile, reaches The Rock Store (water, refreshments, motorcyclist haven) (27.4).

The road continues on mildly rolling terrain for a short distance before heading up a murderous two-mile upgrade which crests near the Seminole Canyon Overlook. The panoramic view of the canyon and surrounding mountains is great! While parked along the roadway on his initial fateful trip, Don commented to the biker in the accompany-ing photo that it must be a tough ride. His slow smile and accompanying response as he pedaled uphill was, "It's all part of the plan." A half mile on flatter terrain puts cyclists at Kanan Dume Road (Kanan Road northbound) (31.0).

Kanan Road to Yerba Buena Road. Continue on Mulholland Highway past Rocky Oaks Park (water, shade, restrooms) and follow a workout upgrade in an open and exposed hilly area. The road becomes progressively steeper, passes Encinal Can-yon Road (32.0), and reaches a summit after about a total one-mile workout. There are periodic peeks at the Pacific Ocean and some of the Channel Islands, on the upgrade, plus nice views into a valley to the northwest from this summit area.

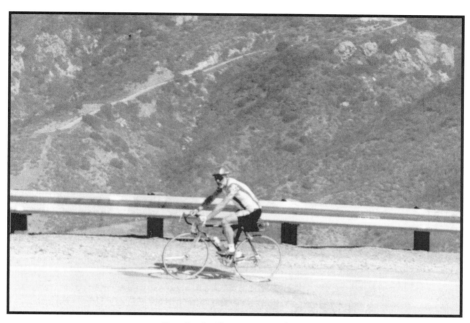

Seminole Canyon overlook

The road rides the crest with continuous views into the canyons and valleys before reaching Decker Road (34.6). The route proceeds left (south) on an extremely winding roadway (5-10 mile-per-hour curves), then enters a light residential valley. In two miles from this intersection, turn sharply right off Highway 23 (Decker Road) onto the Mulholland Highway continuation. Bike a short distance to Yerba Buena Road (37.3).

Yerba Buena Road to Pacific Coast Highway. The earlier hard work pays off on the predominantly downhill final segment. The winding downhill provides an overlook of the GTE Satellite Tracking Station and, in a mile, reaches the valley where the station is sited. In two miles from the Yerba Buena Road junction, Mulholland Highway follows a steep, winding downgrade. The canyon outlet to the coast comes into view in the far distance. After about two miles of exciting downgrade, the road winds through a sparsely populated valley (41.7), passes Camp Bloomfield, and, in 0.2 mile, enters the upper reaches of Leo Carrillo State Beach (as noted by the road sign). There is a half-mile upgrade which graduates from moderate to very steep and reaches a crest with a refreshing ocean view (43.7). In another 0.2 mile, the route reaches the park and the end of a grueling but satisfying trip.

CONNECTING TRIPS: You've got to be kidding! 1) Continuation with the PCH ride (Trip #18B) - near the trip origin, turn either east or west on PCH.

TRIPS #18A-#18C - PACIFIC COAST HIGHWAY: SANTA MONICA TO PORT HUENEME

The entire tour described follows the Pacific Coast Bicentennial Bike Route. The main part of the trip hugs the coastline, following Pacific Coast Highway (PCH) from Santa Monica to an outlet near Point Mugu. The remaining 4.9-mile segment follows Navalair Road inland, turns west on Hueneme Road, and follows that road to Bubbling Springs Linear Park. The total 44.7-mile trip, which is mapped below, is a strenuous one-way shot and a strenuous to very strenuous up-and-back trip. With a short extension into Port Hueneme/Oxnard, the round trip could be turned easily into a "Century" ride.

Trip #18A is relatively flat, but on congested roadway with limited bike room over long stretches. There are, however, some fine coastal views on the route, plus the bonus of tours through Santa Monica, Topanga Beach, and Malibu. Trip #18B is on roadway with a wide, striped shoulder (Class II bikeway but unmarked) and is the most naturally scenic; it is also one mean roller-coaster ride! This tour visits Malibu, Point Dume, and Leo Carrillo State Beach. Trip #18C, the easiest segment of the tour, is on the same quality roadway as Trip #18B. On this trip portion, cyclists visit Sycamore Cove, Point Mugu, the agricultural Ventura County countryside, and Port Hueneme.

TRIP #18A - PACIFIC COAST HIGHWAY: SANTA MONICA TO MALIBU LAGOON

GENERAL LOCATION: Santa Monica, Topanga State Beach, Malibu

LEVEL OF DIFFICULTY: One way - moderate; up and back - moderate
Distance - 10.5 miles (one way)
Elevation gain - periodic moderate grades

HIGHLIGHTS: An excellent scenic stretch of Pacific Coast Highway (PCH), this well-trafficked portion of the Pacific Coast Bicentennial Bike Route is short on bike room but long on outstanding views, landmarks, and sightseeing attractions. Don't bike this one if you are nervous about sharing roadways with high-speed traffic. The relatively flat roadway starts at cozy Palisades Park and, as part of its itinerary, passes near such points of interest as the original J. Paul Getty Museum, Will Rogers State Beach, Topanga State Beach, Big Rock, Las Flores Beach, and Malibu Lagoon State Beach. There are also numerous exploratory adventures that can be taken off this 10.5-mile Class X tour.

TRAILHEAD: From the Santa Monica Freeway, exit at Fourth Street (the last turnoff before the freeway fuses into PCH). Drive 1.25 miles to San Vicente Boulevard and turn left, following this street to its terminus at Ocean Avenue. Park on San Vicente Boulevard near Ocean Avenue. Do not use the pay parking at Palisades Park unless you plan to return within the five-hour meter limit.

From PCH southbound, turn left at Chautauqua Boulevard, then immediately veer right onto Channel Road. Drive 0.3 mile to its terminus, turn right, and proceed across Entrada Drive to Ocean Avenue. Follow this winding uphill 0.3 mile to San Vicente Boulevard.

Bring a filled water bottle. There are a couple of public water sources and scattered commercial sources along the way. Bring a second bottle if you want to squirt water at non-yielding car drivers (just kidding!).

TRIP DESCRIPTION: **Santa Monica to Topanga State Beach.** Bike north-west on Ocean Avenue and follow the steep 0.3 mile downgrade, then continue around the hairpin turn to Entrada Drive. Cross this road and turn left at Channel Road, free-wheeling another 0.3 mile to Chautauqua Boulevard. After a left, turn right in a short distance and follow beach-hugging PCH below the bluffs of northern Palisades Park (entry from Chautauqua Boulevard at Corona Del Mar). There are views of the jagged coastline to the west and the Palos Verdes Peninsula back to the southeast. The winding highway continues to hug the Will Rogers State Beach coastline. Bikers are forced to ride on varying-width shoulder alongside high-speed traffic; this situation continues all the way into Malibu.

The road passes Temescal Canyon Road (1.9) (Temescal Canyon Park with its shade and water is to the north), enters the Pacific Palisades area, passes along a mile-long slide zone, and then reaches Sunset Boulevard and a gas station (2.8). The road

TRIP #18A - PACIFIC COAST HIGHWAY: SANTA MONICA TO MALIBU LAGOON

continues to hug the coast and passes Coastline Road and the entrance to the original J. Paul Getty Museum (3.8). (The new museum has been relocated to the hills above Brentwood.) Bike through an area with a high density of residences in the nearby palisades and past the ocean-side Chart House Restaurant (an old favorite of ours). In a short distance, the road reaches Topanga Canyon Boulevard and Topanga State Beach (4.6).

Topanga State Beach to Malibu Lagoon State Beach. This coastal tour passes another slide area near Big Rock, crosses Big Rock Road (6.0), and reaches the waterfront Moonshadows Bar and Restaurant. Just beyond is Las Flores Canyon Road (6.7) and the entry into a light commercial area sporting a mix of sports shops, boutiques, and eateries.

Bike past Rambla Pacifico and a gas station (7.7), then visit a lovely and mixed hillside/seaside residential area just before reaching Carbon Canyon Road (8.5). The hillsides still contain scattered burned-out structures from the disastrous fires of the early 1990s. Next is a high-density residential area with frequent stop signs. Inviting "pork-out" stops in this area are the Nantucket Light Restaurant (9.6), Malibu Beach Bar and Grill, and La Salsa Tacos El Carbon Restaurant (complete with a giant sombreroed Mexican caricature on the roof).

Continue through the well-trafficked section of town with limited bike shoulder past the Malibu Inn. In a short distance, reach Malibu Surfrider Beach and the Malibu Lagoon Museum. Bike on the bridge over the ocean-side tidepools and land-side Malibu Lagoon. Stop and enjoy the cozy and picturesque lagoon before proceeding to Serra Road and Malibu Lagoon State Beach.

CONNECTING TRIPS: 1) Continuation with the Santa Monica Loop (Trip #2) - at the origin, bike northeast on San Vicente Boulevard; 2) continuation of the PCH: Malibu Lagoon to Sycamore Cove tour (Trip #18B) - at the trip terminus, continue west on PCH; 3) connection with the South Bay Bike Trail (Trip #1C) - bike southeast on Ocean Avenue past Colorado Avenue to Seaside Terrace, turn right, and follow the beach entry route.

Malibu Lagoon

TRIP #18B - PACIFIC COAST HIGHWAY: MALIBU LAGOON TO SYCAMORE COVE

GENERAL LOCATION: Malibu, Leo Carrillo Beach, Point Dume, Sycamore Cove

LEVEL OF DIFFICULTY: One way - moderate to strenuous; up and back -
                           strenuous
                           Distance - 20.1 miles (one way)
                           Elevation gain - continuous moderate-to-steep grades

HIGHLIGHTS: This is the roller-coaster portion of the Pacific Coast Highway (PCH)
route, rich in hills and also in breathtaking coastal scenery. The tour leaves Malibu
Lagoon State Beach and visits Malibu, Point Dume, Zuma County Beach, and Leo
Carrillo State Beach, and ends at Sycamore Cove Beach in Point Mugu State Park. The
hills are many and varied in challenge, with the entire workout trip being on a wide,
striped bike shoulder. A round-trip tour provides what appears to the eye to be two
distinctly different trips.

  Why did God make hills? More knowledgeable bikers than us explain: "So that
bikers can stand up and pump, thereby awaking their backsides."

TRAILHEAD: From Santa Monica, drive on PCH about 12 miles from the Santa
Monica Freeway terminus. At Serra Road, find pay parking at Malibu Lagoon State
Beach or park for free on PCH itself per local parking laws.

  Bring a filled water bottle. Add a second bottle on hot days if you prefer to minimize the number of stops. There are several scattered but reliable water stops on this
challenging trip.

TRIP DESCRIPTION: **Malibu Lagoon to Paradise Cove.** Exit Malibu Lagoon
State Beach and bike past Cross Creek Road and the Malibu Country Mart. The road
moves away from the coast and continues through less-developed countryside with
several beautiful structures built upon the hillside to the north. This refreshing scenery
continues past Webb Way and a gas station (0.4), where the road divides and bikers are
treated to a very nice and wide biking shoulder. This excellent bikeway continues nearly
all the way to Port Hueneme.

  Shortly after, there is a steep upgrade and the beginning of a series of rolling hills
for about the next 15 miles. At the top of the grade to the north is lovely Pepperdine
University campus and Malibu Canyon Road (1.2). The roller-coaster route continues,
and sporadic views open up in about a mile. In another half mile, there is a particularly
steep grade, followed by a nice downhill that returns bikers to near sea level at Dan
Blocker County Beach (3.1). The road is next to a long line of steep palisades in this
area.

  After enjoying the beach scenery, "suck it in" and begin the long and relatively
steep upgrade, passing Latigo Canyon Road (4.7) and reaching the crest in another 0.3
mile. The road moves inland and roller-coasters through more hills, passes posh
Geoffrey's Restaurant (5.5), and follows a downgrade to the Paradise Cove area.

TRIP #18B - PACIFIC COAST HIGHWAY:
MALIBU LAGOON TO SYCAMORE COVE

Paradise Cove to Trancas Beach. In another 1.5 miles of stair-step uphill is the first of three southern road accesses to the Point Dume area, and just after this is Kanan Dume Road (7.6). Note that there are some very scenic coastal coves off these roads, which can be reached with a modest hike. However, for the steady pedaler, continue on this hilly road to Heathercliff Road (gas station) and enjoy the scenic ocean views which open up in this area. Free-wheel downhill past the Corral Beach turnoff (gas station) and return to sea level at Zuma County Beach (water and restrooms) (8.6).

The bike tour generally hugs the coastline from this point until reaching the Point Mugu area. The ocean views are constant and spectacular and the ocean breeze is refreshing any time of year. Pedal alongside scenic Zuma County Beach, then pass Trancas Creek and the local marina, which is the home of the Malibu Yacht Club. In a short distance, pass Trancas Canyon Road and the Trancas Beach turnoff (gas station) (9.7).

Trancas Beach to Leo Carrillo State Beach. Follow a long-overdue flat stretch before returning to the series of rolling hills. There are scattered residences in the area and more great coastal views. Follow the workout upgrade past the El Matador State Beach turnoff (11.7) and continue to Encinal Canyon Road. In 0.2 mile, pass the La Piedra State Beach turnoff and a high-density pocket of expensive beach homes.

Follow the refreshing downhill past Decker Canyon Road and stare straight ahead at yet another challenging upgrade. Pedal past the Malibu Ride and Country Club, the Nicholas Canyon County Beach turnoff (13.9), and follow a half-mile runout which returns cyclists to sea level and Leo Carrillo State Beach; there are restrooms and water at this beach.

Leo Carrillo State Beach to Sycamore Cove Beach. The bikeway follows the steep uphill and passes Mulholland Highway (15.1). At the end of the beach boundary, the route crosses the Los Angeles County/Ventura County Line. Bike on the long upgrade and enjoy the views directly ahead into the Santa Monica Mountains. The road returns quickly to sea level, passes a surfing area, and reaches Yerba Buena Road (16.8). Mercifully, the worst (or best?) is over as the path enters a section of lightly rolling hills.

PCH continues through the hills, with steep palisades just to the inland side. There are excellent views in both directions along the coastline in this area. The route passes the coastal access at Deer Creek Road (18.4), continues through the gentle hills, and reaches the westernmost edge of the extensive Point Mugu State Park. In about one-quarter mile is the entry to the Sycamore Canyon Campground. Just beyond is the access to Sycamore Cove Beach (20.1), which has water, a restroom, a fine beach, and a ranger station. It is also a scenic rest point before returning east or continuing to Port Hueneme.

CONNECTING TRIPS: 1) Continuation with the PCH: Santa Monica to Malibu Lagoon ride (Trip #18A) - at the trip origin, bike east; 2) continuation with the PCH: Sycamore Cove to Port Hueneme tour (Trip #18C) - from the trip terminus, continue west; 3) connection with the Santa Monica Mountains Workout (Trip #17) - at Malibu Canyon Road, turn north (inland).

TRIP #18C - PACIFIC COAST HIGHWAY: SYCAMORE COVE TO PORT HUENEME

GENERAL LOCATION: Sycamore Cove, Point Mugu, Port Hueneme

LEVEL OF DIFFICULTY: One way - moderate; up and back - moderate
Distance - 13.7 miles (one way)
Elevation gain - periodic moderate grades

HIGHLIGHTS: The northern segment of this tour along Pacific Coast Highway (PCH) starts at Sycamore Cove Beach and cruises the scenic coast with a visit to "picture postcard" Point Mugu. The route passes along the Pacific Missile Test Center, then tours the open farmland of eastern Port Hueneme before reaching the Bubbling Springs Linear Park terminus. The tour passes through varied scenic areas on a mix of roadway classes; the highlight area is certainly the scenic coastal portion from Sycamore Cove Beach to Point Mugu. The route is primarily Class II or on a marked roadway with a very wide shoulder.

TRAILHEAD: From Santa Monica, drive on PCH about 32 miles from the Santa Monica Freeway terminus. About a mile beyond the Los Angeles County/Ventura County Line, turn into Sycamore Cove Beach.

Bring a filled water bottle. For the up-and-back trip on a hot day, think about a couple of bottles. There are few water sources between the trip start and end points.

TRIP DESCRIPTION: **Sycamore Cove Beach to Point Mugu.** Exit Sycamore Cove Beach and follow the flat which gives way to a modest steady upgrade. PCH passes a massive natural sand dune built up alongside the cliffs, an impressive sight! Next is a pass-by of the La Jolla Canyon Campground and a seemingly unending line of recreational vehicles, as well as rock-strewn La Jolla Canyon Beach (1.5).

Just beyond, the route meanders along the land-side cliffs about 20 feet above the ocean and passes several scenic locations. The road climbs a grade and returns to the beach near Point Mugu (3.1). The road has been blasted through the rock in this area; once up to and through the resultant portals, there are fine views in both directions. To the west are the first views into the Oxnard/Port Hueneme area, and back to the east is the rugged coastline. Take advantage of the scenic turnouts near Point Mugu.

Point Mugu to Hueneme Road. Pass a rifle range, saltwater marshes of Mugu Lagoon, and bike under the "watchful eye" of the tower-bedecked Mugu Peak (5.1). Cross over Calleguas Creek and continue to the Las Posas Road off-ramp (7.0). Exit at this street since PCH becomes an automobile-only road just beyond, cross over PCH, and follow Navalair Road alongside the Pacific Missile Test Center/Point Mugu Naval Air Station. Follow the fenced-in road past the main entrance gate, the missile model display (7.5), and Wood Road. In another mile, reach Hueneme Road.

Port Hueneme. Turn left and take a country bike ride through a predominantly agricultural area. The Port Hueneme/Oxnard skyline is directly ahead. This is a Class

**TRIP #18C - PACIFIC COAST HIGHWAY:
SYCAMORE COVE TO PORT HUENEME**

X road with a wide bike shoulder and limited traffic. Pass Edison Drive (11.9) and Saviers Road (12.4) and bike through what becomes a mixed residential/light commercial area. Continue about three quarters of a mile, passing "J" Street, and turn left into pleasant Bubbling Springs Linear Park.

This is a fine place to end the trip, as there are restrooms, water, shade, and grass at the park. Another option is to continue biking south another mile along the manicured canal to Port Hueneme Beach Park.

CONNECTING TRIPS: 1) Continuation with the PCH route (Trip #18B) - at the trip origin at Sycamore Cove Beach, bike south.

Beach at Point Mugu

RIVER TRAILS

San Gabriel River in the Seal Beach area

TRIPS #19, #20A, #20B - UPPER RIO HONDO AND LARIO TRAILS

The Upper Rio Hondo Trail (Trip #19) and Lario Trail (Trips #20A and #20B) can be ridden as a complete 28-mile one-way trip. This is a moderate one-way workout and a strenuous round trip. The overall map is provided below. The entire route is a Class I bike trail. In the distant past, there were four street intersections where the biker would have to leave the bike trail in high water. They were in the southern (third) segment of the trip. The upgraded bike undercrossings eliminated any need to leave the bikeway, under any river conditions.

The Upper Rio Hondo Trail explores the segment from its current "origin" at the Peck Road Water Conservation Park (reservoir) through a short stretch of some river bottomland, and ends in the Whittier Narrows Recreation Area (Whittier Narrows Dam, Nature Center, and Legg Lake). Trip #20A (Upper Lario Trail) starts near the Whittier Narrows Dam, follows the lower Rio Hondo just past its conjunction with the Los Angeles River, and ends at Hollydale Park. The lower segment of the Lario Trail (Trip #20B) starts at Hollydale Park and finds its way into Long Beach Harbor and San Pedro Bay.

TRIP #19 - UPPER RIO HONDO TRAIL

GENERAL LOCATION: El Monte, Whittier Narrows

LEVEL OF DIFFICULTY: One way - easy; up and back - moderate
Distance - 8.2 miles (one way)
Elevation gain - short steep grade at
Whittier Narrows Dam

HIGHLIGHTS: This uppermost section of this river trail follows the Rio Hondo from the river's origin to its confluence with the Los Angeles River (and ultimately to Long Beach Harbor). This lightly used segment travels from the pleasant Peck Road Water Conservation Park (reservoir) through the Whittier Narrows Recreation Area to the top of the Whittier Narrows Dam. There is fishing in the park at the trip origin. The lower section of the trip is exceptionally pretty, traveling along natural, forested riverbeds. The entire route is Class I and also qualifies as a nice, fast workout trip.

TRAILHEAD: From the San Gabriel River Freeway, exit at Lower Azusa Road and drive west 1.2 miles to Peck Road. Turn right (north) and proceed 0.6 mile to Rio Hondo Parkway. Turn left into the parking area alongside the reservoir.

From the San Bernardino Freeway, exit north on Peck Road, travel 2.3 miles to Rio Hondo Parkway, and turn left. From the Foothill Freeway, exit south to Myrtle Avenue. Drive 2.3 miles on Myrtle Avenue, which becomes Peck Road, and turn right at Rio Hondo Parkway into the parking lot.

Bring a moderate water supply. There is water at two strategically placed parks near the middle of the trip.

TRIP DESCRIPTION: **Upper River.** Near the southern end of the parking area, follow a short direct trail through an opening in the fence and proceed on a Class I bike trail on the east side of the lake. In 0.4 mile, the route passes the lake spillway where there is a raised diversion trail across the back side (lake side) of the spillway. Our route stays on the main trail on the east side of the lake. Just beyond the spillway, the Upper Rio Hondo Trail actually begins.

TRIP #19 - UPPER RIO HONDO TRAIL

The upper segment of the trip is along the concrete Rio Hondo riverbed through a commercial area. Other than counting the shopping carts in the riverbed, the greatest excitement may be the undercrossings at Santa Anita Avenue (0.9) and Lower Azusa Road (1.2). Soon there is a small rest area next to the El Monte Airport where bikers can watch the small aircraft take off and land (1.4). The stretch along the airport continues for about 0.75 mile, followed by passage under a railroad trestle (2.2), then alongside a raised railway structure and under Valley Boulevard (2.5).

Next is Pioneer Park which stretches for another 0.3 mile along the bikeway. The park has water, restrooms, picnic areas, baseball diamonds, tennis courts, and

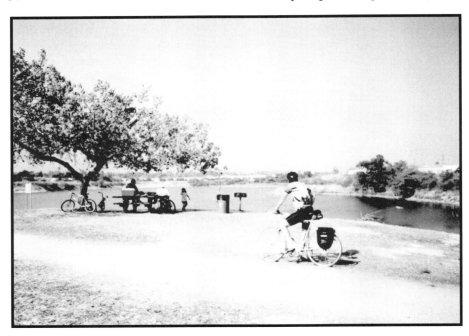

Peck Road Water Conservation Park

playground areas. The architecturally striking El Monte Busway Station and RTD Park and Ride are just east of the park. The path eventually passes under a raised concrete railroad overpass (2.7) and a special bus-lane overpass (2.8), and it passes beside quaint little Fletcher Park before reaching the San Bernardino Freeway (3.0).

Bike the next mile through an area with residences to the left and commercial areas across the river. The bikepath meets Rosemead Boulevard (4.1), then Garvey Avenue (4.2), and later passes a "cable car" river crossing apparatus (4.7).

After more than four miles of concrete, there is a sudden transition to a natural riverbed just beyond this point (5.0). Near the juncture, there is a short spur to the right that provides an overlook of the river transition point. However, our trip follows the main trail and heads south and away from the river. In 0.2 mile, it reaches the northeast end of the Whittier Narrows Recreation Area "A" at Loma Avenue and Rush Street.

Whittier Narrows Recreation Area. Recreation Area "A" is about one-half mile, north-south, by one-fourth mile, east-west. There are numerous spur routes on bikepaths and on the slow, lightly traveled automobile roads in the park. There are restrooms, water, shade, picnic areas, recreational fields, playgrounds, a model airplane flying area, and a model car racing area. Our trip follows the west edge of the park on Loma Avenue.

At the very south end of Loma Avenue (5.8), pass through the opening in the fence. Pedal west, parallel to and on the same level as the Pomona Freeway. In 0.6 mile, the path cuts under the freeway and rejoins the Rio Hondo. This is natural river bottom with lush trees and other greenery. Further downriver, the undergrowth thickens and blocks the river from view (6.7). In half a mile or so of this lovely stretch, the river gives way to an exit trail which takes cyclists up to San Gabriel Boulevard (7.3).

A spur trail just before that exit leads to a wading and rest area below the San Gabriel Boulevard bridge.

Whittier Narrows Dam. To the east on San Gabriel Boulevard is Legg Lake and the Four Corners Trail Intersection (see Trip #26). Our trip heads west on San Gabriel Boulevard over the river to Lincoln Avenue (7.6). Turn left and make another immediate left turn onto an asphalt road blocked to cars. The trail follows above and at some distance from the west bank of the Rio Hondo. This section has scrub brush, an oil well pump or two, and low eroded hills to the west. The trail pulls away from the river at about 0.2 mile from the Lincoln Avenue entrance and comes within close view of that street. Just beyond are the first views of the back side of the Whittier Narrows Dam. In 0.2 mile, follow a steep trail up the back side of the dam and summit the west levee of the Whittier Narrows Dam (8.2).

Stop and enjoy the sweeping views, from the dam's crest, of the San Gabriel Mountains, surrounding hills, local communities, and the lush bottomland of the Whittier Narrows area back upriver. There is a sign noting that this is the origin of the Lario Trail (see Trip #20A). Bike beyond the sign and ride out along the dam for some additional scenery.

CONNECTING TRIPS: 1) Continuation with the Lario Trail (Trip #20A) - pedal south from the Whittier Narrows Dam at the end of the trip; 2) connection with the San Gabriel River Trail (Trips #22C and #22D) - head east on San Gabriel Boulevard as above and, once across Rosemead Boulevard, follow the Class I bikepath to the right into the Whittier Narrows Wildlife Refuge, then cruise on this path past the Four Corners Trail Intersection to the San Gabriel River; 3) connection with the Whittier Narrows Recreation Area/Legg Lake Bike Trail (Trip #26) - head east on San Gabriel Boulevard from the bridge over the Rio Hondo and pedal 0.9 mile on Durfee Avenue (same street, new name) to the Legg Lake parking lot.

TRIP #20A - LARIO TRAIL: WHITTIER NARROWS DAM TO HOLLYDALE PARK

GENERAL LOCATION: Montebello, Downey, Bell Gardens, Hollydale

LEVEL OF DIFFICULTY: One way - easy; up and back - moderate
Distance - 9.0 miles (one way)
Elevation gain - essentially flat

HIGHLIGHTS: This Class I trip starts from atop the Whittier Narrows Dam, travels southward along the Rio Hondo past the river's confluence with the Los Angeles River, and ends at pleasant little Hollydale Park. The river is not the attraction; the attractions are the running streams and holding basins beside the river and the interesting trail diversions that interweave this particular territory. This is an interesting trip right after a heavy winter rain! There are several parks worth visiting. Finally, this is a limited-use stretch; it is a good route for bikers looking for a speedy, unobstructed workout.

TRIP #20A - LARIO TRAIL: WHITTIER NARROWS DAM TO HOLLYDALE PARK

TRAILHEAD: From the Pomona Freeway, exit south at San Gabriel Boulevard, drive 0.8 mile to Lincoln Avenue, and turn right (south). Proceed 0.8 mile to the parking area at the dam west levee/view site. From the San Gabriel River Freeway, exit west on Beverly Boulevard and cruise 1.2 miles to Rosemead Boulevard. Turn right (north) and drive 1.5 miles to San Gabriel Boulevard. Turn left and continue 0.3 mile to Lincoln Avenue. Turn left again and proceed 0.8 mile to the parking area at the dam viewing site.

The route is exposed, with almost no shade other than underpasses and parks. Bring a moderate water supply and refill at the parks.

TRIP DESCRIPTION: Whittier Narrows Dam. Leave the parking area, lift your bike over the low barrier, and proceed up and across the Whittier Narrows Dam's west levee. At 0.4 mile, bike the paved downhill route which exits the south face. The path winds downhill and rejoins the Rio Hondo's west levee beyond the spillway (1.0). The riverbed is solid concrete. More interesting scenery mainly is to the right (west) where there are ravines, equestrian trails, and running streams. (Note: If the route gets confusing over the next several miles, stick to the path nearest the river.)

Grant Rea Park. In 0.4 mile beyond the spillway, a footbridge over the equestrian trails leads to Grant Rea Park. This small park has recreation fields, tree cover, a small barnyard zoo (with common farm animals and then some), and pony-cart rides. Pedal past the bridge and see the red barn and barnyard animals. Further south, there is a footbridge over a ravine (and a diversion route) which leads to Beverly Boulevard (1.7); the area beyond the ravine is marshy with a crush of greenery.

The Middle Section. Further down the reference river path, the bikeway passes Whittier Boulevard (2.2), a railroad trestle (2.4), and a stagnant marshy area. Just beyond are barnyard and horse stalls in a treed rural setting. Pass another footbridge, this one heading to Roosevelt Avenue and Reggie Rodriguez Park (2.8). In 0.8 mile, cross under Washington Boulevard and pass a series of water-holding basins interspersed with equestrian trails. (Bikers can exit the river route by biking a quarter mile south of Washington Boulevard, on the wide paralleling path nearest the bluffs, then following the short and steep diversion trail that leads up to Bluff Road/Frankel Avenue.) Later the bike route leaves the river and races downhill through a tunnel under a railroad bridge before returning to the levee (4.3). Before reaching the tunnel, note the trail exit up the side of the bluffs; this steep path ends at Sycamore Street.

Further south, the trail crosses Slauson Avenue (4.6) and then follows another diversion off the levee, through a railroad tunnel underpass (5.1). Shortly afterward, the path crosses under Telegraph Road and the Santa Ana Freeway. Immediately afterward, the bikepath leaves the levee and crosses a little bridge over the marshes, soon returning to the levee (5.3).

In 0.1 mile, pass a footbridge which leads to Veteran's Memorial Park. The river route then passes alongside the long and narrow Treasure Island Park (5.8). Access to the park (shade, water, picnic facilities) is from the south.

John Anson Ford Park and the River Crossing. The route passes Suva Street (5.9) and Florence Avenue (6.2) before reaching John Anson Ford Park (6.4). This park is an excellent rest stop or alternate turnaround point. It has plenty of shade, restrooms, picnic facilities, a small lake, and even a swimming pool!

Just south of the park, there is a small wooden pedestrian bridge that takes the Lario Trail across the river to the east levee; it is important not to miss this crossing, as the west levee path dead-ends 0.75 mile down the path.

Rio Hondo to the Los Angeles River Confluence. On the east levee, the route passes the Rio Hondo Country Club/Golf Course and little Crawford Park (6.5) which has restrooms, water, and a playground. The next two miles are through areas surrounded by commercial/industrial facilities with little to offer in the way of scenery.

River crossing at John Anson Ford Park

For example, the outdoor "Bandini Planter Mix" factory near Imperial Highway is one of the trip "highlights" in this segment! The route passes Firestone Boulevard (6.8), a trans-river cable car (7.1), Southern Avenue (7.2), Garfield Avenue (7.6), tiny Circle Park, and a railroad trestle underpass (7.9), and reaches the confluence of the Rio Hondo and the Los Angeles River (8.2). Just south of the junction is Imperial Highway (8.4).

    Hollydale Park. A quarter mile beyond Imperial Highway is the north edge of Hollydale Park. This park is a mixture of people-playground and horse-playground. To the north are playgrounds and equestrian show areas which give way to tennis courts and recreation fields to the south (9.0). There is sparse tree cover here, as well as water, providing a chance to rest up for the return trip.

CONNECTING TRIPS: 1) Continuation of the Upper Rio Hondo Bike Trail (Trip #19) - bike the trip north from Whittier Narrows; 2) continuation of the Lario Trail (Trip #20B) - cruise south from Hollydale Park; 3) connection with the Los Angeles River Trail (Trip #21) - cross the Los Angeles River at Imperial Highway; just beyond the bridge on the north side of the street, follow the bike trail sign onto the west levee.

TRIP #20B - LARIO TRAIL: HOLLYDALE PARK TO LONG BEACH HARBOR

GENERAL LOCATION: South Gate, Paramount, North Long Beach, Long Beach

LEVEL OF DIFFICULTY: One way - easy; up and back - moderate
Distance - 10.9 miles (one way)
Elevation gain - essentially flat

HIGHLIGHTS: This Class I trip starts near the midpoint of the Lario Trail at Hollydale Park and proceeds to the trail's end in Long Beach Harbor. It passes several parks on the way south and provides some excellent views, near the lower segment, of the Long Beach city skyline, Long Beach Harbor, and Dominguez Hills, and a long-distance view of San Pedro Hill. In times long past, there were four intersections where the biker was forced to leave the levee (Rosecrans Avenue, Compton Boulevard, Alondra Boulevard, and Del Amo Boulevard) and either bike into the river or cross busy road intersections. Bike undercrossings rebuilt in the early 1990s eliminated any need to leave the Class I path under any conditions.

TRAILHEAD: From the Long Beach Freeway, exit east on Imperial Highway and continue 0.5 mile to Garfield Place (Ruchti Road to the north). Turn right and drive 0.6 mile to Monroe Avenue. Turn right (west) and continue to the parking lot at Hollydale Park.

Bring a moderate water supply or fill up at the parks in the upper part of this tour. There is no near-trail water supply for the last seven miles before reaching the harbor.

TRIP DESCRIPTION: North Segment. At the south end of the park, there is an asphalt entry path up to the Lario Trail. Once up on the Los Angeles River east levee, head south past a horse pasture (0.3) and an old blocked-off railroad bridge (0.7). Continue through a commercial/industrial area with a "lovely" view of the Long Beach Freeway across the river and a concrete riverbed. Next are the awesome multi-level interweaving structures which make up the Long Beach Freeway/Century Freeway interchange (1.1).

The Middle Segment. Pass Rosecrans Avenue and proceed to a long, narrow park that has various athletic courts, playgrounds, play areas, and water (near the south end) (1.4). This is "world famous" Ralph C. Dills Park which runs between Rosecrans Avenue and Compton Boulevard (1.9). Just beyond is the compact Par-3 Compton Golf Course and, in 0.5 mile, Alondra Boulevard.

Cruise by horse stables and a training area (2.7), cross Atlantic Avenue (2.9), and visit another equestrian area. In succession, the bikeway transits below the Artesia Freeway (3.2) and Artesia Boulevard (3.4), passes a "trailer city," and meets up with the ultimate thin strip of park, De Forest Park (3.7). This is another nice rest spot with water (the last readily accessible water until Long Beach). Water and restrooms are at the south end of the park.

**TRIP #20B - LARIO TRAIL: HOLLYDALE PARK TO
LONG BEACH HARBOR**

Beyond the park, the path parallels a marsh for the next 2.5 miles; stop and look awhile, as there are some interesting plants and wildlife. Shortly afterward, the bikepath crosses Long Beach Boulevard (4.6); there is a nice view of Dominguez Hills to the right (west). Pass Del Amo Boulevard, the last of the former "river dippers" (5.5). In 0.3 mile, pass the river confluence with Compton Creek. Proceed under a railroad crossing (6.0), pass the Virginia Country Club, and continue beside a lovely residential area in the hills to the east (6.4). Pedal by the San Diego Freeway (6.9) and Wardlow Road (7.2) where the trip reenters residential surroundings. There is a passenger cable car over the river (7.4) and another group of horse corrals coupled with a training area (7.8).

Southern Segment and the "Real" Los Angeles River. Finally comes the trip juncture where the river bottom transitions from "C" for concrete to "N" for natural (thank goodness!). The most scenic part of the trip follows. Year-round water and wildlife are not too far from the transition point. The route passes under Willow Avenue (8.4) and PCH (9.1). There are views of the harbor area and the Gerald Desmond Bridge. Within another 0.6 mile at Anaheim Street, the waterway transitions into a deep channel that reminds one of a "real" river.

At Seventh Street, there is an excellent view of the Long Beach city skyline and Long Beach Harbor (10.1). In 0.6 mile, the bikepath reaches Ocean Boulevard. There are ski boaters, water skiers, and jet skiers everywhere. Shortly the Lario Trail reaches a gated area with a sign marking the trail's end (10.9). (See Trip #11 for more information about this area.) At this point, there is a nice look at the Queensway Bridge and the Long Beach Harbor area.

CONNECTING TRIPS: 1) Continuation with the Long Beach Shoreline Park tour (Trip #14) - continue south through the parking lot at the Lario Trail terminus and steer toward Queensway Landing (Catalina Boat Terminal); 2) continuation with the upper Lario Trail segment (Trip #20A) - pedal north from the trip origin at Hollydale Park; 3) connection with the Long Beach Harbor: Southeast Basin ride (*Queen Mary*, Harbor Scenic Drive) (Trip #11) - bike to the northwest corner of the Aquarium of the Pacific parking structure (at Shoreline Drive across from South Chestnut Place); stay to the left and enter the separated Class I path on the Queensway Bridge, cross Queensway Bay, and follow the road signs.

TRIP #21 - LOS ANGELES RIVER TRAIL

GENERAL LOCATION: South Gate, Cudahy, Bell

LEVEL OF DIFFICULTY: Up and back - easy
                         Distance - 5.6 miles (one way)
                         Elevation gain - essentially flat

HIGHLIGHTS: This is a short Class I trip along the Los Angeles River, starting just south of its confluence with the Rio Hondo. There is little scenery and broken glass at spots along the bikeway. This may be an excellent trip someday if the route is ever maintained and it is extended northward. Concerned groups like the Los Angeles County Bicycle Coalition (LACBC) are lobbying the city to extend the route southward from the current segment near Griffith Park (see Trip #33). Hopefully, in the farther term, the roughly 15-mile gap between segments will be completed, resulting in a Glendale-to-the-ocean bike trail. However, for now, it is a segment for bikers who want to "see it all" or who want to build up an appreciation for other bike routes.

TRAILHEAD: From the Long Beach Freeway, exit west on Imperial Highway. Turn left (south) at Duncan Avenue and find parking, subject to the local laws. Another option is to park across the river at Hollydale Park. To get there, exit east on Imperial Highway, turn right on Garfield Avenue, and drive about 0.75 mile to Monroe Avenue. Turn right (west) toward the river and drive to road's end.

   Bring a biking partner and a light water supply. No direct-access public supply was found.

TRIP DESCRIPTION: Bike to Imperial Highway, cross it, and pedal right (east) on the north sidewalk over the Long Beach Freeway. Carefully cross the freeway entrance ramp. Turn left (north) at the bike trail sign that appears just before reaching the bridge over the Los Angeles River (0.3) and bike down to the west levee.

   Soon the route passes a viewing point of the river confluence, heads under the Long Beach Freeway (0.6), and then under a railroad crossing. In further succession, pass Firestone Boulevard (1.7), a second railroad crossing, Clara Street (2.7), and Florence Avenue (3.2). Further north, the trail ducks under Gage Avenue (3.8), passes under a railroad trestle, crosses Slauson Avenue, and veers northwest before reaching Atlantic Boulevard and the trip terminus (5.6).

   In the first 3.5-mile river stretch, there is a continuous line of industrial plants, commercial businesses, and mini-junkyards. The one breath of fresh air is just south of Clara Street at Cudahy Neighborhood Park. The environs improve little on the north segment, although the nearby railroad tracks provide some variety.

CONNECTING TRIPS: Connection with the Lario Trail (Trip #20) - at the trip origin, pedal across the Imperial Highway bridge over the Los Angeles River (stay on the north sidewalk); follow the trail sign down to the east levee and bike either north to the Whittier Narrows Dam (Trip #20A) or south to Long Beach (Trip #20B).

TRIP #21 - LOS ANGELES RIVER TRAIL

TRIPS #22A-#22E - SAN GABRIEL RIVER TRAIL

    The San Gabriel River Trail is probably the premier single river trail in this book. The route captures southern California from the sea through the inland valley to the mountains, all in one continuous 39-mile shot. Taken in the winter after a cold storm, this trip is one of the best in every sense. The general area map is provided below.

    The first segment (#22A) explores the river outlet near Seal Beach, then a wildlife area to the north, and ends at super El Dorado Park. The connection segment (#22B) visits no less than five parks and finishes at Wilderness Park in Downey. The next northerly segment (#22C) leaves Wilderness Park, travels alongside some fine San Gabriel River bottom, and ends at one of the tour highlights, the Whittier Narrows Recreation Area. Trip #22D starts at that fabulous recreation area and ends at another, the Santa Fe Dam Recreation Area. The most northerly segment (#22E) leaves from that dam and ends in the foothills at the entrance to San Gabriel Canyon.

TRIP #22A - SAN GABRIEL RIVER: SEAL BEACH TO EL DORADO PARK

<u>**GENERAL LOCATION**</u>: Seal Beach, Long Beach

<u>**LEVEL OF DIFFICULTY**</u>: Up and back - easy
Distance - 5.6 miles (one way)
Elevation gain - essentially flat

<u>**HIGHLIGHTS**</u>: This is the starting segment of one of the most varied and interesting trips in this book. This completely Class I bike route starts at the scenic lower section of the San Gabriel River Trail near the Long Beach Marina and winds up at El Dorado Park. The early part of the trip provides a look at "recreation city" with water, boats, water skiers, and jet skiers. The trip transitions into a nature area rich in wildlife and ends in a park which is so inviting that it could serve as a separate family excursion.

<u>**TRAILHEAD**</u>: Free public parking is available at the Long Beach Marina along Marina Drive in Naples or along First Street in Seal Beach. From Pacific Coast Highway (PCH) in Seal Beach, turn west on Marina Drive (2-3 blocks from Main Street in Seal Beach) and drive roughly half a mile to First Street. In a quarter mile, cross the San Gabriel River and continue a short distance into the marina near Seaport Village for parking. The trailhead is at Marina Drive at the east end (Seal Beach side) of the bridge over the San Gabriel River.

Only a light water supply is needed for this short trip. There are public water sources at the trip origin and terminus.

<u>**TRIP DESCRIPTION**</u>: **The Scenic Lower River Segment.** The first part of the trip provides views of boaters, water skiers, and an interestingly developed shoreline. The natural river basin passes PCH (0.4), the Westminster Avenue access, and the Haynes Steam Plant (electricity generation). At (2.2), a small alternate Class I bikepath leads off to the east along a 1.2-mile shaded route to Seal Beach Boulevard. In this stretch of the river, up to the concrete portion (3.5), one has views of the large bird population that includes pelicans, egrets, and the ever-present seagulls. The trip passes under the Garden Grove Freeway (2.3); just beyond, there is an exit which takes cyclists to College Park Drive and Edison Park. Next is the San Diego Freeway undercrossing (3.5). In this part of the bikepath, there are many "freeway orchards," those freeway-locked areas under the power poles, filled with containerized plants.

The River Crossing and El Dorado Park. In 0.4 mile, cross a signed bikeway/walkway bridge across the river. Do not miss the bridge unless you've decided to change plans and see Coyote Creek (Trip #24). Once over the bridge, there are views across the river to the El Dorado Golf Course and El Dorado Park West. At 0.7 mile from the bridge crossing, reach Willow Street and skirt the edge of the Nature Study Area which is the south end of El Dorado Park East (5.0). Shortly afterward, the bikepath reaches Spring Street and the entry to Areas I and II of the park (5.6).

TRIP #22A - SAN GABRIEL RIVER: SEAL BEACH TO EL DORADO PARK

There are myriad bikepath options within the park. This portion of the trip is worth a good exploration effort in itself (see Trip #16).

CONNECTING TRIPS: 1) Continuation with the San Gabriel River Trail (Trip #22B) - bike north beyond El Dorado Park toward Wilderness Park; 2) connection with the

Belmont Shore/Naples Tour (Trip #15) - from the origin, bike north on Marina Drive to Second Street, turn left (west), and pedal over the bridge to Naples Island; 3) connection with the El Dorado Park tour (Trip #16) - cruise through the park at the trip terminus; 4) connection with the Coyote Creek Trail (Trip #24) - at the eastern end of the bike bridge across the San Gabriel River, stay on the eastern riverbank.

Bridge north of San Gabriel River/Coyote Creek confluence

TRIP #22B - SAN GABRIEL RIVER: EL DORADO PARK TO WILDERNESS PARK

GENERAL LOCATION: Long Beach, Lakewood, Cerritos, Norwalk, Downey

LEVEL OF DIFFICULTY: One way - easy; up and back - moderate
Distance - 9.7 miles (one way)
Elevation gain - essentially flat

HIGHLIGHTS: This segment of the Class I San Gabriel River Trail has direct access to five major parks. In particular, this trip should not be completed without a tour of El Dorado Park. Rynerson Park provides a pleasant diversion from the river route, and Wilderness Park is a fine rest stop with a small pond/lagoon to dip the toes into before returning to the trip origin. There are horse corrals and equestrian trails beside the bike route in some sections. This is a good workout section, as the bike and foot traffic is relatively light.

TRIP #22B - SAN GABRIEL RIVER: EL DORADO PARK TO WILDERNESS PARK

TRAILHEAD: From the San Diego Freeway, turn north on Palo Verde Avenue and drive 0.9 mile to Spring Street. Turn right (east) and continue about 0.8 mile to free parking along Spring Street, just west of the bridge over the San Gabriel River. Other options are to head over the bridge and park in the Nature Center parking area (turn south at the park entrance), or to drive up Spring Street, make a U-turn, and return to the Area II park entrance to the north (right). The latter two options have pay parking.

From the San Gabriel River Freeway, turn west on Willow Street (Katella Avenue in Orange County), continue about one mile to Studebaker Road, and turn right (north). Drive 0.3 mile to Spring Street and turn right. Follow the parking instructions above. For direct entry at Area II (pay parking) from the southbound freeway, exit at Spring Street and turn right at the park entrance.

Bring a light water supply. Plenty of water and many restroom facilities are available at parks along the way. El Dorado Park is a particular delight! Bring some food for the barbecue and enjoy munchies at the park after a "tough" bike ride.

TRIP DESCRIPTION: **El Dorado Park.** From the parking area on Spring Street, ride east over the bridge and turn right (south) at the Nature Center entrance. Make another sharp right and pedal parallel to Spring Street (but in the opposite direction) along the Nature Center roadway. Continue 0.2 mile to the fence along the San Gabriel River bike route. Rather than passing through the fence entry, follow the roadway as it turns to the right and passes under Spring Street. The road enters Park Area II.

Stay to the left rather than bike into El Dorado Park. Pass through the fence and head right (north) along the San Gabriel River Trail (0.6). The first part of the trip parallels Park Area II. The path leaves the river again and follows the roadway under Wardlow Road (1.1). Again, stay to the left and pass through a fence which returns to the river trail (the other option is to bike through Park Area III and rejoin the trail one-half mile later). The path stays beside a stand of trees and passes the end of Park Area III (1.6) near the weapons firing range.

Rynerson Park. Pass a pedestrian bridge (a diversion route which crosses over to De Mille Junior High School) and then pass Carson Street (2.0). For the next 0.7 mile, cruise alongside fun Rynerson Park (formerly River Park) which boasts tree cover, horse stalls and corrals, horse trails, a little footbridge leading to a connecting alternate bike trail (which reconnects near Del Amo Boulevard), baseball diamonds, and water (near the baseball fields). The shady park area ends near Del Amo Boulevard (3.0).

The Middle Trip Section. For the next half mile, the trip highlight is the clever (and in some cases not so clever) graffiti on the concrete river walls. In 0.8 mile, reach little Liberty Park which is effectively a grassy rest area. Just beyond the park is South Street (3.8), followed by a passage below 183rd Street through a narrow tunnel (4.5). (Reduce speed and keep an eye "peeled" for oncoming bikers.) The route then passes more horse stalls.

The path dips down into the riverbed to cross under Artesia Boulevard (4.9). If you miss the marked route, you can walk (crouch) under the roadway. There is a short section where bikes must be walked across a railroad crossing, followed by passage under the Artesia Freeway (5.3). The first of many river spillways is near this junction.

The trail passes the Cerritos Ironwood Golf Course; nearby is the pedestrian bridge that leads across the river to Caruthers Park (5.6). The reference path stays on the east levee. Enter a pleasant, several-mile-long residential stretch beyond Alondra Boulevard, where horses are in many of the backyards (we even spotted a llama). Pass Rosecrans Avenue (7.0), another walk bridge over the river, and bike under a bridge that is part of the Century Freeway (7.8). In 0.3 mile, the path reaches Imperial Highway and later dips down nearer the river, passing below a railroad trestle (8.7).

Wilderness Park. At (9.0), the bike trail passes Firestone Boulevard, then reaches the transition to a natural river bottom after 11 solid miles of concrete. Rio San Gabriel Park is across the river, and a small spillway graces the river bottom. There is some excellent river bottomland north of this area (see Trips #22C and #22D). In about 0.7 mile, the tour reaches a refreshing terminus at Wilderness Park. This is a half-mile strip of park that offers water, restrooms, shade trees, sports and recreation areas, playgrounds, a small pond, and a lovely decorative water fountain.

CONNECTING TRIPS: 1) Continuation with the San Gabriel River Trail south to Seal Beach (Trip #22A) from the trip origin, or north to the Whittier Narrows (Trip #22C) from the trip terminus; 2) continuation with the El Dorado Park tour (Trip #16) at the trip origin.

TRIP #22C - SAN GABRIEL RIVER: WILDERNESS PARK TO LEGG LAKE

GENERAL LOCATION: Downey, Santa Fe Springs, Whittier, Pico Rivera

LEVEL OF DIFFICULTY: One way - easy; up and back - moderate
Distance - 7.7 miles (one way)
Elevation gain - essentially flat (single
steep grade at Whittier Narrows Dam)

HIGHLIGHTS: This pleasant segment of the San Gabriel River Trail starts at Wilderness Park, visits Santa Fe Springs Park, and ends at the trip highlight in the Whittier Narrows Recreation Area. A short diversion at Whittier Boulevard leads to Pío Pico State Historical Park. The Whittier Narrows area sports a ride on the dam levee, a visit to a wildlife refuge area, and a trip at the end to relaxing Legg Lake. This is one of the few river segments that is predominantly natural river bottom, and there are some lush areas that beckon for rest stops. This is 99 percent Class I trail (two street crossings) with light bike traffic south of the Whittier Narrows Dam.

TRAILHEAD: From the San Gabriel River Freeway, exit west on Florence Avenue. A short distance west of the freeway, turn left (south) on Little Lake Road. This road also leads back onto the southbound freeway; therefore, in a few hundred feet, turn right onto Little Lake Road proper. Continue on this roadway to the free parking area at Wilderness Park. From the Santa Ana Freeway, exit west on Florence Avenue. Pass under the San Gabriel River Freeway and follow the directions above.

Bring a moderate water supply. There is no en route water supply between Santa Fe Springs Park and the Whittier Narrows Recreation Area. (Water sources near the recreation area are at Legg Lake and the Nature Center.)

TRIP DESCRIPTION: **Wilderness Park to Santa Fe Springs Park.** From the south end of the parking lot, skirt the south edge of Wilderness Park and follow the path to the river entry. Turn right (north) and bike past Florence Avenue (0.2) and then the first of many spillways 0.2 mile further. There are scattered trees and a great deal of brush along the path, and the riverbed is built up into holding basins. At (0.7), reach Santa Fe Springs Park where there are play areas, shade, recreation fields, and restrooms. Fill up with water here if you are running low.

The Railroad Route and Pío Pico Historical Park. About 0.4 mile from the park, cross Telegraph Road. At (1.4), the bikeway passes the highest spillway (about six feet high) on this segment of the river. In this area, there is a stand of eucalyptus trees and a collection of horse stalls tucked between the river and the San Gabriel River Freeway. At (2.1), pass under a railroad trestle. Soon after, another railroad track comes in from the east and parallels the bike route for several miles. There is a high likelihood of having a train for company on this stretch.

Soon the route passes under another railroad trestle which, in turn, lies below the highly elevated Slauson Avenue overpass (2.3). The riverbed and greenery in the

TRIP #22C - SAN GABRIEL RIVER: WILDERNESS PARK TO LEGG LAKE

riverbed continue, while brush and railroad tracks are to the right. At (3.0), reach Washington Boulevard and the beginning of a long exposed stretch of bikeway. In about 0.6 mile, pass the biker/pedestrian entry at Dunlap Crossing Road. At (4.7), the path meets Whittier Boulevard; it is a 0.2-mile diversion to the right (east) to visit Pío Pico Historical Park and the Pío Pico Museum.

Our route transits a short tunnel under Whittier Boulevard and passes alongside dense brush on the right. At (5.3), the path heads under another railroad trestle; the paralleling railroad tracks fuse and the merged track leaves the river, heading east. In 0.2 mile, pass Beverly Boulevard. Further north, there is a spillway with a collecting basin that is large enough to support a flock of young water frolickers. There is a view into Rose Hills to the east.

Whittier Narrows Dam. The trip reaches a junction where the trail changes from asphalt to dirt at San Gabriel River Parkway (6.1). The dam is viewable at this point. Continue ahead if you have a wide-tire bike and a desire to see Pico Rivera Bicentennial Park and Sports Area. Our reference route follows the parkway and crosses the river to the west side. Pedal north and observe the lush tree-filled river bottom. Pass the Pico Rivera Golf Course (6.7) and make a hard left at the dam base. From this point, there is a short but steep path to the top of the dam (6.9). Stop and take in some of the excellent sights viewable here.

Whittier Narrows Recreation Area. (See Trip #26 map for additional detail.) Cruise down the meandering concrete bikeway on the back side of the dam, cross a water runoff channel, and reach the marked Four Corners Trail Intersection (7.2).

Bike straight ahead and pedal about 0.3 mile to a junction near another water channel. Turn left, crossing over the channel, bike a couple hundred yards through the lush bottomland to Durfee Avenue, and pass through the gate. Turn right (east) and cruise a few hundred feet to the Legg Lake parking area entry within the Whittier Narrows Recreation Area (7.7).

CONNECTING TRIPS: 1) Continuation with the San Gabriel River Trail south to El Dorado Park (Trip #22B) - from the trip origin, bike south; 2) continuation with the San Gabriel River Trail north to Santa Fe Dam (Trip #22D) - from the Four Corners Trail Intersection, turn right (east) at the junction; 3) connection/continuation with the Whittier Narrows/Legg Lake Trail (Trip #26) - from Legg Lake, return to the Four Corners Trail Intersection and turn right (west).

Four Corners Trail Intersection (Susan Cohen Photo)

TRIP #22D - SAN GABRIEL RIVER: LEGG LAKE TO SANTA FE DAM

GENERAL LOCATION: Whittier Narrows, El Monte, Baldwin Park, Irwindale

LEVEL OF DIFFICULTY: One way - easy; up and back - moderate
Distance - 11.4 miles (one way)
Elevation gain - essentially flat (single
steep grade at Santa Fe Dam)

HIGHLIGHTS: This is one of our favorite segments of the river trips. The San Gabriel River in the Whittier Narrows region is river stomping at its best; there are trees, thickets, clear running water, and readily visible wildlife in all. The Whittier Narrows Recreation Area offers a wildlife sanctuary, Legg Lake, vista points from the top of the dam, and a diversion trip to the Pico Rivera Bicentennial Park and Sports Area. The Santa Fe Dam Recreation Area offers an expansive, pleasant picnic and recreation area at the edge of the lake, as well as superb lookout points from the top of the dam. Set aside a few hours and fully explore these territories. The best time to take this trip is within several days of a cold winter storm when the snow level in the nearby mountains is low. The route is nearly 100 percent Class I (one street crossing).

There are also some excellent trip excursions in the Santa Fe Dam area. They range from on-road explorations to the west of the San Gabriel River Freeway and on the west levee to some dirt bike meandering in the flood control basin behind the dam.

TRAILHEAD: From the Pomona Freeway, exit at Rosemead Boulevard south, travel about 0.8 mile to San Gabriel Boulevard/Durfee Avenue, and turn left (east). Drive on Durfee Avenue 0.6 mile and turn left into the pay parking area at Legg Lake. Find a tree under which to park your car. Bring four quarters for the parking area fee.

Bring a moderate water supply. There are rest and water stops directly on the route and at the Santa Fe Dam Recreation Area terminus.

TRIP DESCRIPTION: **Whittier Narrows Recreation Area.** (See the Trip #26 map for additional detail.) Leave the parking area and cross Durfee Avenue a few hundred feet west of the parking area. Pass through the signed gate and pedal down a small asphalt road through an area surrounded by bushes, plants, trees, and brush. In a short distance, there is a junction just beyond a small water channel. The path left leads toward (but bypasses) the Whittier Narrows Nature Center. However, our route proceeds to the right and meets the Four Corners Trail Intersection in 0.3 mile (0.5). There is a nice view into the back side of the Whittier Narrows Dam from this area.

Turn left (east) and follow the path as it turns northward and rejoins the San Gabriel River (0.7). There are permanent horse trails to the left (west) and also "find-your-way" paths in the lush riverbed; both kinds are well used by horse riders, the latter accompanying our path for the next couple of miles. This area has excellent views of Rose Hills to the east.

TRIP #22D - SAN GABRIEL RIVER: LEGG LAKE TO SANTA FE DAM

The Unofficial Recreation Area/San Jose Creek Confluence. Pass the first of many spillways that stair-step their way up the river (1.4). Small children slide down the rounded portion of the spillway into a holding basin below, and even a swimming dog might be seen. In 0.4 mile, pass Peck Road and a second spillway with a large pool backed up behind it. (There are gas stations and restaurants not too far from the river at this exit.)

The trail passes under the Pomona Freeway (2.0) and reaches the third spillway, which usually has some fishermen and a few swimmers using the upstream water pool. In 0.3 mile, pass the confluence with San Jose Creek and one of the most well-used of the unofficial recreation spots on the river. There are inner-tube riders, swimmers, fishermen, horses with riders crossing the river, and even some off-road bicycling.

The Middle Segment. At (2.7), there is a small rodeo ring where bikers have a free chance to watch the trainers work with horses or, with luck, to watch a mini-rodeo. Just beyond is one of the highest spillways on the river (about ten feet high) with a holding basin stretched across the river on the downstream side. The route continues alongside residential areas, passes the Mountain View High School athletic field (3.9), and reaches Valley Boulevard (4.1). There is a small bike rest stop here with a simple pipe water fountain. On a clear day, there is a striking view into the San Gabriel Mountains from this point.

The bikepath travels under a railroad bridge and later meets the Walnut Creek junction (4.3). From this point north, the water level drops significantly and the riverbed is much less interesting. At this junction, to the left (west) of the trail, there is a corral that holds Brahma bulls and a buffalo. Continuing onward, the bikeway passes the San Bernardino Freeway (4.7) and meets another biker rest area at Ramona Boulevard (5.6).

The Gravel Pits. At (6.5), the route passes the first of several large gravel dredging operations (to the right). In 0.2 mile, the trip passes Lower Azusa Road. There is a large, open, water-filled gravel pit to the left (west) (5.9), followed by a "granddaddy" gravel pit across the river to the right (6.4). Also there are several highly visible above-ground mining operations.

Santa Fe Dam. At (7.5), the path crosses under the San Gabriel River Freeway and points cyclists directly into the Santa Fe Dam face. The route passes a power station (7.0), Live Oak Avenue, and appears to dead-end at Arrow Highway (8.8). Cross that street, follow the signed path left, and bike to the base of the dam. Pass through the walker/biker entry opening in the fence and pump a short but steep grade to the top of the dam (9.2).

From the top of the dam in winter, there are views into the San Gabriel Mountains that are awe-inspiring, along with views into the San Jose Hills to the southeast and Puente Hills to the south. The cities of the foothills are spread out all the way to the western horizon.

There is a paved trail left (northwest) that ends just below the west levee terminus. (See the last of the "Santa Fe Dam Excursions" below.) However, our route goes right and continues another 1.9 miles along the top of the dam, providing other fine views, including those down into the Santa Fe Dam Recreation Area. The dam trail descends and ends at the bike trail access gate. The route then proceeds 0.2 mile further to the auto access road into the recreation area (Orange Avenue which is named Azusa Canyon Road south of Arrow Highway). The mileage at this point is (11.4).

Santa Fe Dam Recreation Area. The recreation area behind the dam is a charmer. To get there, make a hard left onto the automobile roadway access just downhill of the auto pay gate. There are bikepaths and a low-speed-limit, lightly traveled paved road that can be linked into a couple of miles more biking. The entire park is built alongside a lake and comes equipped with water and restrooms, picnic areas, a swimming area with a sand beach, playgrounds, fire pits, shaded pagodas (group area at the western end of the lake), boat rental, and a snack bar.

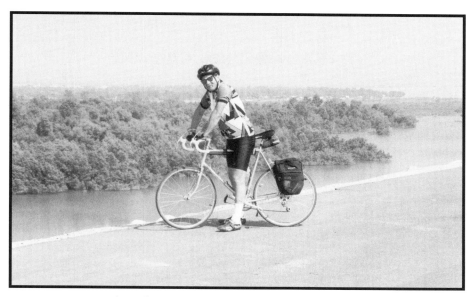

Atop Santa Fe Dam with recreation area below

There are also bicycle roadways beyond the west end of the lake. In periods of low water, fat-tire bikes can be ridden through this maze of dirt trails to the westside dam levee access. (See the last of the "Santa Fe Dam Excursions" below.)

Santa Fe Dam Excursions. At the west base of the dam, just before beginning the climb to the top, there is a trail heading north and west to a tunnel under the San Gabriel River Freeway. On the west side of the freeway, there is a "T" junction. The south fork transitions to dirt in 0.5 mile and follows the Buena Vista Channel west almost to Buena Vista Street; a fence prevents access to that street. The north fork climbs a small levee in 0.8 mile to San Gabriel River Freeway level, then drops down to the Santa Fe Dam Flying Area (model airplanes). Climbing to the opposite levee leads to a ride extension of 0.5 mile, paralleling Duarte Road, to the levee's terminus. At the terminus, the packed-dirt road leading west toward Duarte Road is blocked by the City of Duarte Maintenance Yard, while the eastern path leads into the dirt areas of the main flood control basin. The path south parallels the freeway and loops back to the incoming route in 0.5 mile. The north fork route totals three miles (round trip).

Another choice, once on top of the Santa Fe Dam, is to bike northwest and explore the one-mile west levee, which parallels the San Gabriel River Freeway. The outlet is a downhill into the main flood control basin behind the dam. There are dirt paths winding over the entire basin, including routes leading across to the lakeside recreation area or under the San Gabriel River Freeway and Foothill Freeway. (Do not attempt to bike in this area during rainy periods!)

CONNECTING TRIPS: 1) Continuation with the southbound San Gabriel River Trail to Wilderness Park (Trip #22C) - from the Four Corners Trail Intersection, head south and over the Whittier Narrows Dam; 2) continuation with the northbound San Gabriel River Trail to San Gabriel Canyon (Trip #22E) - at the recreation area auto access, bike north (nearly straight ahead); follow the trail signs.

TRIP #22E - SAN GABRIEL RIVER: SANTA FE DAM TO SAN GABRIEL CANYON

GENERAL LOCATION: Irwindale, Azusa

LEVEL OF DIFFICULTY: One way - easy; up and back - moderate
Distance - 7.5 miles (one way)
Elevation gain - essentially flat (single
steep grade at Santa Fe Dam)

HIGHLIGHTS: This 100 percent Class I trip starts downstream of the Santa Fe Dam, then climbs onto and follows the dam levee. The route cruises from the dam upstream to the end of the San Gabriel River Trail at the Angeles National Forest Information Center in San Gabriel Canyon. Along the way, the path traverses the Santa Fe Dam Nature Area which has a natural river-bottom cactus garden. There are spectacular close-up views of the foothills and surrounding mountains. These views are absolutely great after a cold winter storm. The stretch north of the dam is little used and makes a good workout trip.

TRAILHEAD: From the San Gabriel River Freeway, exit east on Live Oak Avenue and continue 0.9 mile to the junction with Arrow Highway, making a U-turn onto Arrow Highway. Drive in the reverse direction about 0.8 mile to free parking near the dam outlet.

An option is to use pay parking in the Santa Fe Dam Recreation Area. This is particularly useful if you wish to avoid riding up onto the dam and want to start from the recreation area. Exit on Live Oak Avenue (east), as above, but continue one mile past the junction of Live Oak Avenue and Arrow Highway. Turn left (north) at the Recreation Park entrance at Orange Avenue (named Azusa Canyon Road to the south).

TRIP DESCRIPTION: **Santa Fe Dam.** From the free parking area on Arrow Highway, pedal to the bike entry through the fence (to the west of the spillway near the dam base). Follow the bike trail signs and pump the steep roadway to the top of the dam (0.2). At the top, there is a great 360-degree view. Most prominent are the San Gabriel Mountains to the north and the San Jose Hills and Puente Hills to the southeast and south, respectively. The view into the mountains is a real "heart grabber" when the snow level is down to low elevations and the sky is clear.

There is a paved trail left (northwest) that ends just below the west levee terminus. (See the last of the "Santa Fe Dam Excursions" in Trip #22D.) However, our route goes right and continues another 1.9 miles along the top of the dam, providing other fine views, including those down into the Santa Fe Dam Recreation Area. The dam trail descends and ends at the bike trail access gate. The route then proceeds 0.2 mile further to the auto access road into the recreation area (Orange Avenue which is named Azusa Canyon Road south of Arrow Highway). The mileage at this point is (2.3).

TRIP #22E - SAN GABRIEL RIVER:
SANTA FE DAM TO SAN GABRIEL CANYON

Head downhill and turn sharply left below the pay gate to visit the developed park (southern) section of the Santa Fe Dam Recreation Area (see Trip #22D). Our route follows the signed bike route and keeps straight ahead.

Northern Santa Fe Dam Recreation Area. Follow the road to the dead-end at a little walled parklike area (2.8). Turn left and continue tracking the well-marked road 0.2 mile until it turns right (north) again. In 0.2 mile, reach the Wildlife Interpretive Center which has both picnic and tent camping areas near the roadway intersection (3.2). Turn left again and pedal a few hundred feet to the ranger station. There are two bike route options at this point, plus marked walking/nature trails which tour the wildlife area. All routes head west and shortly meet an old north-south asphalt road. Follow the bike trail marker and turn right (north) on that old road.

The roadway passes through an interesting ecological area which is surrounded by a wide variety of cacti. At (3.8), reach the top of a small rise; from here, there is a nice view that includes a good look at the surrounding bottomland and the back side of the Santa Fe Dam, and a view north to the Foothill Freeway. In 0.4 mile, the path returns to the San Gabriel River and passes under the Foothill Freeway just beyond (4.3).

The Gravel Pits. At (4.8), pass a trans-river passenger cable car. In 0.1 mile, pass Huntington Drive/Foothill Boulevard. Next is the Santa Fe Equestrian Staging Area which has restrooms and water (5.2). There is a large above-ground gravel mining/processing works in the background. The riverbed is boulder- and brush-filled with a low spillway breaking the continuity of the scene every half mile or more.

At (5.5), the path goes by an old closed-off railroad bridge. There is a residential area across the river, with the homes continuing up into the nearby foothills. There are more gravel operations along the roadway to the right (east), with one sand and gravel operation lying right next to the trail (6.1). The route also passes a large water-filled gravel pit (6.5).

San Gabriel Canyon Entrance. The trail heads into a progressively more well-defined canyon environment. At (6.8), the route passes Fish Canyon in the hills to the left (west). There is an exquisite series of waterfalls (in winter), several miles back into the canyon, called Fish Falls. (Sorry, this is hiking country only.) At this point on the bike trail, there is also a firing range, the San Gabriel Valley Gun Club. The hills echo the sounds, providing a "Gunfight at the O.K. Corral" aura.

Just beyond, the trail dead-ends at a fence (7.5). A small trail to the right leads to Highway 39 and the Angeles National Forest Ranger Station. There is water and parking here if you want to start from this direction or to use this as a pickup or turnaround point.

CONNECTING TRIPS: 1) Continuation with the San Gabriel River Trail south to Whittier Narrows (Trip #22D) - cross Arrow Highway and bike east a few hundred feet (in front of the spillway); 2) continuation with a very strenuous Class X "gut-buster" up San Gabriel Canyon Road - we observed a few hearty bikers working their way up the several miles of continuous steep grade; 3) connection with the Duarte Bikeway (Trip #64) - exit at Huntington Drive/Foothill Boulevard and bike west a quarter mile to Las Lomas Road.

TRIP #23 - SAN GABRIEL, RIO HONDO, LOS ANGELES RIVERS LOOP: "THE BIG BANANA"

<u>GENERAL LOCATION</u>: Long Beach - San Gabriel Canyon -
Peck Water Conservation Park - Long Beach

<u>LEVEL OF DIFFICULTY</u>: Loop - very strenuous
Distance - 83.5 miles
Elevation gain - essentially flat (three short
steep dam climbs)

<u>HIGHLIGHTS</u>: This trip starts from the Pacific Ocean, visits the foothills of the San Gabriel Mountains, and returns to the ocean in one big loop. The route tours the San Gabriel, Rio Hondo, and Los Angeles rivers. Along the way are some of the finest parks and recreation areas in southern California, e.g., El Dorado Park, Whittier Narrows and Santa Fe Dam recreation areas, and John Anson Ford Park.

Portions of the route are little known to most Angelenos (and Orange "Countians"), such as the San Gabriel Canyon segment and the Upper Rio Hondo segment, including the Peck Water Conservation Park (reservoir). Taken soon after a cool, wet winter storm, this may be the most scenic and inspiring trip in our book!

<u>TRAILHEAD</u>: Refer to the parking instructions for Trip #14.

Bring 2-3 filled water bottles or load up at the trailhead. There are many water stops along the way, but having plenty lessens the number of required stops. Start this trip in the early morning to lessen the effect of headwinds coming off the ocean and to minimize sun exposure.

<u>TRIP DESCRIPTION</u>: The trip description will detail only the new or confusing portions of the loop. The tour starts at Shoreline Park (Trip #14), travels to Marina Drive in Seal Beach (Trip #15), proceeds north up the San Gabriel River (Trip #22), transitions west to Peck Water Conservation Park and returns to Long Beach via the Rio Hondo and Los Angeles rivers (Trips #19 and #20, respectively).

Long Beach to Seal Beach. (Refer to Trip #14.) Exit the Shoreline Village parking area and follow the parking access road that parallels Shoreline Drive. Bike past the overhead walkway along the perimeter of Shoreline Village and turn left at the street's end (0.3). Pedal through the easternmost village parking area on roadway which parallels Shoreline Drive. At the end of the parking lot, follow the bikepath north toward the Villa Riviera Hotel (0.8).

At the first bikepath junction just beyond, turn right and follow the Class I oceanfront path 3.0 miles to its end at Bay Shore Drive. Follow Bay Shore Drive 0.3 mile and turn right on Second Street (see Trip #15 map) (4.1). Cross the two Naples Island bridges and, just past the second bridge, turn right on Marina Drive (5.2). Follow Marina Drive around the marina periphery and, near the Seaport Village entry, turn left (6.3). Just across the bridge (southeast side) is the bike entry to the San Gabriel River (see Trip #22A) (6.4).

TRIP #23 - SAN GABRIEL, RIO HONDO, LOS ANGELES RIVERS LOOP: "THE BIG BANANA"

San Gabriel River. Pedal 3.9 miles to the "Y" river channel junction. Cross the bike/pedestrian bridge across the river (see Trip #22A). Bike along the east levee of the San Gabriel River and make two short passages along the edge of El Dorado Park (13.0). The next major decision point is about 14 miles down the road, where the path crosses to the west side of the river at the San Gabriel River Parkway (see Trips #22B, #22C) (27.1).

The path leads to the top of the dam, then downhill to the Four Corners Trail Intersection (28.2). Turn right (east) and, on the west levee, follow the river to the river outlet at the Santa Fe Dam (36.5). Cross Arrow Highway, turn left (west), and then follow the trail up to and across the dam top. The outlet trail passes the automobile entry fee station, heads downhill, and continues straight ahead (north) (see Trip #22D) (39.1).

The junction to the left enters the Santa Fe Dam Recreation Area. Follow the bike trail signs and rejoin the river on the east levee (41.0). Bike 3.3 miles to the trail's end at the entry to San Gabriel Canyon (see Trip #22E). Reverse the route and return to the base of Santa Fe Dam at Arrow Highway (51.8).

Santa Fe Dam - Peck Water Conservation Park. Bike west on Arrow Highway/Live Oak Avenue 1.9 miles to Peck Road. Turn left (south), ride 0.8 mile on Peck Road, and turn right at Rio Hondo Parkway into Peck Road Water Conservation Park (54.5). Pedal to the south end of the parking lot and follow the small path on the west side of the reservoir. At the spillway, there is a sign noting the start of the formal bike trail (54.9).

Rio Hondo and Los Angeles River. Follow the Upper Rio Hondo bikeway 5.2 miles to Whittier Narrows Recreation Area "A" (see Trip #19). Pedal to the very south end of the recreation area and find the trail that is almost right next to and parallels the Pomona Freeway. Follow the route under the freeway to the point where it leaves the river at San Gabriel Boulevard (61.8).

Ride west on the bridge over the river and bike 0.3 mile to Lincoln Avenue. Turn left, then left immediately again into the bike trail entry. Follow the path 0.6 mile to a point at the western edge of the west levee of the Whittier Narrows Dam (next to Lincoln Avenue). This is the official beginning of the Lario Trail (Trip #20) (62.7).

Cruise east across the top of the dam for 0.4 mile and take the path down the south side (spillway side) of the dam (see Trips #20A and #20B). Pedal 5.4 miles on the west levee of the Rio Hondo and cross the river on a bike bridge near John Anson Ford Park (68.2). The route reaches the Los Angeles River confluence at (70.9).

Continue on the east levee of the Los Angeles River into Long Beach, to the end of the Lario Trail (82.6). With the recently constructed bike undercrossings in this segment of the trip, bikers no longer have to leave the river path in high water conditions (as used to be the case at Rosecrans Avenue, Compton Avenue, Alondra Boulevard, and Del Amo Boulevard). Just past the signed end of the Lario Trail, ride through the parking lot and follow the shoreline around the Queensway (Catalina Cruise) Landing and under the Queensway Bridge. Hug the Los Angeles River shoreline, then turn left at Pierpoint Landing. Follow the walking/biking trail on the north side of Rainbow Harbor and return to the starting point (83.5).

"Small Banana" Trip Option. For a 50-mile version of this trip, park at De Forest Avenue just north of Willow Street (see Trip #20B map) and proceed over Signal Hill to the San Gabriel River. Follow the river trail north to the Whittier Narrows Dam and then to the Four Corners Trail Intersection. Take the left (west) trail and bike to Durfee Avenue/San Gabriel Boulevard. Turn left, then left again (south) at Lincoln Avenue (Trip #26 map) and join the Lario Trail along the Rio Hondo. Cruise the Rio Hondo and Los Angeles rivers back to the starting point (Trips #19, #20A and #20B).

CONNECTING TRIPS: See individual trip writeups.

TRIP #24 - COYOTE CREEK TRAIL

GENERAL LOCATION: Long Beach, Seal Beach, Cerritos, La Mirada

LEVEL OF DIFFICULTY: One way - easy; up and back - moderate
Distance - 14.0 miles (one way)
Elevation gain - essentially flat

HIGHLIGHTS: Another of the river trails, this is a 99.44 percent pure Class I route. It starts at the scenic lower section of the San Gabriel River outlet near the Long Beach Marina and proceeds to the Coyote Creek junction. The Coyote Creek path is well maintained but lightly used. The 10.1-mile Coyote Creek section is not highly scenic, unless one enjoys "window shopping" into backyards of the adjoining homes and apartments. It is a fine workout bikeway, however. The trip passes alongside Cerritos Regional County Park, which is a convenient and pleasant rest point near the center of the Coyote Creek segment. Beyond the Artesia Freeway is the 2.5-mile (most recent) extension through a commercial area to a terminus at Foster Road. A short ride from here leads to shaded Frontier Park.

TRAILHEAD: Free public parking is available on Marina Drive in Long Beach or along First Street in Seal Beach. From Pacific Coast Highway (PCH) in Seal Beach, turn west on Marina Drive (2-3 blocks from Main Street in Seal Beach) and continue roughly half a mile to First Street. In another quarter mile, cross the San Gabriel River and continue a short distance along the marina for parking. The trailhead is located at Marina Drive at the east end of the bridge over the San Gabriel River (across from Seaport Village).

An alternate start point is Edison Park, which starts cyclists much nearer to the Coyote Creek/San Gabriel River junction. From Studebaker Road in southeastern Long Beach, turn east on E. Ninth Street and right (south) immediately after. Continue on that unnamed road to its end at College Park Drive, cross the San Gabriel River, and turn left just beyond into the park. Carefully observe posted parking signs.

Bikers should have a filled water bottle since the trip is waterless up to Cerritos Regional Park. Riders starting at Seal Beach can cycle south about 0.3 mile from the trailhead to use restrooms at the beach. The side trip may also serve as a very pleasant scenic diversion. After the ride, Seaport Village at the marina edge may serve as a nice dining spot, watering hole, or place to shop.

TRIP DESCRIPTION: **The Scenic Lower Segment.** (See Trip #22A for a map of this segment.) The first part of the trip provides views of boaters, water skiers, and an interestingly developed shoreline. The natural river basin then passes the PCH access, the Westminster Avenue entry (1.2), and the Haynes Steam Plant (electricity generation). At (2.2), a small Class I diversion path leads off to the east along a 1.2-mile shaded route to Seal Beach Boulevard. In this stretch of the river, up to the concrete portion at about (3.5), one has views of a large bird population that includes pelicans, egrets, and the ever-present seagulls. The path goes under the Garden Grove Freeway

TRIP #24 - COYOTE CREEK TRAIL

(2.3), passes Edison Park, and then ducks below the San Diego Freeway (3.5). In this portion of the path, there are many "freeway orchards," those freeway-locked areas under the power poles, which are used for growing containerized plants.

Coyote Creek. At (3.9), a marked bridge over the river takes bikers to the connecting portion of the San Gabriel River Bike Trail (Trip #22A). However, at this junction, our route continues along the east side (stay to the right) of the channel and passes the Katella Avenue entry, the San Gabriel River Freeway, and the Cerritos Avenue access (5.2). Nearby, the channel junctions to the north (no easy access at this junction was found), although our reference route stays along the east side of the channel. Two additional small channel junctions to the east are encountered at (5.6) and (7.3). However, both junctions are closed off by locked gates, and the main Coyote Creek path crosses those junctions via small overpasses. The Los Alamitos access is at about (5.6). Pass Ball Road, a small walking-only bridge across the creek at (6.3), and Lincoln Avenue, and bike to Crescent Avenue/Centralia Street.

Exit the bikeway and cross to the west bank. Continue 0.5 mile to La Palma Avenue/Del Amo Boulevard and pass alongside Cerritos County Regional Park. There is water within sight of the bikeway plus a park complete with restrooms, recreational fields, and a limited amount of shade. Pedal along a residential area and pass under Moody Street/Carmenita Road, then South Street/Orangethorpe Avenue (note the fast food establishments and gas stations to the west) (9.2).

In a short distance, bike under the Artesia Freeway and pass alongside residential developments (with scattered shade trees), then cycle past Walker Street/Marquardt Avenue. The path veers left (due north) along the La Cañada Verde Creek fork (the main Coyote Creek fork branches northeast) and continues another 0.4 mile to Artesia Boulevard. The channel dips under the Santa Ana Freeway and Alondra Boulevard, on a recently opened 2.5-mile path extension through a strictly commercial zone. The bikeway passes alongside the Santa Fe Springs Drive-in Theater (12.3), then beelines 1.7 miles to its end at Foster Road.

A short ride east on Foster Road leads to Marquardt Avenue and Frontier Park. The park has shade (a rare commodity on the ride), water, restrooms, a children's play area, and barbecue facilities.

CONNECTING TRIPS: 1) Continuation/connection to the lower and middle portions of the San Gabriel River tour (Trips #22A and #22B) - take major access streets west and cross the San Gabriel River Freeway, noting that the distance between Coyote Creek and the San Gabriel River increases the further north one goes on Coyote Creek; 2) connectors to the lower portion of this trip along the San Gabriel River are described in Trip #22A.

TRIP #25 - WEST FORK, SAN GABRIEL RIVER

<u>**GENERAL LOCATION**</u>: Angeles National Forest

<u>**LEVEL OF DIFFICULTY**</u>: **Glenn Camp Loop**: Up and back - moderate
Distance - 13.4 miles (up and back)
Elevation gain - 450 feet

Cogswell Reservoir Loop: Up and back - strenuous
Distance - 15.0 miles (up and back)
Elevation gain - 800 feet (sheer grade up to reservoir)

<u>**HIGHLIGHTS**</u>: This is one of the most natural scenic rides in our book. This trip follows the meandering West Fork of the San Gabriel River from Highway 39 to Cogswell Reservoir. The route is through a forested canyon along a well-maintained service road and is Class I since it is closed to public traffic. The views of the surrounding canyon, connecting streams, and the abundant floral and wildlife are wonderful. There are plenty of good fishing and swimming holes along the way.

After light rains, there are spectacular small waterfalls over the surrounding bluffs, which fall near the trail; conversely, this trail is dangerous immediately after heavy rains. There are two trip options, one to the mostly flat trip to Glenn Trail Camp, the other a trip extension up the sheer grade to Cogswell Reservoir.

<u>**TRAILHEAD**</u>: Exit the Foothill Freeway at Azusa Avenue (Highway 39) and head north 8.5 miles to the road junction at the north end of the San Gabriel Reservoir. Stay to the left and drive up Highway 39 about 1.5 miles. Cross the bridge over the river. To the left (west), there is a public parking area.

There are public facilities here, so fill up with water (two water bottles if you plan to "dawdle"). Since there are sometimes bacterial problems with the river water in the local mountains, it must be filtered, chemically treated, or boiled prior to ingestion.

<u>**TRIP DESCRIPTION**</u>: **Trail Entry to Bear Creek.** Recross the bridge to meet West Fork Road and lift your bike over the entrance guard (motorized bikes and public cars are not allowed). Begin with a moderate uphill along an open section of the river. In a short distance, there are several small water runoffs that cross the road. (These little dribbles pass a lot of water after a heavy rain!) Pass a small waterfall which is across the river (0.5), then cross a small bridge over the San Gabriel River at the inviting junction with Bear Creek (0.9). (A short hike up Bear Creek leads to some very scenic territory, as well as a "private" camping spot that we call "Pete's Island.") From this bikepath junction, most of the journey is beside a lush tree-lined river with sporadic tree cover and a canyon wall to filter the sun.

At (1.5), recross the river and enter the West Fork Wild Trout Area (no bait, no barbs on hooks, and fish must be thrown back). In one mile (2.6), pass alongside a steep bluff, through a large open area. Another steep bluff is passed in one more mile (3.5), with two small waterfalls flowing over the bluffs. The most westward waterfall cascades down a series of stair steps before dropping within feet of the trail. Just beyond, there is an area where the road is periodically washed out for a few hundred feet;

TRIP #25 - WEST FORK, SAN GABRIEL RIVER

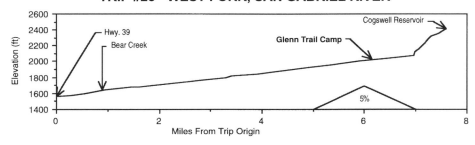

a look up the fractured cliff hints that, during heavy rains, the water is funneled down the cliff side at a frightening rate!

Glenn Trail Camp. In one-half mile, the route enters an area where high canyon walls enclose the trail for about one-half mile. Just beyond, there is a small creek which spills across the road and a solitary, private residence (4.5). Follow the meandering river and cross a small bridge over an unnamed creek (5.7). In one-half mile, reach Glenn Trail Camp, a pleasant rest stop. It has a shaded section near the river and an open field across the trail with picnic tables, fire stoves, and plenty of spots to pitch tents (permits required).

Cogswell Reservoir. Returning to the parking area from this point results in a 13.4-mile round trip. An option is to bike 0.4 mile to the bottom of a steep road which leads up to Cogswell Reservoir (6.6). This road remains as steep as it looks at this point, rising roughly 350 feet in the remaining 0.7 mile up to the spillway. This is steep for walking, and exhaustive for biking for all except those bikers in excellent condition.

On the way up, pass a heliport and a private residential area (quiet please, as a courtesy). Once at the spillway, the way left leads steeply up West Fork, Red Box Road. There is a 360-degree vista from the area just past the junction, with views back down into the river canyon and the reservoir. The trail crosses the dam and ends at the opposite side (7.5) for all but those with mountain bikes. A return to the trailhead from here results in a round-trip distance of 15 miles.

CONNECTING TRIPS: Recreational mountain bikers should try the riverbed recreation area just one-half mile south of this trip origin. For the truly serious mountain biker, continue from the Cogswell Dam up the West Fork, Red Box Road. Another serious option is to head back into the East Fork, San Gabriel River, from the Eldoradoville Ranger Station. For the latter option, check first with the rangers regarding river conditions.

West Fork, near Glenn Trail Camp

INLAND

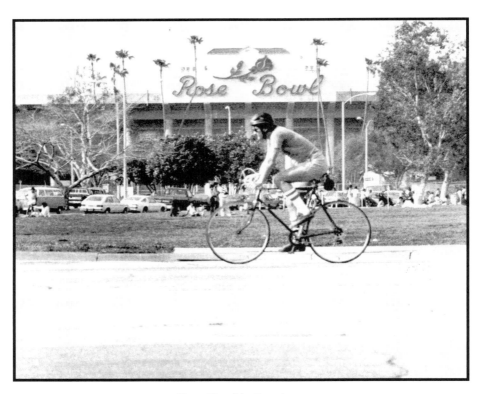

Rose Bowl in Pasadena

TRIP #26 - WHITTIER NARROWS/LEGG LAKE TRAIL

GENERAL LOCATION: Montebello, Pico Rivera (Whittier Narrows Recreation Area)

LEVEL OF DIFFICULTY: Round trip - easy
Distance - 11.2 miles (round trip)
Elevation gain - essentially flat

HIGHLIGHTS: This fiendishly clever route allows exploration of nearly the entire Whittier Narrows Recreational Area on Class I bikeways. It includes a tour around Legg Lake, a visit to the bottomland behind Whittier Narrows Dam, a cruise along the Rio Hondo, and a "secret passage" under the Pomona Freeway to the northern recreation and picnic area. This is a family special that involves crossing only one street and one intersection. Other options are to ride up the east levee of the Whittier Narrows Dam and connect up with the San Gabriel River.

TRAILHEAD: From the Pomona Freeway, exit at Rosemead Boulevard south, travel 0.8 mile to San Gabriel Boulevard/Durfee Avenue, and turn left (east). Drive on Durfee Avenue 0.6 mile and turn left into the Legg Lake pay parking area. Bring four quarters for parking.

The route has plenty of water, so bring a light supply. Food stands are open on weekends at Legg Lake. Bring some bug spray for gnats if you plant to picnic near the lake in the summer.

TRIP DESCRIPTION: **Legg Lake.** The entire lake trip is on well-compacted dirt. It is easy to ride with any type of bike, but some care is needed in a couple of fine-gravel and wet areas. Leave the parking lot and head north toward the lake. Veer right for the counterclockwise tour. Pass a roofed picnic area and a little spillway into the lake, and visit a giant sandy play area with a 10-foot-high cement octopus (0.2).

Shortly the route passes a food stand and boat rental area. There are numerous ducks and geese in the area. Further on, pass a "rocket" playground and some lovely shaded picnic sites situated at the lake edge (0.4). Just beyond is a trail junction. Diverting to the left leads to a bridge crossing between the northernmost lake and the main lake. Our trip heads right and passes around the north lake, through the green, natural, tree-covered surroundings. On this southbound segment, the path meets the other end of the junction route between the lakes at (1.6). This area is one of the fishermen's favorites.

In 0.1 mile, pass a spillway near the western end of the lake, one of the few areas of the lake where motor traffic is visible. Shortly we passed a group of ducks sleeping on the grass six feet away from a busy fisherman. The route turns eastward later and roughly parallels Durfee Avenue (2.1). The final stretch continues to wind along the lake edge and returns to the trip origin in another half mile (2.6).

Dam Bottomland/Wildlife Sanctuary. Leave the parking area and cross Durfee Avenue a few hundred feet to the west. Pass through a signed gate and pedal on a small asphalt road through an area surrounded by bushes, plants, trees, and brush.

TRIP #26 - WHITTIER NARROWS/LEGG LAKE TRAIL

There are many nature exhibits and animals in this area. In a couple of hundred yards, the route reaches a "T" junction just beyond a small water channel. The asphalt trail left heads east towards (but skirts) the Whittier Narrows Nature Center. Our reference route goes to the right and continues about 0.3 mile through lush greenery to the "Center of the Universe," commonly known as the "Four Corners Trail Intersection." This is a pleasant, open area with a nice view of the back side of the Whittier Narrows Dam.

At that intersection, the route to the left (east) meets the San Gabriel River and heads north, while the route dead ahead (south) heads towards the dam and leads to the south San Gabriel River segment. Our route turns right (west) and roughly parallels the dam, passing alongside some very interesting vine-covered trees. In half a mile, there is a view back into Rose Hills (3.7). The trail crosses a small footbridge over a wash and reaches Durfee Avenue in 0.1 mile. The trip remains Class I and continues 0.2 mile to the intersection of Rosemead Boulevard and Durfee Avenue/San Gabriel Boulevard.

Upper Rio Hondo Trail Segment. Cross the intersection to the north side and bike on Class I San Gabriel Boulevard until reaching the bike entry to the Rio Hondo (just before the bridge and on the east levee) (4.1). Ride along a pleasant, natural, tree- and brush-lined stretch of the river. The growth is so dense that the river view does not open up for a quarter mile or so. Pass under the Pomona Freeway (5.0), then parallel that freeway at road level for 0.6 mile before reaching the northern recreation area entrance.

Whittier Narrows Recreation Area "A." The bike entrance to the park is at its south end. Cyclists can cruise both the bikeways and slow-moving, lightly traveled roads within the recreation area. The park dimensions are roughly one-half mile, north-south, and one-fourth mile, east-west, providing plenty of room to roam. The park is moderately treed and has restrooms and water, picnic areas, recreation fields, model airplane flying areas, and model car racing areas. This recreation area, combined with Legg Lake, is certainly on par with recreation/biking areas such as El Dorado Regional Park in Los Angeles County (Trip #16) and Mile Square Park and Irvine Regional Park in Orange County.

CONNECTING TRIPS: 1) Continuation with the Upper Rio Hondo Bike Trail (Trip #19) - bike north on the west park edge on Loma Avenue for the north-heading segment (the south-heading segment of Trip #19 is part of this trip); 2) connection with the San Gabriel River Bike Trail (Trips #22C and #22D) - from the Four Corners Trail Intersection, pedal east to reach the north-heading segment or south toward the dam to meet with the south-heading segment.

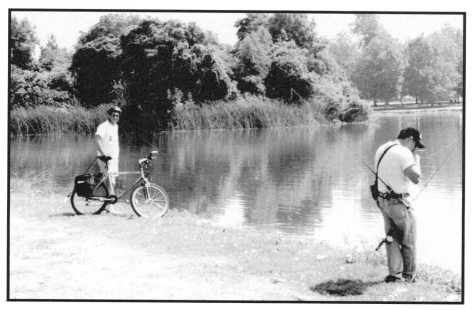

West Shore of Legg Lake (Susan Cohen photo)

TRIP #27 - HACIENDA HEIGHTS LOOP

GENERAL LOCATION: Hacienda Heights

LEVEL OF DIFFICULTY: Loop trip - moderate
                                      Distance - 5.6 miles
                                      Elevation gain - periodic moderate grades

HIGHLIGHTS: This loop trip around the eastern end of Hacienda Heights combines a Class II tour along Colima Road and a Class III tour through local residential areas. There are some views into the San Gabriel Mountains on the route's western segment on Stimson Avenue. Additional trip highlights are Stimson County Park and the Puente Hills Mall. The route is well laid out and well marked and does contain one workout upgrade leading to the southwestern point near Colima Road and Stimson Avenue.

TRAILHEAD: Exit the Pomona Freeway south at Azusa Avenue and turn left into the Puente Hills Mall. The Park and Ride area is near Pepper Brook Way at Azusa Avenue.

Bring a light water supply. The Puente Hills Mall is a nice place for snacks after your tour. Stimson County Park also has water, and so do the public schools on the route, if you're willing to search for it (during non-school periods).

TRIP DESCRIPTION: **Colima Road and the Trip Crest.** Exit the parking area and head south on Azusa Avenue 0.1 mile to Colima Road. A left turn here leads to Schabarum Regional Park (formerly Otterbein Park), where there is some fun hill hiking and possible off-road bicycling (balloon-tire bikes). Our route turns right and cruises down a Class II bikeway next to some heavy car traffic. There are hills to the left (south) with a light mix of commercial and residential development. The route starts uphill (0.4), passing Countrywood Road (0.6) and Dawn Haven Road/Halliburton Road (0.8). The upgrade continues and steepens into a workout grade just before reaching the crest near Punta Del Este (1.4). This is the highest elevation point of the trip.

Stimson Avenue and Stimson Park. The path heads back downhill and flattens out near Stimson Avenue (1.8). Turn right and pedal downhill on a Class II bikepath with some views into the San Gabriel Mountains. There is a long-running downgrade with hillsides to the left and residential areas at road level to the right. The downhill runout continues past La Monde Street (2.6) and flattens out in the vicinity of Stimson Park (3.2). There are restrooms, water, recreation areas, and some shaded, grassy rest spots in this pleasant park.

The Residential Circuit. In 0.2 mile and before reaching the Pomona Freeway, turn right at Garo Street. Note that the marked bikepath also continues down Stimson Avenue. This segment of bikeway is Class III in light-traffic, residential areas. The route turns right (south) at Glenelder Avenue (3.8) and left at Cedarlane Drive in front of a school. Bike down this street and turn right at Fieldgate Avenue (4.2).

Shortly after, turn left on Wedgeworth Drive and pass in front of Wilson High School. There are some nice views into the local hills to the north in this area. The route continues through residential areas past another school and crosses a small creek just beyond (5.1). In 0.3 mile, turn left on Pepper Brook Way, cross Azusa Avenue, and return to the loop starting point (5.6).

TRIP #27 - HACIENDA HEIGHTS LOOP

CONNECTING TRIPS: There are numerous local spurs off the described route. 1) Connection with the Diamond Bar Tour (Trip #42) - from Azusa Avenue and Colima Road, proceed east 3.5 miles on the latter road to Brea Canyon Cutoff; and 2) connection with the San Jose Hills ride (Trip #43) - from Azusa Avenue and Colima Road, cycle east 2.5 miles on the latter road to Nogales Street, turn left (north), and bike another mile to Valley Boulevard.

TRIP #28 - SAN MARINO TOUR

GENERAL LOCATION: San Marino

LEVEL OF DIFFICULTY: Loop - moderate (hill loop)
Distance - 6.8 miles (hill loop)
Elevation gain - periodic moderate grades

HIGHLIGHTS: This stately San Marino tour is not a bikepath or bike route. It is entirely Class X, but is too good not to include. Most of the route is through residential neighborhoods on lightly traveled, mainly wide roadways. There are some hills in the first 1.5 miles, but the biking is primarily flat or downhill beyond that point. The tour highlights stately mansions and well-groomed, upscale neighborhoods. Our route passes by the Huntington Library and Botanical Gardens and provides a selected number of view points into the hills and San Gabriel Mountains.

TRAILHEAD: From the Foothill Freeway, exit south on Sierra Madre Boulevard. Drive 2.5 miles and turn right (west) on Huntington Drive. Continue about one-half mile and turn right at Saint Albans Road. Drive one-half mile further and park on the street near the Lacy Park entrance; be very careful to observe the local parking laws. Note that the park is not open on weekends.

From the San Bernardino Freeway, exit north at Atlantic Boulevard. Continue 2.5 miles to Huntington Drive, turn right (east), and drive 0.75 mile to Saint Albans Road. Turn left (north) and continue as described above.

From the Pasadena Freeway, exit south at Fair Oaks Avenue and drive a mile to Monterey Road. Turn left (east) and drive about 1.5 miles to Saint Albans Road. Turn left and continue several hundred yards to parking just outside Lacy Park.

Bring at least one filled water bottle. We didn't find any public water supply other than at Lacy Park. Also bring a roadmap as a backup, since this is not a marked bicycle path and it is easy to miss the described route.

TRIP DESCRIPTION: **The Hills.** The trip leaves Lacy Park and heads north on Saint Albans Road. In a short distance, turn right on Mill Lane and bike uphill to Virginia Road (0.2). There is an option to turn right here and take the less hilly optional route along Euston Road and Oxford Road. The prettier and more challenging route is to turn left and pedal uphill to Rosalind Road (0.4).

Turn right on Rosalind Road and bike through a rural setting where most residential grounds seem like mini-parks. The road winds downhill, junctions with one segment of Oak Grove Avenue, turns a hard left, and proceeds on another upgrade (0.7).

The route flattens out, then turns right on Orlando Road and proceeds uphill again (0.9). A refreshing downhill segment follows with a nice view into the San Gabriel Mountains. The bikepath continues through well-groomed residential areas, heads up another short upgrade (the last workout for a long time), and passes the Avondale Road loop (1.0-1.1). Cruise along the periphery of the Huntington Botanical Gardens, which shelters several magnificent set-back private residences.

TRIP #28 - SAN MARINO TOUR

Huntington Library and Botanical Gardens. The route proceeds past the Allen Avenue entry to the Huntington Library and Botanical Gardens (1.7). Biking is not allowed within the grounds; note also that the grounds are open only on afternoons, Tuesday through Sunday, with limited public access on Sunday. If you wish to see the Huntington Library, call first for special instructions.

Northeast San Marino. The level route crosses Oxford Road (1.9) and San Marino Avenue (2.0), and it dead-ends at Chester Avenue (2.2). Turn left at Chester Avenue, then right at Lombardy Road, and cruise downhill to Canterbury Road (2.3). Follow this street across busy Sierra Madre Boulevard and bike through a less shaded and less spectacular residential area to Palomar Road (3.1).

"The Southside." Proceed downhill to Huntington Drive, passing the beautiful Saints Felicitas and Perpetua Church (3.4). After crossing Huntington Drive, the route zig-zags a short distance to the left (east) to Bell Haven Road and proceeds downhill about 0.3 mile. South of Huntington Drive is the "other side of the tracks," where the mansions and oversized lots reduce to merely well-groomed, expensive residences. Turn right on Lorain Road (3.8) and bike on flat terrain through more residential areas past busy Del Mar Avenue (4.3), San Marino Avenue (4.7), Virginia Road (5.2), and Saint Albans Road (5.5). In 0.2 mile (just beyond Sherwood Road), veer left (not a hard left) and bike up a light upgrade on Chelsea Road.

The Estates. Cross Huntington Drive (6.0) and follow a short jig-jog to the right (north) to stay on Chelsea Road. Stop and admire some of the lovely estates. The road veers right and dead-ends at Old Mill Road (6.4). Turn left and bike up a mild grade to Mill Lane. The historic El Molino Viejo (The Olde Mill) is just up the hill on Old Mill Road. However, our route turns right on Mill Lane and continues 0.1 mile to Saint Albans Road. Turn right and return to the trip starting point (6.8).

CONNECTING TRIPS: There is an option to visit the San Gabriel Mission and Grapevine Park about two miles south of the West Drive/Lorain Road intersection. About 0.4 mile west of San Marino Boulevard on Lorain Road, turn left (south) on West Drive. West Drive becomes Mission Drive and leads directly into the mission. Connection with the Pasadena Phase I Biking System (Trip #31 map) - at Canterbury Road and Sierra Madre Boulevard, bike north on the latter street 0.75 mile to Del Mar Boulevard.

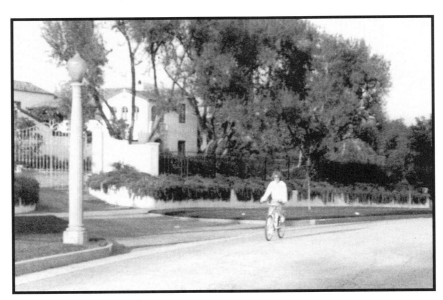

San Marino along Old Mill Road

TRIP #29 - ARROYO SECO BIKE TRAIL

<u>GENERAL LOCATION</u>: Montecito Heights

<u>LEVEL OF DIFFICULTY</u>: Loop - easy
　　　　　　　　　　Distance - 7.5 miles (includes excursion trips)
　　　　　　　　　　Elevation gain - 0.1-mile steep upgrade on trip excursion
　　　　　　　　　　(walk bikes)

<u>HIGHLIGHTS</u>: This bike trip combines an enjoyable ride along the Arroyo Seco and into two parks with excursion trips to several points of interest. The bikeway visits two separate sections of pleasant, shaded Arroyo Seco Park and touches the periphery of massive, hilly, and pretty Ernest E. Debs County Regional Park.

Excursions include visits to Heritage Square (restored Victorian mansions), the Lummis Home and Casa de Adobe (historical sites), and the Southwest Museum. Most of the route is on a marked bikeway (Class I or Class III), with some Class X on mostly lightly traveled roads. A large section of the Arroyo Seco path is flooded during winter storms.

Plan trip timing to be at Heritage Square in the afternoon if you can. Hours and dates of operation vary and should be checked ahead of time.

<u>TRAILHEAD</u>: Exit the Pasadena Freeway east on Avenue 43. Drive two blocks and turn left (north) at Homer Street. Drive to the end of Homer Street and park within the Montecito Heights Recreation Center parking lot.

Bring a light water supply. Water is available at the parks and some of the excursion sites.

<u>TRIP DESCRIPTION</u>: **Arroyo Seco Outward Bound.** Exit the parking lot at the west end and follow the tree-shaded path along the Arroyo Seco. Watch for broken glass near any sections that are around park picnic areas. In 0.3 mile, there is a junction (referred to as the "reference" junction later in the text), with the right-hand path heading up to Avenue 52 within the park. Pedal to the left and down into the Arroyo Seco riverbed. The route leaves the freeway's sounds here and drops into a quiet riverbed that is sheltered by trees for much of the trip. The Avenue 52 overcrossing is in 0.4 mile. In this area, there is a collection of varied types of graffiti that may classify as artwork, and there are some nifty views into the local hills.

The route passes Via Marisol (1.1), Avenue 60 (1.4), and the Avenue 60 on-ramp (1.5), with views of the distant foothills. In 0.1 mile, the path ducks under a railroad trestle, then an off-ramp, followed by the Avenue 64/Marmion Way overpass (1.9). In 0.2 mile, the bikepath climbs out of the river to Arroyo Seco Park where there is a shaded cul-de-sac, the Arroyo Horse Stables, and a nice picnic area with water to the right, about 0.2 mile further down the street (Arroyo Drive).

Arroyo Seco Return Route. Returning from the picnic area, the route backtracks along the Arroyo Seco to the Avenue 60 overpass (3.2). Just before reaching the overpass, take the trail out of the riverbed; follow the path under the roadway to the southernmost segment of Arroyo Seco Park.

TRIP #29 - ARROYO SECO BIKE TRAIL

There is a bikeway/walkway that leads back up to Avenue 60; however, our route tours the pleasant shaded park past picnic areas, tennis courts, and restrooms. Bike through the park and turn right at Via Marisol (3.6). Do not explore the grassy area across that street, even by walking bikes, as there are thorns on the ground that are guaranteed tire and tube wreckers. (We know from experience!)

Cross the Pasadena Freeway and follow the signed Class III bike route as follows: left on Avenue 57 (3.7), right on Carlota Boulevard (3.8), right on Avenue 55 (4.0), left on Glen Ellen Place (4.1), and left on Avenue 52 (4.3). Bike on this Class III road which recrosses the freeway and becomes Griffin Avenue. In 0.7 mile, the route meets the "reference" junction. Turn right and follow the Class I bikepath back to the starting point (5.2).

Excursion Tours. Pedal south on Homer Street. Cross Avenue 43 and bike 0.2 mile to the street's end at Heritage Square (5.6). There are several Victorian mansions here. Return north to Avenue 43, turn left (west), and bike 0.1 mile to the historic cobblestone Lummis Home, "El Alisal" (5.9).

Pedal 0.1 mile on Avenue 43 and turn right (northeast) on Figueroa Street. Follow that street about 0.2 mile just past Woodside Drive to Casa de Adobe, a replica of an 1850s California hacienda (6.2).

Cruise 0.1 mile to Avenue 45 and turn right (northwest), continuing a short distance to Marmion Way (6.4). Turn right again and follow that street 0.2 mile to Museum Drive. Turn left and then angle right almost immediately, following a very steep uphill (probably a walking stretch) to the Southwest Museum (6.6). This museum contains an extensive collection of Southwestern Indian artifacts.

Return 0.9 mile to the park area (7.5).

CONNECTING TRIPS: 1) Connection with the Highland Park Loop (Trip #30) - at the Southwest Museum turnoff, bike north on Marmion Way; 2) connection with the Kenneth Newell Bikeway (Trip #31) - from the trip terminus, head northeast on Arroyo Drive, which becomes Marmion Way; pedal 0.2 mile on Pasadena Avenue to Arroyo Drive, turn left (north), and cruise 1.25 miles to the northernmost section of Arroyo Seco Park.

TRIP #30 - HIGHLAND PARK LOOP

GENERAL LOCATION: Highland Park

LEVEL OF DIFFICULTY: Loop - easy
                                          Distance - 7.6 miles
                                          Elevation gain - periodic moderate grades

HIGHLIGHTS: This mainly Class III loop tours the edge of Montecito Heights, traverses a series of rolling hills through the first half of the trek, and returns via the parks along the Arroyo Seco. There are numerous side trips, including visits to Heritage Square, Casa de Adobe, and the Southwest Museum (see Trip #29). Primarily in a residential zone, most of this trip is on lightly used roads. The areas on either side of the Pasadena Freeway are an interesting contrast, the western side having light tree cover and a high-density residential area, while the east is heavily treed, somewhat residential, and full of lovely parks.

TRIP #30 - HIGHLAND PARK LOOP

TRAILHEAD: Exit the Pasadena Freeway east on Avenue 43. Drive two blocks and turn left (north) at Homer Street. Continue to the end of Homer Street and park in the Montecito Heights Recreation Center parking lot.

Bring a light water supply. Water is available at the parks and at several gas stations on the route.

TRIP DESCRIPTION: **Western Segment.** Exit the Montecito Heights Recreation Center area and bike south on Homer Street. Turn right on Avenue 43 (biking south leads to Heritage Square) and pedal over the Pasadena Freeway 0.3 mile to Figueroa Street (stay on Figueroa Street to visit Casa de Adobe and Sycamore Grove Park). Turn right and bike 0.1 mile to Avenue 45, turn left, and then turn right on Class III Marmion Way. Follow the mild upgrade past Museum Drive (0.7) (turn left here to visit the Southwest Museum). Turn left at Shanley Avenue, then right at Malta Street. Cruise to Avenue 50 and turn left (1.4).

Pedal on this Class III road through the residential community situated in rolling hills, cross York Boulevard, and turn right, one street beyond, at Meridian Street (2.4). Follow the 0.8-mile upgrade through this quiet residential area which crests near Milwaukee Avenue. Cruise 0.7 mile and turn sharply right at Avenue 63, skirting the covered water reservoir and passing shady, green Garvanza Park. Turn left at Repton Street, right on Avenue 66, and then bike to York Boulevard (4.4).

Eastern Segment. Turn left (southeast), cycle past San Pascual Avenue, and cross over the Pasadena Freeway, using the signed walkway. Stop on the bridge and admire the riders training their horses in the equestrian area below. Turn left and bike up shady Sycamore Avenue, which fuses with Arroyo Verde Road, and turn right again at Monterey Road (4.9). Pedal uphill through the well-treed area with large rustic residences just above the northern Arroyo Seco Park segment. After a 0.3-mile climb, coast downhill to a level near Avenue 60. Turn right and pedal almost to the bridge over the Arroyo Seco (5.6).

Cross Avenue 60 and pass through the motorized vehicle barrier, using a walk/bike ramp. Follow the Class I path through the lovely southern segment of cozy Arroyo Seco Park, which has restrooms, shade, tennis courts, and many inviting rest spots. At Via Marisol (6.1), cross over the Pasadena Freeway and bike on several well-marked Class III zig-zags, recrossing the freeway at Avenue 52 (6.7). The road veers right and becomes Griffin Avenue. Bike 0.7 mile along Griffin Avenue and turn right at the marked Class I junction trail that leads down into the Arroyo Seco. Pedal this path 0.2 mile back to the parking area (7.6).

Griffin Avenue Spur. There is an option at the 7.4-mile point to remain on Griffin Avenue. Follow this road 2.3 miles on Class II road to its terminus at Mission Road at the back side of the Los Angeles County/USC Medical Center. This segment has some moderate grades and a winding road primarily in residential areas with reasonable bike room.

CONNECTING TRIPS: 1) Connection with the Arroyo Seco Bike Trail (Trip #29) - at the trip origin, bike south on Homer Street; 2) connection with the Kenneth Newell Bikeway (Trip #31) - at San Pascual Avenue, turn left (north) and continue about one mile to the northern segment of Arroyo Seco Park.

TRIP #31 - KENNETH NEWELL BIKEWAY

<u>GENERAL LOCATION</u>: Pasadena

<u>LEVEL OF DIFFICULTY</u>: One way- easy (north to south); moderate (south to north);
up and back - moderate
Distance - 6.8 miles (one way)
Elevation gain - periodic moderate upgrades

<u>HIGHLIGHTS</u>: One of the premier inland trips, this popular, well-marked bikeway explores an interesting north-south slice of Pasadena, with picturesque old homes near the starting point. It follows a pleasant tree-shaded residential area along the Arroyo Seco, passes the Rose Bowl, visits Devil's Gate Reservoir and Oak Grove County Park, and ends at Jet Propulsion Laboratories (JPL).

Most of the route is on roomy, lightly traveled Class III bikeways, with one workout upgrade (south to north) that places this trip at the "moderate" difficulty rating upper limit. An additional option is to link this route with the Phase I inner-city bikeway system.

<u>TRAILHEAD</u>: From the Pasadena Freeway southbound, exit west on York Boulevard (Pasadena Avenue to the east). Drive 0.2 mile to San Pascual Avenue and turn right. Continue about 0.75 mile beyond Comet Street and just short of the Arroyo Seco overcrossing. Park in the Arroyo Seco Park lot. From the northbound direction, exit at Marmion Way, turn left, and follow that street over the freeway. Stay on a road now named Avenue 64 and go to York Boulevard. Turn right and drive to San Pascual Avenue. Turn left (north) and continue to the Arroyo Seco Park lot, as described above.

Bring a moderate water supply. There are strategically located public water sources at Brookside Park near the Rose Bowl and at Oak Grove County Park near trip's end, as well as at both start and finish.

<u>TRIP DESCRIPTION</u>: **Classic Residential Pasadena.** Exit the parking area and turn right (north). Soon the Class III path crosses in succession the Arroyo Seco, Stoney Drive near a recreation field, and the San Pascual Stables. The rural area path climbs a short and steep uphill which crests at the San Pascual Avenue terminus at Arroyo Boulevard (0.2). Turn left (north) and pedal past a collection of lovely fenced estates with their turn-of-the-20th-century homes. The bike route here is in a tree-shaded, rural, serene setting. Cruise past Madeline Drive (0.5) and junction to the right at Grand Avenue (0.7). The path is well marked at this junction, as well as at all upcoming junctions.

Cycle a moderate upgrade for 0.3 mile, which becomes rather steep in the next 0.1 mile. Turn left at California Boulevard (1.2) and turn right in another 0.1 mile at California Terrace. Bike the slow, steady uphill in the shaded, classic residential area to Arbor Street (1.6). Turn left and, very shortly, turn right back onto Arroyo Boulevard. The path is now alongside the Arroyo Seco and offers a look down into Lower Arroyo Park. Just beyond, the route passes historical La Casita Del Arroyo, a replica of an early southern California hacienda (1.8).

Brookside Park. In 0.2 mile, pass under the majestic Colorado Boulevard bridge. Up the hill from this area there is a view of the classic Federal Building. Nearby, but

1 - ARROYO SECO PARK
2 - LOWER ARROYO PARK
3 - NORTON SIMON MUSEUM
4 - BROOKSIDE PARK
5 - ROSE BOWL
6 - DEVIL'S GATE RESERVOIR
7 - LA CANADA HIGH SCHOOL
8 - OAK GROVE COUNTY PARK
9 - JET PROPULSION LABS (J.P.L.)
10 - CALIF. INSTITUTE OF TECHNOLOGY
11 - PASADENA CITY COLLEGE

••••••• ALTERNATE BIKE ROUTE

PHASE 1 BIKEWAY SYSTEM

KENNETH E. NEWELL BIKEWAY

TRIP #31 - KENNETH NEWELL BIKEWAY

out of view, is the Norton Simon Museum of Art. In another 0.1 mile, pass under the massive Ventura Freeway bridge with a "window" view to the mountains, achieved by sighting through the bridge supports northward and down the canyon. The route heads steeply downhill for 0.2 mile, flattens out, and passes under Holly Street (2.3). The flat roadway continues past the southern portion of Brookside Park, which has a nice picnic area and water (2.5).

Rose Bowl. In 0.3 mile, cross Seco Street, jog to the right, and head north beside the east side of the Rose Bowl. This area has recreation fields and restrooms (3.0). Cross Rosemont Avenue and bike on a workout upgrade through tree-lined residential areas past Westgate Street and Everts Street (3.7). The upgrade eases and proceeds 0.2 mile to a great turnout/vista area that overlooks the Brookside Golf Course and offers a look at the local hills. Then cross Washington Boulevard and pedal to a crest at La Cresta Drive (4.5).

The "Maze." Cross over the Foothill Freeway and turn left at N. Weimar Avenue, just before W. Woodbury Road (4.9). Follow a well-marked route on N. Yucca Lane to Yucca Lane and turn right again. Pass over W. Woodbury Road. Turn left on Woodbury Road near a cul-de-sac, right on N. Arroyo Boulevard, and left on La Cañada Verdugo Road (5.2). Cruise downhill to the road's end at a cul-de-sac (5.4).

Devil's Gate Reservoir and Oak Grove County Park. Follow the Class I path across Devil's Gate Reservoir (5.7) and bike downhill above the reservoir area. There are excellent views into the San Gabriel Mountains here. Cruise past a little shady park (with benches) into the main area of Oak Grove County Park. Continue 0.3 mile along the park periphery past a junction to the right (west) which leads to the lower picnic area. At (6.3), the route meets Oak Grove Drive. Turn right and bike 0.5 mile to JPL (6.8).

CONNECTING TRIPS: 1) Connection with the Arroyo Seco Bike Trail (Trip #29) - from the junction of San Pascual Avenue and Arroyo Drive, pedal 1.25 miles south on Arroyo Drive/Pasadena Avenue and turn left at Marmion Way; turn right in 0.2 mile at Arroyo Verde Road and proceed to the Arroyo Seco; 2) connection with the Highland Park Loop (Trip #30) - at the trip origin, bike one mile south to York Boulevard; 3) connection with the Pasadena inner-city bikeway shown on the eastern portion of the trip map - bike east at California Boulevard or Colorado Boulevard.

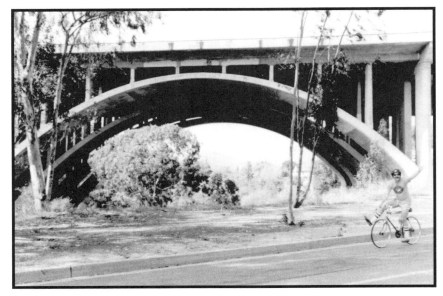

Ventura Freeway overpass

TRIP #32 - ARCADIA LOOP

GENERAL LOCATION: Arcadia

LEVEL OF DIFFICULTY: Four loop trips - moderate to strenuous; Highland Oaks
segment of Rancho Oaks Loop is strenuous
Distance - 29.4 miles (not including the 3.0-mile
strenuous Rancho Oaks segment)
Elevation gain - periodic moderate grades
(Rancho Oaks Loop); single extended
steep upgrade (Highland Oaks segment)

HIGHLIGHTS: The delightful Arcadia bikeway system consists of four well-laid-out, well-marked loops. Most of the route is Class III on lightly used roads with plenty of bike room. The system is mainly flat, except for the northern portions of the Rancho Oaks Loop, particularly the steep upper segment of Highland Oaks Drive. Bikers can follow individual marked loops or free-lance among them. Rancho Oaks Loop is the longest and most varied, with such points of interest as the Los Angeles County Arboretum, Santa Anita Race Track, Arcadia Park, Wilderness Park, and elegant residential neighborhoods in the foothills.

TRAILHEAD: From the Foothill Freeway, exit south at Michillinda Avenue. Follow Colorado Street to Michillinda Avenue, turn right (south), and drive one mile to Huntington Drive. Turn left and continue 0.4 mile to Golden West Avenue. Turn left and find parking in this residential area, subject to local parking laws. From the San Bernardino Freeway, exit north on Rosemead Boulevard and drive about four miles to Huntington Drive. Turn right and continue 0.75 mile to Golden West Avenue. Turn left and park as stated above.

    Bring plenty of water unless you are willing to search or beg and borrow along the way. There may be water at some of the parks that we did not visit.

TRIP DESCRIPTION: Individual loops should be biked in the direction shown, since the bikepath signs are only posted in one direction. Bring a map on this trip as a backup, whether following the signed routes or "free-lancing." Below are highlight descriptions of each loop.

    Hugo Reid Loop. The shortest of the four loops, the counterclockwise 3.0-mile route cruises a pleasant, quiet, well-manicured residential area bordered by Baldwin Lake and the Los Angeles County Arboretum on the east. This area is neatly tucked away, isolated from the busy roads to the north, west, and south. Peacocks wander this territory at will. This loop has some light upgrades and views into the San Gabriel Mountains, particularly from Altura Road looking back.

    Lucky Baldwin Loop. This counterclockwise 6.8-mile loop enfolds a major portion of the Hugo Reid Loop. From the parking area, cross Huntington Drive to a modest residential area, pass Tripolis Park (0.3), and meander as far south as Camino Real. The route goes north at El Monte Avenue (2.1) on a Class II route and turns left

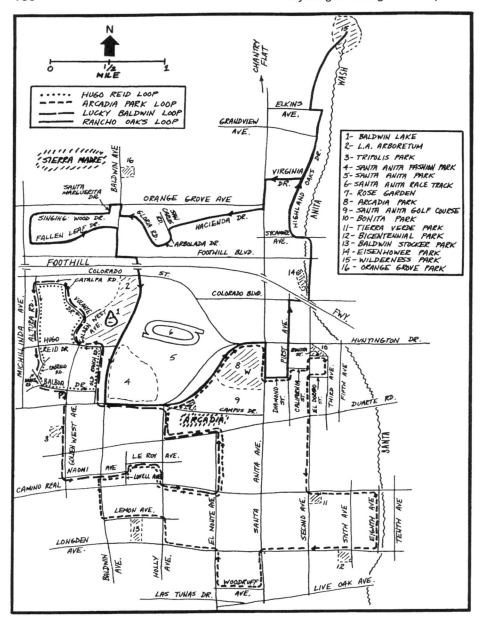

TRIP #32 - ARCADIA LOOP

(west) at Duarte Road, returning to Class III biking. The path zig-zags north and west, passes Holy Angels Church, and crosses Huntington Drive near the exquisite Rose Garden (2.9).

The bike route passes directly south of the Santa Anita Raceway with its great mountain backdrop. The path cruises past Santa Anita Fashion Park (shopping center) (3.4), crosses Baldwin Avenue, and heads north on Old Ranch Road (3.8). Just beyond this junction, the bikepath shares a common route with the Hugo Reid Loop, returning to the starting point (6.8).

Rancho Oaks Loop. The longest of the loops, this counterclockwise 9.9-mile favorite is described starting at Hugo Reid Drive and Baldwin Avenue. The parking previously described is near this starting point, or bikers can park at Santa Anita Fashion Park. Start south on Baldwin Avenue and turn left on Huntington Drive (0.8). The path follows that road as it passes the Santa Anita Race Track, the Rose Garden (1.2), and swings north alongside Arcadia City Park which has recreation and picnic areas, trees and grassy rest spots, water, and restrooms.

Turn right (south) at Santa Anita Avenue (2.3) and pass an arts and crafts exhibit area. A left turn at Diamond Street leads to a series of jig-jogs which lead to a Foothill Freeway undercrossing at Colorado Boulevard (3.5). Cruise by Eisenhower Park and a shopping center near Second Avenue and Foothill Boulevard, then bike over to Highland Oaks Drive (4.2). The route goes uphill on a workout grade, then heads toward the mountains, through a residential area, and meets Virginia Drive (4.7). An option here is to bike about 1.5 miles further on Highland Oaks Drive on a steep, gutsy uphill to rustic Wilderness Park (trees, picnic areas, restrooms, nature trails); this is a strenuous to very strenuous workout! The compensations are great vistas and a feeling of accomplishment.

For everyday mortals, the bike route turns left, heads uphill for a short distance, and works its way to some exceptionally impressive residential areas starting south of Orange Grove Avenue and Santa Anita Avenue at Hacienda Drive (5.2). At Baldwin Avenue (6.7), the bikepath jig-jogs over to Santa Margarita Drive and proceeds mostly downhill through some of the most elegant and impressive residential areas in Los Angeles County. The Singing Wood Drive/Fallen Leaf Drive area is stocked with mansions and large, elegant homes on huge, immaculately tended lots.

Everyday reality returns as the path heads right at Baldwin Avenue (8.6) and proceeds downhill to Foothill Boulevard. Baldwin Avenue continues about 0.2 mile to the east and soon passes under the Foothill Freeway. The bike route passes one entrance to the Los Angeles County Arboretum just south of Stanford Drive (9.4) and returns to the starting point (9.9).

Arcadia Park Loop. This 9.7-mile clockwise route starts at Huntington Drive and Holly Avenue, which can be reached from the described trailhead parking area. Other options are to start at one of several parks on the route. This is the flattest route of the group, mainly confined to less spectacular territory than other loops. Most of the route passes through residential areas which are liberally sprinkled with parks.

Bike along Huntington Drive, passing the Santa Anita Race Track, the Rose Garden, and swing north alongside Arcadia City Park. Turn right at Santa Anita Avenue (1.1) and left at Diamond Street. The route goes through a series of jig-jogs, passing Bonita Park (1.9), and heads south on Second Street. Then head left at Camino Real and pass Tierra Verde Park (3.2). The path reaches its easternmost edge at Eighth Street (3.7) and loops back west on Longden Avenue, passing Bicentennial Park (open playground and tennis courts) (4.3).

The bike tour turns left (south) on Santa Anita Avenue, passes near the southern Arcadia city limits on Woodruff Avenue (5.4), winds its way north and west on Class II El Monte Avenue, and returns to Class III Longden Avenue (6.4). Then it turns right (north) on Holly Avenue, left on Lemon Avenue, and passes Baldwin Stocker Park (6.9) with picnic areas, restrooms, and a playground.

Soon the path turns right (north) on Baldwin Avenue and heads to Camino Real (7.6). From this point, the route shares a path with the Lucky Baldwin Loop. The path jig-jogs north and east, eventually reaching El Monte Avenue (8.9). To return to the starting point (9.7), proceed north on El Monte Avenue, left (west) on Duarte Road, and north again on Holly Avenue.

CONNECTING TRIPS: There are numerous combinations of possible routes just within the four loops described.

TRIP #33 - GRIFFITH PARK

GENERAL LOCATION: Hollywood Hills, Griffith Park

LEVEL OF DIFFICULTY: Griffith Park Drive Loop - moderate to strenuous
Distance - 8.8 miles (loop)
Elevation gain - single long, moderate-to-steep grade

Zoo Drive Up-and-Back Trip - easy
Distance - 8.2 miles (up and back)
Elevation gain - periodic light grades

Los Angeles River Trail - easy
Distance - 3.2 miles (one way)
Elevation gain - essentially flat

HIGHLIGHTS: This is a pleasant ride in a rural setting through one of Los Angeles County's finest parks. One option is the loop route which includes Griffith Park Drive and a half-mile strenuous upgrade. (This is the reference option described below.) Another option is to take the Zoo Drive route up and back, avoiding Griffith Park Drive completely, or plan a route that includes all but the strenuous upgrade.

There is an option to bike a 3.2-mile trail along the Los Angeles River. This ride can be used as an option to the Zoo Drive/Crystal Springs return or biked in addition to the basic Griffith Park ride. The trail provides a different perspective of the Griffith Park area, as well as some scenic river bottom and a taste of man's "levee artistry."

Regardless of the option, the tree-lined route passes numerous picnic areas and sightseeing attractions (Los Angeles Zoo, Travel Town, and the Griffith Park Merry-Go-Round). Griffith Park Drive is effectively a Class III roadway, while the remainder of the bikepaths are Class II. The Zoo Drive up-and-back option is a nice family ride for all but inexperienced or very young bikers.

TRAILHEAD: Exit the Golden State Freeway at Los Feliz Boulevard and turn west. Drive a quarter mile and turn right (north) at Crystal Springs Drive. Park in the area just off the roadway, preferably in a shady spot.

TRIP #33 - GRIFFITH PARK

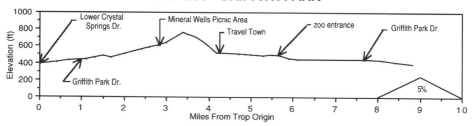

Bring a light water supply. There is plenty of water in the main picnic areas surrounding Crystal Springs Drive near the Griffith Park Drive junction, and there are water fountains and restrooms at most park attractions, although bikers must leave the bike trail to gain access.

TRIP DESCRIPTION: **Lower Crystal Springs Drive.** Leaving the parking area, Crystal Springs Drive starts on a mix of moderate upgrades and flats. In 0.1 mile, pass the Los Feliz Passenger Station, the point of departure for rides on the mini-railroad. Continue above and alongside the Golden State Freeway until it transitions to an area above grassy knolls and horse stables (0.8). The entire Griffith Park area is crisscrossed with great horse trails. Shortly, the roadway passes alongside the Visitor's Center/Ranger Station and, just beyond, meets the junction with Griffith Park Drive (1.1).

Mineral Wells Picnic Area. Bike straight ahead (north) on Crystal Springs Drive for the easier family bike route. For the reference loop trip, turn left (west) on Griffith Park Drive and bike up a short steep upgrade. Cruise past the car roadblock and around the edge of the Cedar Tree Picnic Grounds parking area. Pass above the Griffith Park Merry-Go-Round and a pleasant, grassy, shaded picnic area (1.5) which extends for about a quarter of a mile.

At the junction north of the picnic area, bear left and pedal alongside the golf course. Pass the Boy's Camp turnoff (2.4), golfer's clubhouse/restaurant, and driving range (2.6), then head uphill to the Mineral Wells Picnic Area (2.8), one of the most natural and scenic picnic areas in the park.

The "Roller Coaster." Beyond the picnic area, the route steepens. For the next half mile, bikers face a gritty uphill that levels off near a developed area. This segment

Merry-Go-Round at Griffith Park

leaves some question as to whether the route is moderate or moderate to strenuous. Just beyond the flat, the route twists and winds steeply downhill, passing Mount Holly-wood Drive (3.5) and then leveling out in 0.6 mile.

Travel Town. Just beyond is the turnoff to Travel Town (4.2) with miniature train rides, as well as stationary, life-size steam trains. The roadway continues past Travel Town, makes a turn to the right (east), and becomes Zoo Drive. Zoo Drive passes alongside the live "Steamer" area (4.3), a small open picnic area (4.5), Riverside Drive (5.3), and the Pecan Grove Picnic Area (5.4).

Los Angeles Zoo and the Return Loop. In 0.3 mile, there is a junction where the bikeway splits. A left turn leads around the edge of the Los Angeles Zoo parking lot, while the reference route proceeds straight ahead. The road passes under a walking bridge (6.1) and continues along a eucalyptus-lined route which passes through two golf courses. In a short distance, pass alongside the eastern edge of the Cedar Tree Picnic Area and later return to the Griffith Park Drive junction (7.7). The final segment follows Crystal Springs Drive southbound through a series of small rolling hills back to the parking area (8.8).

Los Angeles River Trail. This 3.2-mile Class I trail can be used as a separate trip or connected to the Griffith Park ride. It is the northern segment of the Los Angeles River Trail. There is an ongoing drive by groups such as the Los Angeles County Bi-cycle Coalition (LACBC) to, one day, connect this to the southern segment described in Trip #21. Recently, the river trail has been extended to Fletcher Drive, with the hope of continuing it into the Civic Center area.

The trail entry is on the south levee at Riverside Drive. The night-lighted route cruises east, with nifty Griffith Park and Forest Lawn vistas southward. It pulls away from the Ventura Freeway and passes the park's soccer fields just before bending south at the 0.5-mile point. Just beyond the Ventura Freeway undercrossing, there is a walker/biker entry from North Zoo Drive.

Beyond about (1.2), look across the river and observe the cat faces articulately painted on the water outlet ports which dot the levee face. From this point, which is directly alongside the Golden State Freeway, the river bottom blossoms with heavy vegetation. At (2.5), there is an equestrian crossing for riders coming from Griffith Park via a tunnel under the freeway. Los Feliz Boulevard and the end of the river segment is at (3.2). Just before the Baum Bridge entry, take the right fork to reach that street. To return to the park, turn right (west) and carefully cross three freeway on/off-ramps to reach Riverside Drive in about a quarter mile. All that remains is for cyclists to turn right again and return to their parked car on what is now Crystal Springs Drive.

Note that the ride can be extended along the Los Angeles River by taking the Baum Bridge over Los Feliz Boulevard and continuing on the west bank to exits at Glendale Boulevard and Fletcher Drive. Just a few hundred yards south of the Baum Bridge, there is an elevated walk/bike path which crosses the river to the east bank. At this same juncture, there is also an elevated westbound walk/bike path which outlets at the Griffith Park Recreation Center along Riverside Drive.

CONNECTING TRIPS: 1) There are other connecting trips in the Hollywood Hills area, but these routes are extremely hilly and on Class X roadways, and are only for ex-perienced bikers in excellent condition; 2) connection with the Burbank Bikeway (Trip #36) - at Zoo Drive and Victory Boulevard, follow the latter street across the freeway.

TRIP #34 - ELYSIAN PARK

GENERAL LOCATION: Elysian Park (Central Los Angeles)

LEVEL OF DIFFICULTY: Loop - moderate to strenuous
Distance - 6.4 miles
Elevation gain - single steep grade

HIGHLIGHTS: Elysian Park provides a natural setting tucked away in the middle of the city of Los Angeles. The trip boasts parks, trees, hills, and vistas, all in a lightly traveled area (barring a major event at nearby Dodger Stadium). The key word is vistas. Few places in Los Angeles County provide more spectacular views per bike mile. While "gut-busting" on Angels Point Road, there are rewarding vistas back into the park area, the hills across the Los Angeles River, and the Los Angeles city skyline, and views to the south that include Dodger Stadium. The price paid is some strenuous hill climbing and an entire route on Class X roadway. There are options to link additional loops and thus expand the trip mileage.

There are numerous additional park service roads and trails for hikers and mountain bikers. Check with the park headquarters to confirm which are open for use.

TRAILHEAD: From the Harbor/Pasadena Freeway, exit at Stadium Way and follow that roadway southwest and parallel to the freeway (do not drive up into Dodger Stadium). Continue about 1.25 miles past the point where Stadium Way takes a 90-degree bend to the northwest. At Academy Road, drive straight into the park on Chavez Ravine Road (do not take the jog to the right, which is the continuation of Stadium Way). From the Golden State Freeway, exit at Stadium Way. Drive 1.5 miles to Academy Road and turn right. Just beyond, turn right into the Chavez Ravine Road parking area.

Bring a moderate water supply. Bikers will use plenty of water, and resupply is available at several sites within the park.

TRIP DESCRIPTION: **Elysian Park Road (West) and Grace E. Simons Lodge.** Leave a well-treed picnic area with benches, barbecues, a playground, restrooms, and water, and cycle south along Stadium Way. Just across Academy Road, there is a similar picnic area that is slightly more hilly. In 0.1 mile, there is a smaller park area with a blocked uphill entry to Old Lodge Road.

Just beyond, the route turns right (northwest) and heads uphill on Scott Avenue (0.2). In another 0.1 mile of steep uphill, the path turns right on Elysian Park Road and parallels Stadium Way.

Continue on a moderate upgrade, on a shaded roadway with views down into the picnic area, and cross Academy Road (0.6). This is a favorite parking area for folks taking a workday lunch break or just "playing hooky." The path reaches a crest (0.9) and soon passes a small arboretum and picnic area with water. In 0.1 mile, there is a short diversion trip to a nice group picnic area and the Grace E. Simons Lodge. The path proceeds downhill past a small picnic/playground area and returns to Stadium Way (1.3).

The "Workout" and the Vistas. The route crosses that street and begins a strenuous 0.9-mile winding grade on Angels Point Road. This is the toughest part of

Legend:
1- GRACE E. SIMONS LODGE
2- ANGELS POINT
3- POINT GRAND VIEW
4- ELYSIAN RESERVOIR
5- BUENA VISTA HILL PARK
6- BUENA VISTA MEADOW
7- RADIO HILL
8- PARK HEADQUARTERS
9- ELYSIAN ADAPTIVE REC. CENTER
10- L.A. POLICE ACADEMY

TRIP #34 - ELYSIAN PARK

the trip! The first of several vista points is 0.2 mile beyond, with a nice park overlook. Following is a great 180-degree view that includes the "back side" of the Los Angeles Civic Center (1.7). This is Angels Point, where there is access to a lookout kiosk and picnic area. Next are views down into the Police Academy Firing Range and across to the Hollywood Hills (2.0) and, at the crest, a fine overlook of Dodger Stadium and the San Gabriel Mountains (2.2).

Following a flat stretch and steep downhill, the route reaches a junction with Solano Canyon Drive (2.7). Stay to the left and enjoy the excellent view down into the Los Angeles River and across to the local hills. In 0.2 mile, there is another junction. Turn left again and bike on Grand View Drive to an automobile turnout with an exceptional 180-degree view into the Los Angeles Civic Center (3.3). Appropriately, this is Point Grand View.

Elysian Reservoir and the "Other" Elysian Park. Grand View Drive begins a steep and winding downhill, passing the Elysian Reservoir (4.0) and a small shaded park area with restrooms. Soon there is a short but steep upgrade that leads to a junction with Park Row Drive. Turn left and cross over the Pasadena Freeway to the park's southeastern section. There is a short but steep spur trip up Buena Vista Drive to a tree-walled cul-de-sac on Buena Vista Hill (4.4). For the very determined, there is a steep half-mile spin down Park Row Drive to the North Broadway exit. (Take the left fork at the first junction on the downhill and take the right fork at the second junction.) Another pleasant diversion is to follow Meadow Road over to the Buena Vista Meadow Picnic Area.

However, our trip returns over the bridge and continues straight ahead on Park Row Drive on a steep 0.3-mile upgrade. Just beyond the crest, the route reaches a junction (4.9) and bears left, following the arrow pointing to the Solano Canyon Information Center. There is a short downhill to another junction. Turn left onto Solano Canyon Drive and bike past several plush picnic areas, tennis courts, and water fountains to reach the Academy Road intersection (5.5). The Park Headquarters is on the east side.

Los Angeles Police Academy. Turn right (northwest) and pedal up a steep 0.3-mile upgrade past the Elysian Adaptive Recreation Center. Just beyond the crest, pass Academy Drive and the Los Angeles Police Academy (5.9). In another 0.2 mile, the roadway turns hard right and descends 0.3 mile further to Stadium Way. Proceed across Stadium Way to the parking area (6.4).

CONNECTING TRIPS: For those in the mood for further exercise, there are numerous alternate routes within the park, including the Dodger Stadium "spoke."

Elysian Park with Dodger Stadium in background

TRIP #35 - GLENDORA BIKEWAY

GENERAL LOCATION: Glendora

LEVEL OF DIFFICULTY: Loop - moderate
Distance - 8.3 miles
Elevation gain - periodic moderate grades

HIGHLIGHTS: This predominantly Class III tour is essentially a loop trip around the South Hills of Glendora. The route has nice views into the local foothills and San Gabriel Mountains, particularly on the northern trip segment. The main route is well laid out and well marked, primarily in residential neighborhoods on lightly traveled roadways, and has many potential spurs and connectors which were not investigated by the authors.

TRAILHEAD: From the Foothill Freeway, exit north at Grand Avenue, continue about half a mile north to Foothill Boulevard, and turn right (east). Drive 0.5 mile to Wabash Avenue, turn left, and then turn right at Meda Avenue in 0.2 mile. Continue into the Finkbiner Park area and park on Minnesota Avenue, subject to the posted laws.
    Bring a moderate water supply. There is water at the origin, at South Hills Park (spur trip), and at some of the schools on the route. (Use the schools only during off-school hours.)

TRIP DESCRIPTION: **The North Segment.** From the park, ride west to Wabash Avenue and turn right. Follow this Class III roadway as it passes through a residential neighborhood, past Bennett Avenue, Whitcomb Avenue, and a market, and reaches Leadora Avenue (0.4). Turn right (east) and begin a steady uphill while taking in the foothills and San Gabriel Mountains to the north. The Class III path continues past Live Oak Avenue and a school (0.9), crosses Little Dalton Wash (1.1), and dead-ends at Loraine Avenue (1.4) near the crest.
    Turn right (south) and bike on a moderate downgrade one-half mile past a school to Foothill Boulevard. Turn left and follow a tree-lined and busier roadway on a Class II bikepath, crossing Big Dalton Wash (2.4) and Valley Center Avenue and then passing by Glendora High School (2.5). Start uphill and pedal to a crest just short of Lone Hill Avenue (3.0). Instead of proceeding up the nasty-looking hill straight ahead, breathe a sigh of relief and turn right at Lone Hill Avenue.
    East Segment. Follow a long downhill on a Class III route in a more exposed, more residential area than the Foothill Boulevard area. There is a slight uphill just before Alosta Avenue (3.5) and, in 0.4 mile, pass under the Foothill Freeway. There is a San Dimas Wash crossing just beyond, and the route is now alongside some large agricultural fields. The South Hills are clearly visible to the right (west) in this area.
    South Segment. The bike route turns right at Gladstone Street (4.5) and proceeds on a flat Class II road alongside open fields. In half a mile, cross Valley Center Avenue and again enter a residential area. The bike route crosses Sunflower Avenue (5.5), the San Dimas Wash, and Gladstone Park (5.8), and it reaches Glendora Avenue in 0.7 mile.

TRIP #35 - GLENDORA BIKEWAY

West Segment. Turn right (north) and pass under the Foothill Freeway, cross the Big Dalton Wash (7.0), pass Baseline Road, and meet up with Mauna Loa Avenue (7.3). A right turn here leads 0.3 mile to South Hills Park and a dead end. There is a small, grassy playground with a restroom, together with lots of local hills to hike.

However, our Class III route heads down Glendora Avenue past Alosta Avenue where the road narrows considerably. In 0.2 mile, the route junctions. Follow the bike sign right to S. Vista Bonita and right again (east) on E. Ada Avenue. Pass through a shaded residential area to Wabash Avenue and turn left (7.9). Cross Foothill Boulevard, pass the Glendora Ranger Station (8.1), ride across the Little Dalton Wash, and turn right on Meda Avenue. Ride through the park to the starting point (8.3).

CONNECTING TRIPS: Numerous spurs off our basic trip were observed. Bikepath signs were noted on Bennett Avenue, Live Oak Avenue, and Alosta Avenue, and extensions to our basic route were found at Loraine Avenue, Foothill Boulevard, Gladstone Street, and Glendora Avenue. Connection with the Baseline Road tour (Trip #45) - at Lone Hill Avenue and Gladstone Street, continue east on the latter road.

TRIP #36 - BURBANK BIKEWAY

GENERAL LOCATION: Burbank

LEVEL OF DIFFICULTY: Peripheral loop - moderate to strenuous
Distance - 14.8 miles
Elevation gain - continuous moderate-to-steep
grades in foothills, essentially flat elsewhere

HIGHLIGHTS: This 15-mile extravaganza is one of the better inner-city tours in our book. The Burbank Bikeway actually consists of four separate Class III inner loops and a fifth, peripheral loop. The latter loop is described here. The route initially tours the foothills below the Verdugo Mountains in the northeast trip sector; there are several nice parks and excellent San Fernando Valley views. The long and sometimes steep upgrades in this area are also what give the trip the borderline "strenuous" label.
    The route drops out of the foothills, passes through "Beautiful Downtown Burbank," and proceeds southwest as far as the Los Angeles Equestrian Center along the Los Angeles River. The path follows past the Disney Studios and NBC Television Studios, visits the relaxing, lightly trafficked residential area on Burbank's west side, and then returns to the trip origin via busy Buena Vista Street.

TRAILHEAD: From the Golden State Freeway, exit at Buena Vista Street. From the northbound freeway exit, turn south on Buena Vista Street (back toward the freeway) and turn left (east) on Winona Avenue. Drive several blocks to Keystone Street and find parking, subject to the posted parking laws. From the southbound exit, turn left upon reaching Buena Vista Street and drive north back under the freeway; turn right on Winona Avenue and continue as above.
    Bring a moderate water supply. There are water sources strategically located throughout the trip.
    Follow the route map carefully, as some turns are not clearly marked (e.g., at the intersections of Kenneth Road/Providencia Avenue and Santa Anita Avenue/Lake Street). In addition, bring a street map as a backup, should you lose your way. Because some of the route is tricky, this trip is written with more than the usual number of turns described.

TRIP DESCRIPTION: **The Foothills.** From the Winona Avenue intersection, pedal north (toward the hills) through a shaded residential area on Keystone Street. Then proceed on varying grades of uphill for 0.9 mile before reaching Scott Road. Turn right and puff another 0.2 mile before reaching a level area below Brace Canyon Park.

TRIP #36 - BURBANK BIKEWAY

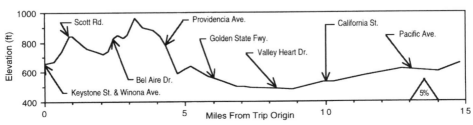

Just beyond is Haven Way, a diversion route up to the park; the park has shade, restrooms, a picnic area, recreation fields, a playground, and a mesh of walkways/bikeways. However, our route continues downhill on Scott Road, turns left on Kenneth Road (1.3), curves southeast, and heads moderately downhill to Cambridge Drive (2.1).

Now the fun begins! Pump up a steep grade 0.3 mile to Bel Aire Drive. A nice lady living at this corner intersection watched us struggle up the hill and offered our tired, weary group of bikers some ice water, which we gladly accepted! Just across the street, there is a rest area at Bel Aire Park.

Turn right on Bel Aire Drive and cruise downhill through this impressive residential area past UCLAN Drive (yes, UCLAN), then pedal a steep uphill which crests at Delaware Road (2.9). Turn left and climb another "gut-buster" for 0.3 mile; it crests near the junction where Delaware Road fuses into Sunset Canyon Drive. There are scattered views into the San Fernando Valley from here, particularly on clear days. Bike on a more moderate set of rolling hills through rural territory, passing the De Bell Golf Course (3.3) and Palm Park (3.7), and reach Providencia Avenue (4.3).

Downhill to Downtown. Turn right on Providencia Avenue and bike steadily downhill, enjoying the view of the Hollywood Hills and Griffith Park straight ahead. Turn left (east) at Kenneth Road (4.6) and turn right at the next street, which is Cedar Avenue, skirting pleasant little Miller Park. Turn right at Sixth Street (4.8) and left at Verdugo Avenue in 0.2 mile. The route now enters one of the busier commercial areas of town, passing Glenoaks Boulevard and reaching First Street (5.6). Turn right and bike to busy Olive Avenue, turning left and pedaling on a narrow sidewalk over the Golden State Freeway (6.0).

The Southern Segment and The Studios. Ride 0.3 mile to Lake Street, turn left, bike to Santa Anita Avenue, and then make a right (6.5). Cruise to the end of the street, turn right on Verdugo Drive, and follow that street a short distance before turning left on Verdugo Avenue (6.9). Bike 0.2 mile and turn left on Virginia Avenue, continuing to its terminus at Oak Street. Turn right, pedal one block to Mariposa Street, and turn left on that tree-lined residential roadway (7.4).

The route continues another half mile through this pleasant residential area and crosses Riverside Drive where the road narrows significantly. The roadway continues a short distance and ends at the Los Angeles River, at the western edge of the Los Angeles Equestrian Center. Turn right on Valley Heart Drive and return to Riverside Drive (8.4), following that road left (west). The bikeway passes the Disney Studios, goes under the Ventura Freeway (9.0), and cruises the southern segment of Johnny Carson Park (formerly Buena Vista Park). There is a shaded rest area here with water and views across the Los Angeles River into Forest Lawn, the Hollywood Hills, and Griffith Park.

At the park's edge, go right at Bob Hope Drive (formerly S. Catalina Street) and bike back under the freeway to the main body of Johnny Carson Park. A creek runs through the park, which has shade trees, restrooms, and picnic tables. Across the street are the NBC Television Studios with their KNBC helicopters and television vans nearby (9.3).

The Residential Western Segment. Bike on Bob Hope Drive to its terminus at Alameda Avenue and turn left (9.6). Pedal almost to the Olive Avenue intersection; however, just short of that junction, use the Olive Avenue pedestrian crossing which leads across to Fairview Street. Ride on that street for a short stretch and follow the one-way entry to Whitnall Highway as it angles left under the high-tension power poles (9.9). Follow Whitnall Highway to its end at California Street (10.0), turn right, and

Burbank-based NBC Studios

cruise by Verdugo Park with the California Swim Stadium and a park with restrooms, tennis courts, barbecue facilities, and a children's playground.

The remainder of the trip is through lightly trafficked residential areas with well-marked routes back to the trip origin. The highlights of that segment are provided below.

The route zig-zags its way northward and westward, reaching its westernmost point along Valley Street (12.1). At Valley Street and Allan Avenue is Valley Park with shade, restrooms, tennis courts, picnic benches, and a recreation field. The route then works its way northward on Maple Street, reaching Pacific Avenue (13.2). At that junction, there is a terrific view of Valhalla Memorial Park and its gigantic mausoleum. This area is directly under the Burbank Airport flight path (an interesting contrast, is it not?).

The Return Leg. The bikepath travels by pleasant little Pacific Park with its shade trees, restrooms, tennis courts, and picnic tables (13.3). Cruise through a mix of residential and light commercial zones with splendid views into the nearby Verdugo Mountains and the more distant San Gabriel Mountains. Our route heads north on busy Buena Vista Street (14.0), passes under the Golden State Freeway (14.6), turns right on Winona Avenue, and returns to the trip origin (14.8).

CONNECTING TRIPS: 1) There are numerous combinations of routes just within the five loops mentioned; in addition, there is a linking Class I trail which parallels the Golden State Freeway between Cohasset Street and Morgan Avenue; 2) connection with the Griffith Park ride (Trip #33) - at Mariposa Street and Riverside Drive, turn left (east) on the latter street, continue to Victory Boulevard, and turn left; 3) connection with the Glendale Bikeway (Trip #62) and Verdugo Mountains Loop (Trip #63) - from Sunset Canyon Drive and Providencia Avenue, continue east roughly one mile to the entrance to Brand Park (just beyond Western Avenue).

TRIP #37 - MULHOLLAND DRIVE

<u>GENERAL LOCATION</u>: Santa Monica Mountains

<u>LEVEL OF DIFFICULTY</u>: One way - strenuous
Distance - 13.0 miles
Elevation gain - continuous steep upgrades

<u>HIGHLIGHTS</u>: This roller-coaster tour along the crest of the Santa Monica Mountains provides some of the more spectacular vistas into the San Fernando and San Gabriel valleys. There are views north across the valley to the San Gabriel Mountains and south to the ocean and the Palos Verdes Peninsula that are breathtaking! A potential drawback of this Mulholland Drive tour is that it is open and very hilly, i.e., sun-exposed and very physically exhausting. In addition, this Class X two-lane roadway is narrow in some areas, with little or no separate shoulder for biking, and some sections are poorly maintained.

The one-way mileage is provided above. This trip can be started from either end. Our tour starts with an up-and-back of the western Mulholland Drive segment and covers the region from Sepulveda Pass to the end of the paved section of Mulholland Drive. This up-and-back is included as a "hint" that it might be wise to test a short segment before committing to the entire trip.

<u>TRAILHEAD</u>: From the San Diego Freeway northbound, exit at Rimerton Road and make a right turn. Continue about a quarter mile to the Park and Ride area. From the southbound lanes, exit at Rimerton Road and turn left. Drive on the bridge over the freeway to the parking area.

Bring a large water supply and plenty of sun-protection gear. There is water at Coldwater Canyon Park, Vista Point, and Laurel Canyon Park, all concentrated in a two-mile stretch. Avoid this route during the week, particularly during the rush hours.

<u>TRIP DESCRIPTION</u>: **Western Segment.** From the Park and Ride area, cycle back to Rimerton Road and turn left, crossing over the San Diego Freeway and above the Mulholland Tunnel. Follow the uphill-downhill tour on an upgrade past Curtis School and, just beyond, stop and admire one of many excellent overlooks of the San Fernando Valley/Encino area (0.7).

Bike past the Bel-Air Church (note the great view from the north-facing parking lot) and cruise the workout through a lovely residential area to Calneva Drive/Park Lane Circle (1.4). The area now takes on a less developed, more rural setting and begins a steady uphill climb for the next half mile. Near the top of the grade at the Encino Hills Drive junction is the end of the paved section of Mulholland Drive (2.1). Beyond is mountain bike territory! Return to the San Diego Freeway overpass. (The one-way trip mileage starting from Encino Hills Drive is used in the discussion below.)

Eastern Segment - Skirball Center Drive to Coldwater Canyon Park. Cross back over the freeway and begin a short but steep uphill that is followed by a steep, winding downhill (2.6). Pass Woodcliff Road (3.1), cruise through some moderate rolling hills, and pass several overlooks into Stone Canyon Reservoir to the south (3.4). In succession, the tour crosses Nicada Drive and Beverly Glen Boulevard (4.3).

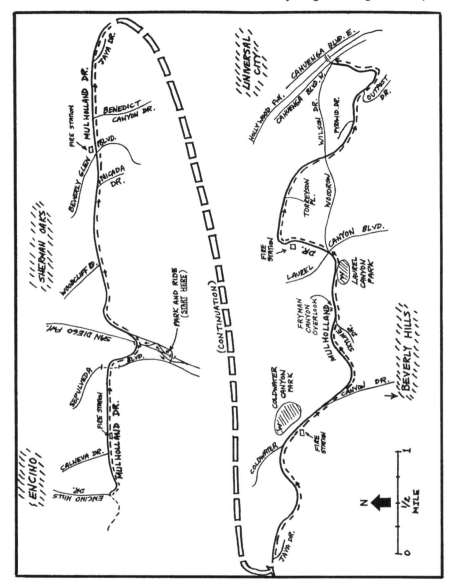

TRIP #37 - MULHOLLAND DRIVE

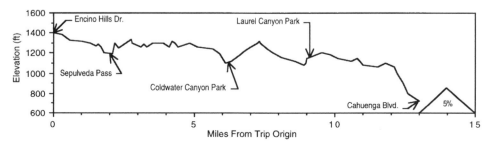

The journey proceeds uphill for about half a mile, crosses Benedict Canyon Drive (4.7), and then continues the "rolling hills tradition." There are interesting views into the San Fernando Valley to the left (north) and the canyons and canyon residential communities to the right. In the stretch just beyond Java Drive is the first of several well-separated "peeks" into the "back side" of central Los Angeles (6.2). The tour heads uphill, soon merges with Coldwater Canyon Drive, and passes near pleasant, shady Coldwater Canyon Park, the home of the "Tree People" (6.5).

Coldwater Canyon Park to Laurel Canyon Park. The bike route continues for about half a mile as a merged roadway; at this point, Mulholland Drive splits off to the left (east, if there is a single direction one can define on this winding road!). The roadway approaches a large radio tower placed high on the hillside and opens up into a view area with a turnout; hike out just beyond the parking area and take in one of the most sweeping, spectacular views of the San Fernando Valley and surrounding mountains (7.6).

There is a short downhill and a flat before reaching another valley vista in about one mile; this is the Fryman Canyon Overlook (and a water stop). Another section of very winding, steep downhill follows, leading to pleasant Laurel Canyon Park (9.1) and shortly to Laurel Canyon Boulevard (9.3).

Laurel Canyon Park to Cahuenga Boulevard. Just across this intersection, the route starts up a steep, steady, winding grade. Near the crest, there is an inspiring view of Universal City (10.1). In half a mile, near Torreyson Place, is the official "Universal City Overlook" with another fine view. Head downhill, cross Woodrow Wilson Drive (11.1), and then start a steep upgrade with views into the downtown Los Angeles area.

At 0.4 mile from the Woodrow Wilson Drive intersection, there is a spectacular view into the central Los Angeles area and beyond! The road heads very steeply downhill through a series of curves and switchbacks, recrosses Woodrow Wilson Drive, passes Outpost Drive (12.3), and meets up with another fine view at the "Mulholland Scenic Vista Turnout" (12.6). The highway snakes its way steeply downward 0.7 mile before reaching the trip's end at Cahuenga Boulevard West.

Los Angeles Civic Center from east of Woodrow Wilson Drive

CONNECTING TRIPS: Connection with the Old Sepulveda Hill Climb (Trip #5) - from the Park and Ride area, cross over the San Diego Freeway at Rimerton Road; continue west to the intersection with Sepulveda Boulevard.

TRIP #38 - SEPULVEDA BIKE BASIN

GENERAL LOCATION: Encino

LEVEL OF DIFFICULTY: Loop - easy
                          Distance - 9.1 miles
                          Elevation gain - essentially flat

HIGHLIGHTS: This popular bike route is comprised of two separate loops within the Sepulveda Dam Recreation Area, a 3.8-mile western loop and a 5.3-mile eastern loop. Most of the route is Class I and, with use of the Balboa Boulevard bike undercrossings, street travel is restricted to one short 0.3-mile segment. The bikeway tours pleasant tree-lined routes in many areas, cruises around the Balboa Sports Center and several golf courses, and has several open areas with spectacular views into the mountains to the east and south. There are several nice "R & R" areas along the route, including Woodley Avenue Park.

TRAILHEAD: From the Ventura Freeway, exit north on Balboa Boulevard. Cross Burbank Boulevard, continue several hundred yards further, and turn left into the tree-lined parking area. From the San Diego Freeway, exit west on the Ventura Freeway and drive about 2.5 miles to Balboa Boulevard. Continue as above.

    Bring a light water supply. Water is strategically located along the route.

TRIP DESCRIPTION: **West Loop.** Exit the parking lot and head north on a Class I bike route. Directly north, there is a nice view into the hills at the base of the Santa Susana Mountains. Pedal past a small restroom facility and cruise alongside a large recreation area that is the eastern edge of the Balboa Sports Center. A short distance beyond, there is a junction with a bikepath segment heading across the recreation field (west) (0.2). Continue north along Balboa Boulevard and, in 0.1 mile, cross the bridge over the Los Angeles River. A look into the river reveals bikers on the Balboa Boulevard bikeway undercrossing. To the east, there are views into the Verdugo and San Gabriel Mountains.

    Continue north along open fields and turn left at Victory Boulevard (0.7). Pass the USN/USMC Reserve Training Center and enter an open area with a panoramic view south to the Santa Monica Mountains. Bike past the cannon in front of the California National Guard Armory at Louise Avenue (1.3). Next is the San Fernando Valley Youth Center (there are biking activities for youngsters here) and an open agricultural area (1.5). Turn left at White Oak Avenue (1.7) and cross over the Los Angeles River.

    Just beyond, the bikepath shifts over to the west side of White Oak Avenue (Class II) and proceeds 0.3 mile through a residential area to Oxnard Street. The bike route turns left and returns to a Class I path alongside a small wash (2.2). This segment continues along open fields to the left and passes the entry to the Encino Velodrome (2.7).

TRIP #38 - SEPULVEDA BIKE BASIN

In 0.2 mile, the bikeway curves to the right (south) and passes a junction with the path which crosses the recreation field (3.0). Cycle past the junction to a picnic/play area with shaded picnic tables (3.4). A short distance beyond is Burbank Boulevard, where the bike route turns left (east) and crosses Balboa Boulevard on a pedestrian crosswalk (3.8).

East Loop. This loop starts along the well-treed Balboa Golf Course, snakes through a parking lot along Burbank Boulevard, and passes the Balboa Park Clubhouse

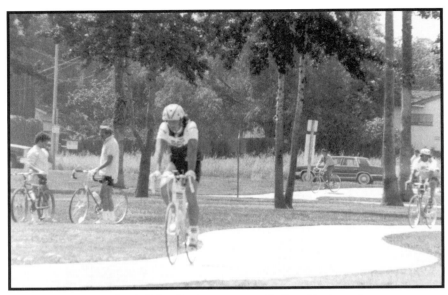

Sepulveda Bike Basin entry near Balboa Boulevard

(4.2). This is a convenient place to stop for water, food, or any number of "attitude arrangers." Just beyond, the path continues to maneuver between the golf course and Burbank Boulevard.

At 0.8 mile from the East Loop starting point, the path crosses Hayvenhurst Avenue. In 0.3 mile, there is a roadway to the Hjelte Sports Center, an interesting diversion. The reference route continues alongside the Encino Golf Course into an area where there are views into the San Gabriel Mountains (5.3). In another 0.1 mile, there is a short upgrade just prior to crossing the Los Angeles River. At Woodley Avenue (5.6), there is an option to continue 0.4 more mile on a Class I path along Burbank Boulevard to the top of the Sepulveda Dam. However, this trip turns left on Woodley Avenue and continues past open fields into an area with an unobstructed 360-degree viewing area (6.0).

In a short distance and to the east of Woodley Avenue is Woodley Avenue Park, where there are restrooms, cricket fields, and an archery range (6.2). The route passes the entrance road to the Woodley Lakes Golf Course (6.8) and turns left at Victory Boulevard (6.9). There is an option to turn east and bike about half a mile to the dam edge. Also, there is a Class III connector on Woodley Avenue which continues about 6.5 miles north to Granada Hills. However, the reference route proceeds on a relatively exposed stretch alongside open fields, passing a mini-rest area with water at Hayvenhurst Avenue (7.3). In succession the path passes a lone rest bench, crosses over the Bull Creek channel (7.7), and meets Balboa Boulevard (7.9).

Turn left (south) and follow a short path loop that leaves Balboa Boulevard for a short distance (8.1). In 0.3 mile, the route meets the Los Angeles River. Take the Balboa Boulevard undercrossing to the west side of Balboa Boulevard and backtrack a short distance to the starting point (9.1).

CONNECTING TRIPS: 1) There are numerous spurs off the main route, as mentioned in the trip writeup; 2) connection with the Chatsworth-Northridge-Granada Hills

Loop (Trip #55) - at Woodley Avenue and Nordhoff Street, turn south on the former street and bike 3.25 miles to Victory Boulevard; 3) connection with Trip #59 (Woodland Hills-Tarzana Loop) - at the intersection of Oxnard Street and White Oak Avenue, turn right (west) on the former street.

TRIP #39 - CHATSWORTH TOUR/ BROWN'S CREEK BIKEWAY

GENERAL LOCATION: Chatsworth

LEVEL OF DIFFICULTY: Loop - easy
Distance - 6.3 miles
Elevation gain - essentially flat

HIGHLIGHTS: This tour explores the Chatsworth area in the western San Fernando Valley. It combines a Class I segment along Brown's Canyon Wash with a Class X tour on lightly traveled roadways. The tour visits two excellent parks, Chatsworth Park North and Chatsworth Park South. There are interesting hills and rock formations there, as well as pleasant, shaded rest areas. There are also fine views into the surrounding hills throughout the trip.

TRAILHEAD: From the Ronald Reagan Freeway, exit south at De Soto Avenue, continue about 1.5 miles to Lassen Street, and turn right (west). Drive about one-half mile to the Brown's Canyon Wash overcrossing and find parking nearby on Lassen Street. From the Ventura Freeway, exit north at Topanga Canyon Boulevard and continue about 5.5 miles to Lassen Street. Turn right and drive about 0.4 mile to Brown's Canyon Wash.

Bring a light water supply. This is a short trip, with water available along Brown's Creek Bikeway and at both Chatsworth Parks.

TRIP DESCRIPTION: **Brown's Creek Bikeway.** From Lassen Street, follow the Class I bikepath which is on the east side of Brown's Canyon Wash. This is the Brown's Creek Bikeway. The path immediately passes a tightly packed group of kennels with a large canine greeting committee. The exposed path continues alongside the back side of a light industrial/commercial area. The bikeway leaves the wash diagonally, crosses Devonshire Street (0.4), and returns to the wash just north of that street.

The bikeway passes a nursery and then cruises through a neighborhood with apartments on the left and homes to the right. There is one section where bikers can pluck citrus off the trees that overhang the bikeway (but don't do it, okay?). Further north, there is an aromatic area that is surrounded by small pens of farm animals and an area with riding horses (0.9). Shortly, the path crosses Chatsworth Street and proceeds through a residential area. Near Chatsworth Street, there is a mini-rest area with a bench, shade, and a water fountain (1.1). In 0.2 mile, the path fuses with Variel Avenue, where there is another mini-rest area (figure this one out!).

TRIP #39 - CHATSWORTH TOUR/BROWN'S CREEK BIKEWAY

Chatsworth Street/Chatsworth Park North. Just beyond, the bikeway ends at Rinaldi Street (1.4). The route proceeds left (west) on that wide, lightly traveled roadway, passes trail-marked hills (foot or bicycle trails) in 0.2 mile, and heads left at Canoga Avenue (1.8). There are nice views into the surrounding hills to the west and north in this area. The path turns right on Chatsworth Street (2.4) and reaches Topanga Canyon Boulevard in 0.3 mile. Turn right (north) if a visit to Stoney Point Park and Stoney Point is on your agenda; there are some magnificent rocks, in this area, that attract many climbers and onlookers.

Our route crosses Topanga Canyon Boulevard, passes some horse stables and a parking lot to the left (2.9), and reaches a dead end at Chatsworth Park North (3.0). Follow the bikeway/walkway around the tree-dotted park and investigate the rocky outcroppings at its periphery. There are picnic benches, barbecues, and recreation areas, as well as a lovely lush field in the northernmost section of this park. Follow the path past the restroom and ride into the southern edge of the parking area. Just beyond the lot is the terminus (origin) of Valley Circle Boulevard (3.2).

Chatsworth Park South. Follow Valley Circle Boulevard 0.4 mile and turn right at Devonshire Street. Bike on that roadway as it changes name to Shadow Oak Drive. This is Chatsworth Park South. This larger park has lighter tree cover, but has nice picnic facilities, large grassy fields, tennis courts, hiking trails into the hills, and a recreation center (4.0).

Return Segment. Return to Valley Circle Boulevard and turn right (south). This segment leads to a more rural area of town and passes alongside the pretty, well-maintained Oakwood Cemetery (5.1). Just beyond is Lassen Street, where the bike route turns left (5.3). The tour transitions from rural to light commercial/industrial surroundings and returns to the starting point at Brown's Canyon Wash (6.3).

CONNECTING TRIPS: 1) Connection with the Chatsworth-Northridge-Granada Hills Loop (Trip #55) - the two routes share common roadway in the Chatsworth Street and Valley Circle Boulevard areas; 2) connection with the Santa Susana Pass ride (Trip #56) - from Brown's Creek Wash at Chatsworth Street, bike east one-third mile to Topanga Boulevard and turn left; in about one-half mile on the left (west) is Santa Susana Pass Road.

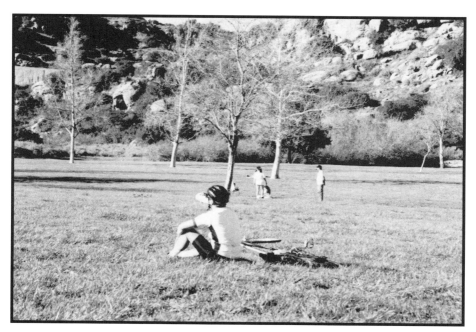

Chatsworth Park South below the rock outcroppings

TRIP #40 - TORRANCE TOUR

GENERAL LOCATION: Torrance

LEVEL OF DIFFICULTY: Loop - moderate
                                    Distance - 14.3 miles
                                    Elevation gain - periodic easy-to-moderate grades

HIGHLIGHTS: A fine city ride, this 14.3-mile loop tours the periphery of the larger Torrance bikeway system. The tour starts at the Torrance Civic Center, visits northern Torrance, cruises the scenic Torrance Boulevard area of eastern Torrance, and then beelines south to the Skypark Office Center area. This is followed by a 1.3-mile segment on action-packed PCH and a return via the pleasant residential area along Anza Avenue. The tour is of mixed classes, though predominantly Class II.

TRAILHEAD: From the San Diego Freeway, exit south at Crenshaw Boulevard and drive two miles to Torrance Boulevard. Turn right (west) and continue one mile to Madrona Avenue/Prairie Avenue. Turn right, then turn right again at the first entry, which leads to a large parking area near the Torrance Recreation Center. From the Harbor Freeway, drive west on Torrance Boulevard 3.5 miles to Madrona Avenue/Prairie Avenue. Turn right and continue as above.

Bring a filled water bottle. There is water at the Torrance Recreation Center and at scattered parks which are generally off the described route. There are also numerous gas stations along the way.

TRIP DESCRIPTION: **Northern Segment.** Follow the Class I path on the east side of Prairie Avenue to the intersection, then bike across Prairie Avenue on Class II Torrance Boulevard. Pass the stately Marriott Hotel, then Hawthorne Boulevard, and shift over to the Class I sidewalk path just past Village Lane. Shift back to the Class II Torrance Boulevard path in 0.1 mile and turn right at Anza Avenue (1.0). Bike on the Class II route (the path is shared with parked cars for 0.7 mile) through a residential area. Pass the small shopping center at Del Amo Boulevard and turn right on Class X 190th Street in 0.6 mile (2.3).

Pass a larger shopping center and bike on the tree-lined road segment, continue across Hawthorne Boulevard, and then pass under a railroad bridge. Pedal on the road with generally wide bike shoulder and pass Columbia Park (recreation fields, a playground, picnic benches, water, a few trees). Pass Prairie Avenue (3.6), the Mobil Torrance Refinery entrance, then shift over to the Class I sidewalk path. Follow that path 0.9 mile to Crenshaw Boulevard, then return to the Class X path and bike to Van Ness Avenue (5.0).

Southbound: 190th Street to Pacific Coast Highway (PCH). Follow the Class III road alongside the Mobil Refinery; there is a wide bike shoulder for most of the Van Ness Avenue segment. Bike through an industrial/commercial area past Del Amo Boulevard (5.9) and cruise 0.4 mile to the point where Van Ness Avenue jogs left. Continue straight ahead on little Class X Arlington Avenue 0.1 mile to Torrance Boulevard and turn right.

Pedal on the Class II path (which is shared with parked cars) through the pleasant tree-lined residential/light commercial area past Crenshaw Boulevard and a couple of

TRIP #40 - TORRANCE TOUR

gas stations (6.9). Continue 0.6 mile, turn left on Class X Maple Avenue, and bike 0.8 mile south on that lightly traveled residential street to Sepulveda Boulevard. Continue past the shopping center and turn right at the first street, Nadine Circle.

Follow Nadine Circle 0.4 mile through the residential area to 229th Place, turn right, pass the Torrance and Levy Adult Schools, and turn left on Madison Street (9.0). Continue to Lomita Boulevard and pedal against the traffic on the Class II path; cross Lomita Boulevard (no traffic signal) and rejoin Madison Street by cycling east. Coast past the well-groomed Skypark Office Center, pedal under the Torrance Airport flight path, and follow the 0.2-mile upgrade to PCH.

Pacific Coast Highway. Turn right at PCH and follow the Class II path on this busy road across Hawthorne Boulevard (10.2), pass a cluster of fast-food businesses, and go 0.4 mile to Anza Avenue. Pass a pair of shopping centers and a donut shop (we could spend a lot of time talking about one of Don's big weaknesses, but we won't). Follow the upgrade past South Torrance High School, then bike another 0.3 mile on the short upgrade just before reaching Calle Mayor (11.4).

The Return Segment. Turn right and follow the steep downhill past the shopping center entry. Turn left in 0.6 mile at Anza Avenue and follow the Class III road through the residential area to the short uphill segment at Sepulveda Boulevard. The route transitions to Class II and continues another 0.7 mile to Torrance Boulevard (13.3). Turn right, veer right again, and follow the small road which parallels Torrance Boulevard. In 0.3 mile at Ocean Avenue, the bikeway transitions to Class II on Torrance Boulevard and continues across Hawthorne Boulevard, Prairie Avenue/Madrona Avenue, then returns to the trip starting point (14.3).

CONNECTING TRIPS: 1) Connection with the South Bay Bike Trail (Trip #1A) and Palos Verdes Peninsula Loop (Trips #6A and #6B) - at PCH and Calle Mayor, bike southwest on the latter street 1.25 miles to Palos Verdes Boulevard; turn north for Trip #1A and south for Trip #6A or Trip #6B; 2) connection with the Gardena/Dominguez Channel ride (Trip #41) - at 190th Street and Yukon Avenue, bike north 1.5 miles on Yukon Avenue to Alondra Park.

TRIP #41 - GARDENA BIKEWAY/DOMINGUEZ CHANNEL

GENERAL LOCATION: Gardena

LEVEL OF DIFFICULTY: **Gardena City Loop** - easy
Distance - 7.0 miles
Elevation gain - essentially flat

Dominguez Channel Round Trip - easy
Distance - 5.2 miles (round trip)
Elevation gain - essentially flat

HIGHLIGHTS: **Gardena City Loop.** A well-marked Class III loop that explores the city of Gardena, this described trip is part of a larger city bikeway system. With the exception of the Van Ness segment, the bikeway is generally on relatively slow-moving residential or light commercial streets. The route is only modestly scenic, but does offer some nice parks which are scattered along the route.

Dominguez Channel and Alondra Park. There is also a Class I bikepath to the west along the Dominguez Flood Control Channel, which is not directly connected to the Gardena loop. This 1.6-mile path starts at 135th Street and Crenshaw Boulevard and works its way south to its terminus at the Alondra Park entrance. There is an excellent Class I park tour beyond this park entry point.

TRIP #41 - GARDENA BIKEWAY/DOMINGUEZ CHANNEL

TRAILHEAD: **Gardena City Loop and Dominguez Channel.** From the San Diego Freeway, exit east at Artesia Boulevard and drive 1.5 miles to Van Ness Avenue. Turn left (north) and drive 2.5 miles to 135th Street. Continue to 132nd Street and turn right. Find parking near Rowley Park (water, shade, recreation fields, basketball courts). From the Harbor Freeway, exit west at Rosecrans Avenue and drive 1.75 miles to Van Ness Avenue. Turn right (north) and drive 0.75 mile to 132nd Street, then continue as above.

Bring a light water supply; there are public water sources at the parks along the trail.

TRIP DESCRIPTION: **Gardena City Loop.** The outer city loop in the accompanying trip map is described below. The western segment starts along narrow and highly trafficked Van Ness Avenue, but leaves the busy road and cruises residential territory beginning at 154th Street. An Army Reserve Center and Freeman Park are nearby.

Once across busy Redondo Beach Boulevard, the bikeway passes the civic center area on the 162nd Street southern trip segment. A miniature public Japanese Garden and the Rush Memorial Gymnasium are on this stretch. The eastern trip segment jig-jogs its way north through a residential area and passes near the Victorian-architectured Saint John's Lutheran Church (163rd Street and Budlong Avenue). After recrossing Redondo Beach Boulevard, the bikeway continues on a tree-lined segment of Budlong Avenue and passes the back side of the Normandie Club (24-hour gambling) near Rosecrans Avenue.

The route heads west at 139th Street, traversing a predominantly industrial area with relatively light traffic, and returns to Van Ness Avenue in about 1.25 miles. A short half-mile cruise to the north leads back to Rowley Park.

Dominguez Flood Control Channel. From Van Ness Avenue and 135th Street, bike west 0.5 mile along the latter street to a bridge just before reaching Crenshaw Boulevard. Pass through the entrance gate on the south side of 135th Street and bike 0.5 mile on the back side of an industrial area to Rosecrans Avenue. Cross Rosecrans Avenue to the southwest side of the intersection and switch over to the west levee of the Dominguez Channel. Pedal through a residential area with street crossings at 147th Street (1.3), Compton Boulevard (1.6), and Manhattan Beach Boulevard (2.1). Note that there are roadway dividers on the latter two busy streets, which make the crossings relatively easy; however, keep an eye on the traffic!

Alondra Park. Once across Manhattan Beach Boulevard, follow the Class I path to the right of the divider fence into Alondra Park. (The gated and locked downhill path to the left leads to the channel floor.) Once inside the park, stay to the left, pass a restroom facility, and follow along the periphery of El Camino College through the

Feeding the fowl at Alondra Park

green and shaded park. Veer right just before reaching Redondo Beach Boulevard (2.6) and follow the loop around the Alondra Park lake. Bring a few slices of bread and make friends with the ducks and geese! Bike past the large reservoir/swimming pool and follow the loop around the lake's west side, returning to Manhattan Beach Boulevard (3.1). Return to Rowley Park by reversing the incoming route (5.2).

Note: Alondra Park is certainly the tour highlight. An excellent option is to "set up camp" at this park and start the Dominguez Channel ride from there. In addition, the channel ride can be extended one mile north to 120th Street. The main concern with this segment is that cyclists must leave the channel and bike to the pedestrian crossings at both 135th Street and El Segundo Boulevard.

CONNECTING TRIPS: There are numerous local spurs off the Gardena City Loop.

TRIP #42 - DIAMOND BAR LOOP

GENERAL LOCATION: Diamond Bar

LEVEL OF DIFFICULTY: Loop - moderate
Distance - 10.4 miles
Elevation gain - periodic moderate grades

HIGHLIGHTS: This pleasant, predominantly Class II loop trip starts at rustic Sycamore Canyon Park and proceeds through a mix of flats and rolling hills on Diamond Bar Boulevard through Brea Canyon. Next is a short pump over the Puente Hills and a return via Colima Road/Golden Springs Drive. There are varied views of the Puente Hills throughout the trip and an excellent view of the valley below and the San Jose Hills from the Brea Canyon Cutoff summit.

There is an interesting workout diversion tour up Grand Avenue which provides a dandy view of Diamond Bar. The Diamond Bar Loop easily can be connected to the San Jose Hills ride if the biker is interested in extending this hillside tour.

TRAILHEAD: The Orange and Pomona freeways merge for about a two-mile stretch near Diamond Bar. Exit at Grand Avenue, turn right (east), and drive 0.4 mile to Golden Springs Drive. Turn left, then continue one-half mile to the Sycamore Canyon Park entrance on the right and find public parking. The park has restrooms, light tree cover, picnic facilities, a children's playground, and a baseball field.

Bring a filled water bottle, especially on hot days. We found public water sources at Sycamore Canyon Park and at the Los Angeles Royal Vista Golf Course. There are also gas stations peppered along the route.

TRIP DESCRIPTION: **Golden Springs Drive Eastbound.** Before leaving the park, investigate the upper segment where there is a hiking trail through a lightly forested area. Turn right onto Golden Springs Drive and bike on the modest grade which crests and heads downhill to Diamond Bar Village with eateries and shopping. In 0.1 mile, turn sharply right onto the wide expanse of Class II Diamond Bar Boulevard (0.6).

TRIP #42 - DIAMOND BAR LOOP

Diamond Bar Boulevard. Follow this road uphill through the treeless canyonlike setting to the crest at Tin Drive. Coast the downhill past Steep Canyon Drive to Grand Avenue where all four corners are filled with shopping centers (1.9). Coast downhill on the long, slight grade past several small shopping plazas, then follow the steeper descent which leads to Mountain Laurel Road (2.6). Note the homes on the ridge above; we'll say more about the ridge area in "The Grand Avenue Diversion Trip."

Continue on the mile-long downgrade through a residential setting past Pathfinder Road, Shadow Canyon Road (4.0), and the Country Hills Town Center (shopping center), then bike uphill to the crest at Cold Spring Lane. Just beyond, the road passes Brea Canyon Road with a shopping complex and gas stations, then tunnels under the Orange Freeway; the road name changes to Brea Canyon Cutoff.

Brea Canyon Cutoff. The route passes below the house-bedecked Puente Hills, on Class X roadway with a wide biking shoulder. Follow the 0.75-mile workout stairstep upgrade through the exposed canyon past Pathfinder Road (5.3). Just beyond at the summit in this more lightly developed area, there is an excellent view into the valley below and the San Jose Hills across the valley. Next follow the steep, mildly winding downhill which lets out at Colima Road near a small business complex with both sit-down and fast-food eateries (6.9).

Colima Road - Golden Springs Drive Eastbound. Turn right (east) and bike on the Class X road with wide shoulder between the two segments of the Los Angeles Royal Vista Golf Course. Continue past the Los Angeles Royal Vista Restaurant and an area of the golf course to the right with a convenient water fountain (7.2). Just beyond, the road becomes Golden Springs Drive. Near Calbourne Drive, there is a return to Class II bikeway. Ride on the flat, pass Lemon Avenue, and begin the 0.3-mile uphill to an area with fast food restaurants and gas stations. Pass Brea Canyon Road (8.5) and ride under the freeway interchange on Golden Springs Drive.

Just beyond is the stair-step upgrade which becomes testy just before reaching Gateway Drive. Here, there are both the freeway and lightly developed hills to the left and commercial complexes to the right. In the next 0.6 mile is a ride on varying degrees of grade, and it reaches the crest at Grand Avenue at a shopping/industrial complex (9.9). To the north is the Diamond Bar Golf Course, and just beyond is the Diamond Bar Country Club. Enjoy the view of the San Gabriel Mountains from this elevated area. In 0.3 mile, turn right and return to Sycamore Canyon Park (10.4).

Grand Avenue Diversion Trip. One look at the street map convinced us to bike up Grand Avenue east of Golden Springs Drive; the ride on the ridge at the summit appeared to be too good to pass up. So we biked up steep Grand Avenue on a 0.7 mile workout to Shotgun Lane, only to find that the road access to that street is gated: private property! However, we continued up to Summit Ridge Drive, turned left, and biked 0.3 mile to the Summit Ridge Park turnoff. A short distance uphill is the park with water, restrooms, picnic tables, and a tremendous view of the surrounding hills and valleys. The total round trip is 2.2 miles. (More-ambitious cyclists can continue north on Summit Ridge Drive or follow Grand Avenue into the city of Chino Hills.)

CONNECTING TRIPS: 1) Connection with the Hacienda Heights Loop (Trip #27) - at Brea Canyon Cutoff and Colima Road, turn west at the latter road; 2) connection with the San Jose Hills ride (trip #43) - at Brea Canyon Road, bike north 1.5 miles to Valley Boulevard; 3) connection with the Bonelli Regional County Park tour (Trip #44) and the Baseline Road tour (Trip #45) - from the intersection of Golden Springs Drive and Diamond Bar Boulevard, bike north on the latter street, which becomes Mission Boulevard and meets little Humane Way in 2.5 miles; follow that road to Valley Boulevard and turn left (north) at the first major intersection (Ganesha Boulevard) beyond the Corona Expressway.

TRIP #43 - SAN JOSE HILLS

<u>GENERAL LOCATION</u>: Walnut, City of Industry

<u>LEVEL OF DIFFICULTY</u>: Loop - moderate
Distance - 12.9 miles
Elevation gain - periodic moderate-to-steep grades
(Amar Road and Temple Avenue)

<u>HIGHLIGHTS</u>: This is a dandy trip for "hillies." From Nogales Street to La Puente Road to the outlet at Temple Avenue and Valley Boulevard (6.7 miles), bikers are treated to a steady diet of ups and downs in the San Jose Hills. The trip is mostly on Class II and Class X roads with plenty of biking room. There are splendid views into the valleys and across to the Puente Hills at the higher elevations. For variety, the remaining half of the trip is in the valley flatlands.

On a hot, smoggy day, this workout might budge the strenuous difficulty rating. Bikers that are more adventurous might explore the surrounding hillside, residential communities, particularly on La Puente Road, Lemon Avenue, western Amar Road, and northern Grand Avenue.

<u>TRAILHEAD</u>: From the Pomona Freeway, exit at Brea Canyon Road and drive north 1.5 miles to Valley Boulevard. Turn right and continue one-half mile to Grand Avenue. Turn left, drive 0.6 mile to Snow Creek Drive, and turn right into Snow Creek Park. From the Orange Freeway south of Diamond Bar, exit at the Pomona Freeway westbound and turn off at Brea Canyon Road. Continue as described above. From the Orange Freeway north of Diamond Bar, exit at Temple Avenue and drive 0.7 mile to Valley Boulevard. Turn left, proceed 2.25 miles to Grand Avenue, and turn right (north). Continue to Snow Creek Drive, as described above.

Bring a filled water bottle (two for hot days). There is water at Creekside Park near the halfway point, which is reached via a testy uphill; however, no easily accessible (on-route) public water sources were found.

<u>TRIP DESCRIPTION</u>: **Grand Avenue.** Explore the well-designed little Snow Creek Park before hitting the road. There are shade trees, picnic benches and a picnicker's pagoda, water, restrooms, a sunken baseball field, and little Snow Creek on the park periphery. Return to Grand Avenue and bike downhill through the hills. In 0.4 mile, pass La Puente Road, then continue downhill 0.3 mile to Valley Boulevard.

Valley Boulevard Outbound. Turn right and bike on the Class X road with wide biking shoulder through the flat and wide valley. The road parallels the Southern Pacific tracks, and there is a reasonable likelihood of having a choo-choo for company along this stretch. The area along the tracks has scattered industry for the next several miles; this is part of the City of Industry (surprise!). Ride through varying and sparsely populated and developed areas (mixed residential and commercial) past Brea Canyon Road, transit a short span beyond Suzanne Road where the bike shoulder narrows, and reach Pierre Road with its small shopping plaza and gas station (1.8). In 0.7 mile, pass Lemon Avenue with a gas station, a small shopping center, and a few rolling hills. Bike

TRIP #43 - SAN JOSE HILLS

past Fairway Drive and a shopping plaza, then Sentous Avenue with a gas station and mini-mart (3.2), and cycle another 0.4 mile to Nogales Street and yet another shopping complex.

Nogales Street. So you're wondering, where are these San Jose Hills? Class X Nogales Street provides the introduction. Bike one-half mile in a residential setting to

La Puente Road, using the sidewalk in this stretch if you are nervous about taking up a lane of traffic. However, our trip starts uphill on tree-lined (now Class II) Nogales Street, reaching the crest in 0.4 mile. The residential road continues on the flat for a short distance then starts a mild, steady uphill to Shadow Oak Drive (4.9).

Just 0.4 mile to the left is Shadow Oak Park, while well-equipped Creekside Park can be reached by turning right and biking 0.7 mile on a testy uphill. Our reference route stays on Nogales Street and follows another steady uphill which steepens and continues 0.4 mile to Walnut Plaza (shopping center). Pump another 0.2 mile to Amar Road (5.5).

Amar Road - The Hillside Tour. Turn right (east) on the Class II road and pedal through shadeless residential territory. There are barren hills to the left and scattered peeks down into the valley on the right. Follow another steady upgrade which steepens, then reaches the crest at (6.6). For the next two miles to Grand Avenue, the route transitions from this steady upgrade to rolling hills.

Bike past scattered residential pockets beneath plush hillside homes and enjoy the periodic views down into the valley. The road passes Lemon Avenue (7.1), then roller-coasters through a less-populated area before reaching a little valley with a small, tightly packed community. In a short distance, Amar Road reaches the Grand Avenue intersection (8.7).

Temple Avenue and the Downgrade. Pedal by a gas station and continue on the road now named Temple Avenue. Pass the Mount San Antonio College Wildlife Sanctuary, then the campus entrance, and follow the steady upgrade alongside the campus. The uphill continues through more open country across Bonita Drive, and the route transitions to Class X with a wide shoulder. What follows is a workout steady uphill to the crest 1.2 miles from Grand Avenue. Enjoy the view from the crest, then bike downhill on divided highway through less-developed country. Pass on the periphery of California State Polytechnic University campus on tree-lined (with a short stretch of narrowing) roadway, cross San Jose Creek, and bike to Valley Boulevard (10.8).

Valley Boulevard - Return Segment. There is a small shopping center one-fourth mile further on Temple Street at Pomona Boulevard. However, the reference route turns right onto Class X Valley Boulevard and continues through open and exposed valley country. There are scattered residential pockets along the way with a mix of industry and some farmland. There are also continuous views of the relatively barren Chino Hills to the left. Pass the gas station 1.5 miles from Temple Avenue and reach Grand Avenue in another 0.6 mile. Turn right and puff up the workout upgrade 0.7 mile, returning to Snow Creek Park (12.9).

La Puente Avenue Option. On the outbound segment, cyclists can turn west off of Grand Avenue onto La Puente Avenue and enjoy a Class II roadway which continues to Nogales Avenue. This alternative is not as flat as Valley Boulevard, but is more scenic and does reduce the trip length by about a mile.

CONNECTING TRIPS: 1) Connection with the Hacienda Heights Loop (Trip # 27) - at Valley Boulevard and Nogales Street, head south for one mile to Colima Road; 2) connection with the Diamond Bar Loop (Trip #42) - at Brea Canyon Road, bike 1.5 miles south to Golden Springs Drive and turn left; 3) connection with the Bonelli Regional County Park tour (Trip #44) and the Baseline Road tour (Trip #45) - from the Temple Avenue/Valley Boulevard intersection, bike north on the latter road 1.7 miles to the first intersection just past the Corona Expressway (Fairplex Drive) and turn left.

TRIP #44 - BONELLI REGIONAL COUNTY PARK

__GENERAL LOCATION__: San Dimas, Pomona

__LEVEL OF DIFFICULTY__: Loop - moderate
Distance - 8.9 miles
Elevation gain - periodic moderate grades in
      eastern side of park

__HIGHLIGHTS__: A pleasant spin around Puddingstone Reservoir, this tour offers a wide variety of terrain and attractions. Sally Bond, our triathlete reviewer, notes that it is also part of the course for one of the Los Angeles County Triathlon series. This is a varied class ride with wide bike shoulder on most of the Class III and Class X segments. The route traverses rolling hills through Picnic Valley, winds along the east shoreline by Raging Waters, visits the North Shore picnic area and beach, cruises by Brackett Field on a flat road, and returns for a hilly tour through the scenic East Shore area. There are numerous vistas overlooking the reservoir. The picnic areas are in a naturally scenic and well-groomed part of Bonelli Park. There are several short grades on this tour which "push" this trip out of the easy category; however, there is an easy two-mile mini-loop which circumnavigates Picnic Valley.

__TRAILHEAD__: From the San Bernardino Freeway, exit north onto Fairplex Drive. Drive 0.75 mile to Via Verde, turn left, and continue 0.75 mile to the east entrance of Bonelli Park. Pay the entry fee and drive one-half mile to the nearest parking. From the Orange Freeway, exit at Via Verde and turn east. Drive one-fourth mile to the west park entrance. Continue another mile and make a hard left into the parking area.

An option is to park in the Raging Waters lot and enjoy some exciting water rides at the trip's end. A free option is to park on Via Verde, just west of the Orange Freeway.

Bring a light water supply, as there is water throughout the park. There is a three-mile waterless stretch in the Brackett Air Field/Mountain Meadows Golf Course area. Look out for thorns, particularly off the established roads. Our tour group picked up several of these little devils at unknown locations and eventually had flat tires! (Once the thorns are pulled out, plan on repairing a tube.)

__TRIP DESCRIPTION__: __Picnic Valley.__ Bike west on the Class I path, near the parking lot, which follows along Via Verde. For the next half mile, the route passes a large pagoda, playgrounds, and picnic areas. The charming grass and treed areas along the path are all part of Picnic Valley, and the path heads downhill. The path crosses under a park roadway and then veers right and heads downhill again along Lakeside Drive. Next it passes above a sailboat launch area where there is an excellent view of the lake, and reaches a parking entry where the Class I path ends (1.2).

__Raging Waters.__ Pass the parking entry (stay to the left) and follow the Raging Waters sign to the right at the next road junction. (A left at this junction leads to the Equestrian Staging Area.) Bike next to Puddingstone Reservoir to a picturesque overlook with the reservoir to the right and Raging Waters to the left. Several different water rides can be viewed (and visited), including the ultimate downhill ride, the

TRIP #44 - BONELLI REGIONAL COUNTY PARK

seven-story-high "Dropout" (2.0). At the Raging Waters road junction just beyond, turn right and bike uphill to the powerboat launch area (2.6).

Puddingstone Drive. For the next mile, Class II Puddingstone Drive passes a series of excellent picnic areas and a site with a miniature sand beach. The road crosses Walnut Avenue (3.2) and begins a short uphill just before reaching the outskirts of

Brackett Air Field. Bike alongside the airport and admire the longhorn cattle in the hills to the north, pass the control tower, and turn right on Fairplex Drive (4.5).

Los Angeles County Fairgrounds and Mountain Meadows Golf Course. Follow the Class I path (west side of street only) one-half mile along the Los Angeles County Fairgrounds and turn left, staying on Fairplex Drive. (A right turn leads to Brackett Field.) Note that there is a nifty spot directly below the flight path in this area. Pedal a Class X stretch 0.3 mile to the McKinley Avenue split, then veer right to remain on Fairplex Drive (5.3). Bike on the mild Class II road uphill along the golf course for one-half mile, then turn right at Via Verde and follow the steeper upgrade to the Bonelli Park east entry gate.

East Shore. An option is to continue one-half mile on Via Verde and return to the parking area. However, this reference ride follows the road right on a steep upgrade which passes the Puddingstone Hot Tubs (public tubs with nice vistas) (6.6); this grade levels in a short distance. Bike into the East Shore RV Park and turn right at the corner market.

Stay to the right and follow the winding downhill into the lower RV park (7.4), turn left at any of the small streets, and follow the road toward the reservoir. Bike below the tent camp area, pass through the bike entry near the lake edge, and join up with the pleasant Class I path along the lake. This area has one of the premier lake views; it is a particularly nice location from which to watch the powerboats and jet skiers (8.1). Continue uphill on the path to the inviting East Shore picnic area, following the trail inland to the road (8.5), and then turn left. Cycle 0.2 mile to Via Verde, turn right, and return to the parking area (8.9).

CONNECTING TRIPS: 1) Connection with the Glendora Bikeway (Trip #35) - follow Via Verde west to San Dimas Avenue, turn right and bike 2.5 miles to Gladstone Street, and then turn left; 2) connection with the Baseline Road tour (Trip #45) - at Lakeside Drive and Via Verde, continue west on Via Verde.

East shore of Puddingstone Reservoir

TRIP #45 - BASELINE ROAD

GENERAL LOCATION: San Dimas, La Verne, Claremont

LEVEL OF DIFFICULTY: Loop - moderate
Distance - 22.3 miles
Elevation gain - periodic moderate grades

HIGHLIGHTS: This very scenic loop explores Ganesha Park and Bonelli Regional County Park, cruises the foothills of the San Gabriel Mountains, and visits three fine cities to boot. Most of this tour is on Class X roads with relatively light traffic and with wide biking shoulder. There are hill, valley, and mountain vistas scattered throughout this trip. Also, there are numerous interesting diversion trips, throughout the loop tour, which are identified in the detailed trip writeup.

TRAILHEAD: From the San Bernardino Freeway, exit at Dudley Street in Pomona. Turn north and continue as the street changes name to Via Vista Drive. Follow this winding road one mile into Ganesha Park; continue toward the north end of the park, on what is now Paige Drive, and find parking. Ganesha Park is a pleasant base of operations. There are hiking trails, dense tree cover, picnic areas, a swimming pool, children's playgrounds, and restrooms.
    Bring a filled water bottle (two if you want to bike without leaving the described route). There is water at several parks which are generally reached with short diversions off the main route.

TRIP DESCRIPTION: **Ganesha Park to Bonelli Regional County Park.** Leave the picnic area near the swimming pool and return to Paige Drive heading north. Bike uphill about 0.3 mile to McKinley Avenue. Turn left and pump uphill, above the Los Angeles County Fairplex, on Class III bikeway. In 0.5 mile on McKinley Avenue, the road crests and continues a short distance to Ganesha Boulevard (0.9).
    Turn left and bike one-half mile on the mild upgrade on Class III roadway alongside the Mountain Meadows Golf Course. Turn left at Via Verde and follow the steeper upgrade to the Bonelli Park east entrance gate (2.9). Bike in the hills of the large and pleasant park on Via Verde and, in one-half mile, reach a spur leading to a parking area. (See the Trip #44 map for more detail.) There are options to stay on Via Verde or to bike the paralleling Class I path through the tree-shaded picnic area known as Picnic Valley. The reference route stays on Via Verde for another 0.9 mile on rolling hills before reaching the park's west entrance gate at Lakeside Drive (4.4). Continue west a short distance, pass over the Orange Freeway, and reach San Dimas Avenue.
    Western Trip Segment. Turn right and bike a 0.4-mile flat to an area with an exceptional view north into the valley area. Follow this Class X road on the steep downgrade with barren hills to the east. Coast downhill past Avenida Loma Vista (5.5) alongside the Orange Freeway; the road curves east and passes under that freeway in 0.4 mile. Cycle through the rolling hills in a small canyon and pass an area with a view of Raging Waters. Soon, the road curves back to the north and levels, goes by Ben's

TRIP #45 - BASELINE ROAD

Bait Shop (bait and cold liquid refreshments), and then passes a gas station. The route continues across Arrow Highway and reaches Bonita Avenue just beyond (7.2).

Turn right (east) and pedal 0.8 mile on this palm-lined road, passing several small shopping plazas before reaching San Dimas Canyon Road. Turn left and bike on another Class X road with wide shoulder. The road heads uphill through an area with San

Gabriel Mountains views directly ahead, crests, then returns downhill and passes Allen Avenue. In a short distance is the State Highway 210 undercrossing and a more rural area with Baseline Road just beyond (9.0). There is a spur-trip option to continue north 0.4 mile to San Dimas Canyon Park for water, restrooms, shade, recreation fields, picnic areas, and a nature center.

Baseline Road. However, our reference route goes a few hundred feet north to Foothill Boulevard, turns right, and then left in 0.3 mile to reconnect with Baseline Road. This Class X road continues its full course along the base of the San Gabriel Mountains. Bike through the surrounding residential area, pass Wheeler Avenue (10.6) and Fruit Street (11.5), and navigate through rolling hills past an out-of-place road curve (12.0). Later, there is a light but steady upgrade that levels near Mountain Avenue (14.4); there is a nifty (and steep) diversion trip on this road into the hillside residential area. However, the reference tour continues on Baseline Road through the residential area 0.5 mile to Indian Hill Boulevard.

Indian Hill Boulevard. Turn right, cross above the freeway, and follow yet another Class X road through the quiet and tree-shaded residential area. The refreshing downhill leads past Cahuilla Park (water, shade) and Claremont High School, then crosses Foothill Boulevard shortly (15.9). The road narrows as it continues through the treed, rural residential setting past inviting Memorial Park (water, restrooms, shade, grass, playgrounds).

Bonita Avenue. The return west on this road passes through a residential area up to Mountain Avenue, then transitions into a more industrially oriented region up to the La Verne city limit (17.9). The flat, lightly traveled Class X road returns to the tree-lined residential area and proceeds to "D" Street (19.9). There is an old-fashioned but well-maintained shopping complex here with a donut shop (Don's weakness!).

The Return Segment. Turn left (south) on "D" Street, cruise by the University of La Verne, and cycle 0.3 mile to Foothill Boulevard. Turn left, then turn right again at the next intersection ("E" Street). Just south of Arrow Highway, the street name changes to Fairplex Drive. Pedal past the Pomona Raceway between Brackett Field and the west side of the Los Angeles County Fairplex, turning sharply left to stay on Fairplex Drive. Continue 0.3 mile to the McKinley Avenue intersection (21.4) and bike straight ahead to stay on that street. Now, simply return to Ganesha Park by retracing the outgoing route. The total tour is 22.3 miles.

Diversion Trips. There are several additional interesting areas to explore in the Claremont area. There is an interesting workout in the Mills Road-Pomelo Drive-Padua Avenue region (Mills Road becomes Baldy Road and can be continued on the gut-wrenching uphill to Mount Baldy, for expert bikers only!). There is some excellent tour biking available in the area bounded by Foothill Boulevard, Indian Hill Boulevard, Arrow Highway, and Claremont Boulevard; in this zone are Pomona College, Claremont College, Claremont Men's College, Scripps College, Harvey Mudd College, and Pitzer College.

CONNECTING TRIPS: 1) Connection with the Diamond Bar Loop (Trip #42) and the San Jose Hills ride (Trip #43) - from the intersection of Fairplex Drive and Via Verde, bike south 1.5 miles on the former road to Holt Avenue; turn right and follow that street as it becomes Valley Boulevard 1.75 miles to Temple Avenue; continue south for the San Jose Hills trip and turn left on Temple Avenue to reach Diamond Bar Boulevard and the Diamond Bar Loop trip; 2) connection with the Bonelli Regional

County Park tour (Trip #44) - at Lakeside Drive and Via Verde, turn north on the former street; 3) connection with the San Dimas Canyon Road tour (Trip # 65) - at the intersection of San Dimas Canyon Road and Baseline Road, follow the former road north into the foothills.

TRIP #46 - LA MIRADA BIKEWAY SYSTEM

GENERAL LOCATION: La Mirada

LEVEL OF DIFFICULTY: Loop - easy
Distance - 9.8 miles
Elevation gain - periodic easy-to-moderate grades

HIGHLIGHTS: All too often, those little green spots on our maps wind up being wayside parks with some tumbleweeds and a drinking fountain! Not this tour! This is a well-designed route on primarily Class I/Class II bikeways, with the trip highlights being Creek Park and La Mirada Park. After cruising a few miles on the city streets, the route follows a natural and refreshing Class I path alongside La Mirada Creek, then visits the green rolling knolls and recreation areas of La Mirada Park. Both inviting parks have their own networks of excellent walking/biking trails.

TRAILHEAD: From the Santa Ana Freeway, exit north at Valley View Avenue and continue 1.8 miles to Foster Road (just beyond Rosecrans Avenue). Turn right and drive 0.3 mile to Gardenhill Drive; turn left and continue 0.2 mile to the parking area in front of the Gardenhill Park Community Center. Gardenhill Park has a playground, trees, picnic benches, and barbecue facilities, as well as water and restrooms.

Bring a light water supply. There is water at the parks and numerous gas stations along the way.

TRIP DESCRIPTION: **The City Streets.** Exit the park and turn right, biking through the residential area a short distance to Foster Road, and then turn right again. Continue a short distance and turn left (south) on Valley View Avenue. Follow the mild stair-step upgrade on this Class II path 0.5 mile to Rosecrans Avenue (0.8). Turn left and cruise through the residential setting past Biola Avenue; a left turn here leads to Biola University.

Our reference route remains on Rosecrans Avenue and continues 0.5 mile to La Mirada Boulevard (1.8). Turn right and cruise by the La Mirada Civic Theater and the La Mirada Mall. In 0.4 mile, turn left at Santa Gertrudes Avenue where there is a small collection of businesses (including some pleasing eateries). Pass Rosecrans Avenue (3.9) on this Class II route and bike the short workout upgrade to the point where there is a clear view of the Los Coyotes Hills.

Pedal alongside the La Mirada Golf Course through modest rolling hills, pass Foster Road, and reach Imperial Highway (5.1). Bike 0.3 mile on Class X road and, near the bottom of the first grade, cross the street to the Class I bike entry.

TRIP #46 - LA MIRADA BIKEWAY SYSTEM

La Mirada Creek Park. Follow the path through the grassy park alongside La Mirada Creek. The path follows the creek a short distance on both north and south sides. Keep a wary eye for rotating sprinklers in this area; Don was thoroughly zapped by one of these gadgets at one of the bridge crossings. (Don never was too bright!) Follow the tree-lined bikeway to the park's edge and transition to Las Flores Avenue. There are horse corrals, chicken, geese, and even rabbits in this area.

Bike to Imperial Highway (6.2); just before reaching this street, follow the dirt path back down to the creek and pass through the short tunnel under Imperial Highway. This is the southern segment of La Mirada Creek Park. Meander along the creek through this serene environment, following the small bridges which cross the creek. At the last creek crossing before reaching the next tunnel, take the paved path to the left up to the residential area. The path leads down to the Oakwood Lane cul-de-sac, and that road leads to La Mirada Boulevard. (An option is to stay on the creek path and take the tunnel under La Mirada Boulevard. Cross the creek at the tunnel outlet and climb up to La Mirada Boulevard just south of the Oakwood Lane junction.)

La Mirada Park. Turn left (south) on La Mirada Boulevard and bike 0.2 mile to Foster Road. Turn left and, in a short distance, make a right turn into the parking area (7.4). (Note that there are many paths throughout the park, and only a sample route is described. The general rule is to maintain a southerly heading and head for Alicante Road.) Follow the Class I path that is dead ahead on the short workout upgrade into the La Mirada Park vicinity. There are numerous recreation fields in this green and scenic area.

Follow the path until it passes near Adelfa Drive, then take the junction to the right, toward the swimming pool and tennis courts. Near the lowest set of courts, follow that path to the right, turn left at its terminus, and cycle down to the small lake. This is a pleasant rest spot with a wide variety of friendly waterfowl. Walk a short distance across the grass to Alicante Road and turn right (8.1).

The Return Leg. Bike past the well-manicured Olive Lawn Cemetery to La Mirada Boulevard. Turn right (north) and follow the rolling hills past the water fountain at La Mirada City Hall, continuing to Tacuba Drive (9.1). Turn left and bike on the Class III street through the quiet residential area. Cruise 0.5 mile to Biola Avenue and turn left; follow that Class II route to Gardenhill Drive. Pedal through well-groomed residential territory past Gardenhill Elementary School and return to the Gardenhill Park Community Center (9.8).

CONNECTING TRIPS: 1) Connection with the Coyote Creek Trail (Trip #24) - from the Valley View Avenue/Foster Road intersection, take the latter road west 0.75 mile to the trail's upper entry; 2) there is also an interesting hilly connecting tour of the Los Coyotes Country Club vicinity, and it passes through an area of plush residential estates; continue east on Rosecrans Avenue past the Santa Gertrudes Avenue intersection, turn right at Beach Boulevard, and then left at the first street, which is Los Coyotes Drive.

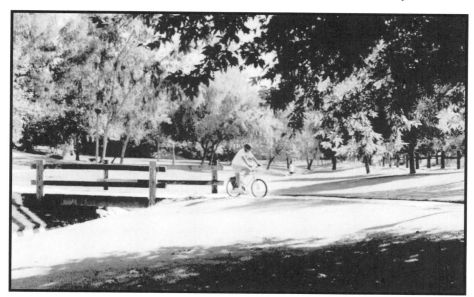

La Mirada Creek Park

POTPOURRI

First Street near City Hall

TRIP #47 - SKYSCRAPER TOUR

GENERAL LOCATION: Los Angeles Civic Center

LEVEL OF DIFFICULTY: Loop - moderate
Distance - 10.8 miles
Elevation gain - periodic moderate grades on
Beverly Boulevard/First Street

HIGHLIGHTS: At its best, this is an early Sunday morning tour. Start between 7 a.m. and 8 a.m. and plan to spend several hours riding and browsing. Traffic during the week is murderous and our recommendation is: "Save it for Sunday." The tour is on a mix of roads with much of the route on Class II or Class III paths, or unmarked roads with a wide, marked car-parking area.

This little beauty provides a fine morning cross-section of the Los Angeles scene. The tour starts at scenic MacArthur Park, then heads into central Los Angeles, visiting the Los Angeles Convention Center, skyscraperville, and the Los Angeles Wholesale Flower Terminal. Next is a short tour through "Street People's Los Angeles," Koreatown and Little Tokyo, El Pueblo De Los Angeles Historic Park, and Union Station. The return leg passes through the Los Angeles Civic Center and returns to the trip origin via the rolling hills of Beverly Boulevard.

For the truly adventurous, this is a "can't miss" trip.

TRAILHEAD: From the Santa Monica Freeway, exit north at Vermont Avenue and drive 0.75 mile to Wilshire Boulevard. Turn right, continue 0.75 mile (past Lafayette Park) to Park View Street, and turn right. Find parking at the west edge of MacArthur Park, subject to the posted laws. (There is no parking time limit on Sunday and no meter fees; there is no posted guideline on the latter rule, but we were not ticketed.) From the Harbor Freeway, exit west at Sixth Street and drive 1.25 miles to Park View Street. Turn left, cross Wilshire Boulevard, and park as above. From the Hollywood Freeway, take the Alvarado Street turnoff southbound and drive 1.1 miles to Wilshire Boulevard. Turn left at Park View Street.

Bring a filled water bottle or two if you do not want to rely on the scattered water sources. There are very few public restrooms along the route. An option is to start the tour from Lafayette Park (Wilshire Boulevard and Hoover Street). This option adds about one mile to the reference tour. Also, some of the inner city roadway is in a rough or torn-up state due to Metro Rail construction. Road conditions can be checked with the Los Angeles Department of Transportation.

TRIP DESCRIPTION: **MacArthur Park.** Tour the park before leaving on the trip to the civic center. It has a small but beautiful manmade lake with water fountains. There are bikeways/walkways throughout the treed park, which allow easy access to the park's north side. In this grass-laden hilly park, there are observation and picnic benches, an outdoor theater, and a mixed array of walkers, joggers, sitters, and a few "overnight campers."

TRIP #47 - SKYSCRAPER TOUR

Eastward into the Big City. Bike the periphery of the park, heading southeast on Seventh Street. Turn right on Alvarado Street, follow the mild upgrade near Eighth Street, and cycle on Class II-like bikeway to Olympic Boulevard. Note that "Class II-like" is used on this tour to mean unsigned roads with a marked lane for car parking and adequate bike space within the lane. Turn left on Olympic Boulevard (0.6) and pedal on flat Class II roadway through a light commercial section with scattered residences. Bike under the Harbor Freeway and turn right at the first street, Byram Street (1.3).

Convention Center to Los Angeles Wholesale Flower Terminal. Turn left again at 11th Street and pass in front of the Los Angeles Convention Center. There is a view of the civic center skyscraper complex to the left in this area. Turn left onto Class II Figueroa Street and pedal to Ninth Street where the marked bikepath ends. Cycle north into the "teeth" of skyscraper country and follow the short upgrade to Wilshire Boulevard (2.2). Turn right and bike on the road that is almost totally shadowed by the surrounding high-rise buildings.

Pass Hope Street and the First Interstate Bank Building, the scene of the deadly and spectacular 1988 fire. Bike to the street's end at Grand Avenue, turn right, and then left again at Seventh Street. Turn left in a short distance and travel one block north to Pershing Square, listen to a "fire and brimstone" speech from one of the locals (subject is variable), and backtrack to Wilshire Boulevard.

Follow the continued Class X road past venerable Clifton's Cafeteria and cruise 0.4 mile to Los Angeles Street, where the commercial buildings dwindle in height and the sunshine returns (3.1). Turn right at Maple Avenue and pass the quaint Los Angeles Wholesale Flower Terminal. This local "flower capital" bustles at 5:30 a.m. on Monday, Wednesday, and Friday. Turn left at Eighth Street, bike a short distance to San Pedro Street, and turn left (northeast) (3.3).

"War Zone" to Koreatown. Traveling north on San Pedro Street provides a study of poverty and filth (we are providing the "full" Los Angeles tour!). There is trash everywhere and a large number of folks milling around, many of whom are street people. In 0.6 mile, reach Fourth Street and the southern terminus of Koreatown. The environment transitions to one of cleanliness and order just by crossing from the south side of Fourth Street to the north side. At Second Street in Little Tokyo, cross the street and follow the diagonal bikeway/walkway through the nifty little shopping center. Stop and observe Los Angeles City Hall, which is framed by the buildings in the mall.

Northward to Union Station. Cross First Street and head northwest on Class II bikeway, with Parker Center to the right. Turn right on Main Street, pass under the City Hall-City Hall East walkway, and continue to the Temple Street intersection (4.4). On the west side is the interesting U.S. Courthouse, and to the east, the Los Angeles Mall and pleasant Fletcher Bowron Square. Just beyond is the Los Angeles Children's Museum.

Cross over the Santa Ana Freeway and enter the birthplace of Los Angeles. Directly ahead is the expansive El Pueblo De Los Angeles Historic Park, which includes the old Mission Church to the left and the charming Los Angeles Plaza to the right (4.6). Just north of the plaza, paralleling Main Street, is renowned Olvera Street. Pedal north on Main Street, turn right on Sunset Boulevard/Cesar E. Chavez Avenue, and then right again on Alameda Street. Bike a short way to the classic Union Station railroad passenger terminal. Return to Cesar E. Chavez Avenue and bike west.

Chinatown and the Los Angeles Civic Center. Continue west 0.2 mile to Broadway and turn right. Bike through Chinatown on the busy Class X road with two lanes and no bike shoulder – bike in the middle of the right lane in this stretch all the way to College Street (5.9). Turn left on the Class II bike route and pedal a moderate upgrade 0.2 mile to Alpine Street. Turn right and bike the testy upgrade which crests and heads downhill to its terminus at Figueroa Street.

Turn left and stare into the Los Angeles Civic Center, then bike downhill under the Santa Ana Freeway. Turn left at Temple Street, pump uphill to the crest at Grand Avenue, and cruise by the Music Center complex. Continue downhill to Hill Street (7.1) and turn right. Bike further downhill over the top of the Los Angeles subway to First Street and turn right again.

The Return Segment. Cycle a short distance on this Class II street and begin the short workout upgrade to a point with views of the Los Angeles area skyline, both east and west. Pass the north side of the Los Angeles Music Center and bike downhill under the Harbor Freeway (7.9).

This tour is different from most of our tours, as we saved the most testy hills until last. This is a great opportunity to work off all those goodies which were consumed at the landmark sites along the way. Follow the short uphill to the crest from which there is a grand view of three more hills. Just before reaching the Glendale Boulevard overpass, turn right and bike down the paralleling road to Glendale Boulevard, cross that street, and bike back up to Beverly Boulevard (previously First Street); trust us, its easier! Climb the steep grade which crests at Belmont Avenue. Continue up another shorter upgrade, then pedal downhill to Alvarado Street (8.9).

Turn left (southwest) and bike on Class II-like roadway through the commercial/industrial area. Cycle through lightly rolling hills past Third Street and continue another half mile to Sixth Street and the edge of MacArthur Park. Bike northwest through the park, pass the outdoor theater, and pedal through the tunnel to the park's south side. Follow the path up to Park View Street and return to the starting point (9.8).

CONNECTING TRIPS: Connection with the Exposition Park/USC Campus tour (Trip #48) - at the intersection of Olympic Boulevard and Figueroa Street, turn southwest on the latter street and bike 1.75 miles.

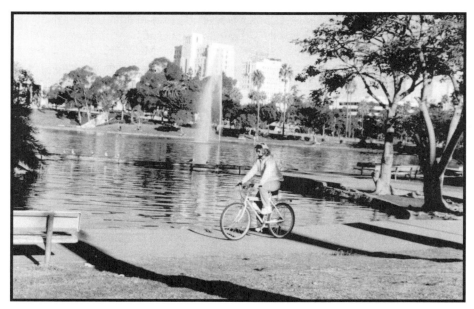

MacArthur Park

TRIP #48 - INNER CITY BIKEWAY SYSTEM

<u>**GENERAL LOCATION**</u>: Central Los Angeles, Exposition Park, USC Campus

<u>**LEVEL OF DIFFICULTY**</u>: Loop - easy
Distance - 3.8 miles
Elevation gain - flat

<u>**HIGHLIGHTS**</u>: **Central Los Angeles.** There is a system of predominantly Class III bikeways spread throughout the central city area, as is shown in the accompanying tour map. The problem is that these routes are so little used by bikers, that drivers appear oblivious to the fact that these are shared roadways. This was particularly true on the north-south Hoover Street and Broadway routes. Also, most routes are on busy, fast-moving roadways.

We have only biked selected segments of this system, but will generalize: For bikers who are uncomfortable biking with heavy traffic on roadways with limited biking room, use these routes only as connectors to other rides, but not as primary routes. We have included the "Inner City Bikeway System" for completeness.

Exposition Park-USC Campus. There is an interesting and scenic tour available in the Exposition Park-University of Southern California area. The area is shown in the mini-tour map below. Take this tour any time when there is not a major event at either the Coliseum or the Sports Arena. Allow extra time beyond that needed for biking to visit the following: the Science and Industry Museum, the Museum of Natural History, and the Rose Garden in Exposition Park, as well as the USC Campus.

<u>**TRAILHEAD**</u>: **Exposition Park-USC Campus.** From the Harbor Freeway, exit west at Martin Luther King Jr. Boulevard and turn right (north) in 0.6 mile at Vermont Avenue. Drive 0.3 mile to N. Coliseum Drive and turn right. Find parking subject to posted laws.

Water is plentiful on this tour.

<u>**TRIP DESCRIPTION**</u>: **Exposition Park-USC Campus.** A sample Class I peripheral route is shown in the mini-tour map below. However, we recommend a freeform tour which includes many of the scenic interior bikeways/walkways.

Exposition Park. Bike north on Menlo Avenue 0.2 mile and turn right on Exposition Boulevard. Cycle past one of several treed rest/picnic areas and pass the striking main entrance to the Museum of Natural History. Follow the wide walkway past the north edge of the exquisite Rose Garden (0.4), then continue a short distance to the aircraft displays behind the Aerospace Museum.

Turn right at Figueroa Street and pedal on the walkway passing the IMAX theater and the main entry into the Museum of Science and Industry and the African American Museum. Pass the Sports Arena and turn right at Martin Luther King Jr. Boulevard (1.0). Follow the wide sidewalk to Hoover Street and turn right. Turn left at the next street (E. Park Drive) and bike alongside the classic Los Angeles Swim Stadium. Turn onto Menlo Avenue and cruise along the periphery of the gigantic Coliseum before returning to the trip origin (1.6).

TRIP #48 - INNER CITY BIKEWAY SYSTEM

USC Campus. Cross Exposition Boulevard at Watt Way and turn left immediately (1.8), pass the Computer Science Center, and then turn right at McClintock Avenue. Enjoy the varied architectures which are found throughout the entire campus, while biking past the Andrus Gerontology Center, Bloom Way, the tennis stadium at Child's Way, the track stadium, Howard Jones' Field, and the swim stadium, complete with giant hot tub (2.2).

Turn right at 34th Street, pedal past the Carson Motion Picture Studio, the water fountain at Trousdale Parkway, and continue to the end of the street (2.7). Backtrack a short distance and turn sharply left onto Hoover Way. Pass towering Phillips Hall and follow the picturesque roadway to Child's Way (3.2). Turn right and bike through the stately common with its lovely water fountain, then turn left again at Trousdale Parkway. In a short distance is the popular USC (and UCLA) landmark, Tommy Trojan.

1 - COLISEUM
2 - MUSEUM OF NATURAL HISTORY
3 - ROSE GARDEN
4 - MUSEUM OF SCIENCE AND INDUSTRY
5 - AFRICAN AMERICAN MUSEUM
6 - AEROSPACE MUSEUM
7 - L.A. SPORTS ARENA
8 - L.A. SWIM STADIUM
9 - HOWARD JONES FIELD
10 - SWIM STADIUM
11 - UNIVERSITY VILLAGE MALL
12 - SHRINE AUDITORIUM
13 - PHILLIPS HALL
14 - TOMMY TROJAN

Rose Garden at Exposition Park

Continue pedaling to Exposition Boulevard. Cross this road and turn right, then bike just beyond the Rose Garden and turn left. Turn right again at State Drive and bike to Menlo Avenue. Turn left and return to the trip origin (3.8). NOTE: Don is a UCLA graduate, so inclusion of this tour should be considered "beyond the call of duty."

CONNECTING TRIPS: Connection with Tour de Los Angeles (Trip #49) - at the intersection of Trousdale Parkway and Jefferson Boulevard (near the water fountain), bike east on Jefferson Boulevard, then turn north on Figueroa Street; continue to Venice Boulevard.

TRIP #49 - TOUR de LOS ANGELES

GENERAL LOCATION: Ballona Creek, Central Los Angeles, Los Angeles River, Long Beach, San Pedro, Palos Verdes, South Bay

LEVEL OF DIFFICULTY: Loop - strenuous
Distance - 71.7 miles
Elevation gain - periodic moderate-to-steep grades in San Pedro and the Palos Verdes Peninsula; flat elsewhere

HIGHLIGHTS: This nifty 70-mile-plus "looper" cruises Ballona Creek, travels inland into the heart of the city of Los Angeles, and then follows the Los Angeles River to Long Beach. Next, the tour visits the scenic Palos Verdes Peninsula before heading north on the South Bay Bike Trail, returning to the origin at Fisherman's Village in Marina Del Rey. For cyclists wanting a true slice of the Los Angeles area, do this tour. Most of the route is on Class I or Class II path. Because of heavy traffic in the central Los Angeles area, this trip is best saved for weekends.

TRAILHEAD: Follow the Marina Freeway to its terminus and continue west to Lincoln Boulevard. Turn left (south) on Lincoln Boulevard and go about half a mile to Fiji Way. Take Fiji Way to the parking area at Fisherman's Village or use the overflow parking lot between the village and Lincoln Boulevard.

Bring a couple of bottles of water to minimize water stops, even though there is water at several parks along the way. Also bring an automobile roadmap as a backup to cover straying from the described route.

TRIP DESCRIPTION: **Ballona Creek to Central Los Angeles.** The trip description will detail only the new or confusing portions of this loop. Refer to the trip numbers cited in the text for additional detail. This tour starts at Fisherman's Village and continues northeast along Ballona Creek to Kronenthal Park (Trip #4) (6.6). Bike east on National Boulevard, which fuses shortly with Class III Jefferson Boulevard. In 0.9 mile, turn left at Redondo Boulevard and bike on Class III bikeway with a wide shoulder under the Santa Monica Freeway. Cycle past Washington Boulevard to Venice Boulevard (gas station) and turn right (8.9).

TRIP #49 - TOUR DE LOS ANGELES

Pedal on Class II roadway through a mixed commercial/residential area, follow the short and mild upgrade, and pass under West Boulevard. At Crenshaw Boulevard, the path transitions to Class III, and the bike shoulder varies from skimpy to modest from this juncture to downtown Los Angeles. (This was our least favorite segment of the trip.)

Continue through varied areas of residential, commercial, and limited industrial development past Normandie Avenue (11.7). On the northeast corner is Normandie Recreation Center (water, recreation fields). The Rosedale Cemetery and Loyola High School are nearby; this area is definitely the highlight of the Venice Boulevard segment. Pedal past Vermont Avenue, pass under the Harbor Freeway, and cruise through the run-down commercial district to Figueroa Street (13.6).

Central Los Angeles to Los Angeles River. Follow the Class X roadway through another 1.8 miles of an old commercial area to Hooper Avenue. The route is Venice Boulevard to Broadway, left to 16th Street, 0.5 mile to San Pedro Street, left to 15th Street, 0.3 mile to Griffith Avenue, left to 14th Place, 0.3 mile to Central Avenue, right to 15th Street, and 0.3 mile to Hooper Avenue.

Turn right, pass under the Santa Monica Freeway, and turn left (east) at Washington Boulevard in 0.2 mile. In 0.4 mile at Alameda Street, the road passes "truck city" where there are hundreds of trucks clustered near the local railway complex. In half a mile, turn right at Santa Fe Avenue (16.5) and continue south for 0.7 mile. Turn left at 38th Street, which fuses into Bandini Boulevard in a short distance. This is a well-surfaced, wide road which crosses Soto Street and reaches a gas station in 0.4 mile, passes a large meat processing plant (P.U.!), and then crosses the Los Angeles River. The road parallels the river, continues another three miles to the Long Beach Freeway undercrossing, and reaches Atlantic Boulevard just beyond (20.7). Recross the Los Angeles River and bike to the bicycle entry point on the southeast side of the bridge.

Los Angeles River. Follow the river 5.3 miles south to Imperial Highway (Trip #21), cross over the river to the east levee, and cruise 10.0 miles south to Anaheim Street (Trip #20B) (36.0).

San Pedro. (See Trip #9 map.) Cross the river and bike 2.5 miles west on Class X Anaheim Street to Alameda Street; the region is effectively early 20th-century industrial. Turn left and bike one mile until reaching the Los Angeles Harbor area. The street becomes Harry Bridges Boulevard, continues another 1.25 miles to the Harbor Freeway, and then turns sharply south on what is now John S. Gibson Boulevard. (A Class I path is on the harbor side of the street.) Cycle 1.75 miles to Channel Street and turn right, leaving the harbor area (42.5).

Follow Channel Street a short distance to Gaffey Street and turn left. Pedal a steady half-mile upgrade to Class III Summerland Avenue. Turn right and bike a series of testy upgrades to Western Avenue. There is water at Peck Park to the right, but our route turns left and continues through rolling hills to 25th Street (46.0).

Palos Verdes Peninsula. Turn right and follow 25th Street, which becomes Palos Verdes Drive South, and bike the southern part of the peninsula (see Trip #6C). Follow the road as it turns north and becomes Palos Verdes Drive West, continuing to Malaga Cove Plaza (Trip #6B) (57.8).

South Bay Bike Trail. (See Trip #1A map.) Go east to Palos Verdes Boulevard, turn left, and bike 0.9 mile to Calle Miramar. Turn left toward the beach, veer left on Via Riviera, and continue about 0.1 mile across Paseo De La Playa to the beach parking lot. Coast down the bikeway/walkway to the South Bay Bike Trail origin. Cruise north 12.7 miles to the trip starting point at Fisherman's Village (Trips #1A and #1B). The total tour is 71.7 miles.

CONNECTING TRIPS: See individual trip writeups.

TRIP #50 - AVALON, SANTA CATALINA ISLAND

<u>GENERAL LOCATION</u>: Avalon, Santa Catalina Island

<u>LEVEL OF DIFFICULTY</u>: Loop - moderate to strenuous
Distance - 9.7 miles
Elevation gain - steady, strenuous upgrades on Wrigley
Terrace Drive and Chimes Tower Road area

<u>HIGHLIGHTS</u>: We visited Catalina for this fantastic tour on our wedding anniver-
sary…very romantic! We strongly recommend that you make the trip just for the sake
of biking the Avalon area. Visit Santa Catalina Island, bike this scenic route, and return
the same day; however, a more relaxing option is to stay overnight and spend the next
day telling the locals how you "smoked" the tourist golf-cart crowd with your bikes!

The described tour leaves the channel boat landing and tracks scenic Pebbly Beach
Drive along the coast, then follows an inland road to Mount Ada, cresting just above
the Inn on Mount Ada (former Wrigley residence). Next is a tour of Avalon proper, a
visit to Avalon's Casino, a workout pedal to the Chimes Tower, and a traverse of the
hills to Avalon Canyon Road. From this point, there is a nifty uphill ride to the Wrigley
Memorial and Botanical Gardens and a restful return to the Cabrillo Mole.

<u>TRAILHEAD</u>: Avalon can be reached by several channel boat carriers from San Pe-
dro, Long Beach, or Newport Beach, and by small air carriers from coastal airports.
During summer or holiday periods, make round-trip reservations at least one or two
weeks in advance. Bikers can transport bikes on most boat lines for a small fee; check
with the line of your choice if interested in this option. Another possibility is to rent a
multi-speed bike (18-speed preferred for the trip described) in Avalon proper. Visitors
planning overnight trips to Catalina during peak season should not arrive in Avalon
without confirmed room reservations.

Bring a filled water bottle. There are abundant public water sources in the flats of
Avalon (where it is not needed) and no water in the hillside mountainous areas (where
it is needed).

<u>TRIP DESCRIPTION</u>: **Pebbly Beach Road.** From the Cabrillo Mole, turn left on
Pebbly Beach Road and bike on the flat road with the ocean immediately to the left and
the cliffs to the right. Pass the cruise ship anchorage (many Mexican-bound cruise
ships visit Santa Catalina Island), the Amphibian Air Terminal (this mode of travel has
fallen off dramatically in recent years), and the Buffalo Nickel Restaurant at Pebbly
Beach. This is a 0.9 mile-stretch of continuous ocean viewing. Cycle another 0.2 mile
to a small residential-industrial complex and, just beyond, branch to the roadway which
heads inland and uphill.

The Inn at Mount Ada (Former Wrigley Residence). Turn right and shift
into the "granny gears" on this one-way highway stretch (keep an eye peeled for kamikaze rental golf carts going the wrong way!). The small road progresses on a series of
switchbacks through a treed, semi-arid canyon area, follows an uphill, traverses the

TRIP #50 - AVALON, SANTA CATALINA ISLAND

side of Mount Ada, and then reaches one of several scenic viewpoints in about one-half mile. In about one mile from the initial branch point, the road reaches a crest with a spectacular overlook of Avalon and the harbor (2.3).

Just beyond is the private entry to the Inn at Mount Ada. The majestic former Wrigley Residence is visible at different angles from the street, now named Wrigley

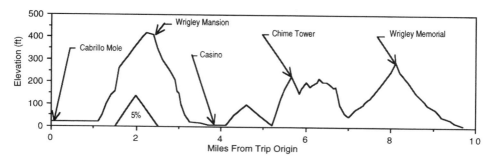

Road. There are additional spectacular harbor views as the narrow (now two-way) street switchbacks down to the city of Avalon at Clemente Avenue (3.2).

City of Avalon. Turn right, then immediately left at Beacon Street. Cycle one-fourth mile on this residential street to Metropole Avenue and turn right. Follow the mixed commercial/residential road to the Metropole Market Place and turn left (3.7). To the right is the Busy Bee Restaurant, with some delightful outdoor dining under umbrellas and alongside the harbor.

However, our route goes left and passes Solomon's Landing (one of our dinnertime favorites, with a bakery and deli), then proceeds on Crescent Avenue to Casino Way. Follow this road below the cliffs past the Casino Landing and the Catalina Island Yacht Center. Just beyond is the landmark Casino of Avalon. Turn right and tour the Casino periphery, passing the Catalina Island Museum entrance and the Casino Dock Café, and reach the scuba dive area at Casino Point.

Avalon Harbor from Mount Ada

Cruise around the Casino and follow the beach pathway to developed Descanso Beach (4.1). Bike the short uphill to Saint Catherine Way, turn right, and follow the testy upgrade through lovely tree-covered Descanso Canyon. We followed the road for a half mile and turned around, although more-adventurous bikers can follow the road another half mile to the dead end at condo city in Hamilton Cove. Return to Solomon's Landing and turn right at Marilla Avenue (5.2).

Chimes Tower. Turn right and pump 0.1 mile up steep Marilla Avenue. The reward is a right turn at Vieudelou Avenue and another steep upgrade for 0.2 mile. Pump past Old Stagecoach Road and bike on continued steep uphill to a majestic vista point just below the Zane Grey Hotel (original home of Zane Grey). Bike a short distance on continued steep uphill on a one-way road to the Chimes Tower and yet another scenic viewpoint (5.5). (Note that more-ambitious bikers can take the one-way Old Stagecoach Road-Chimes Tower Road loop and bike downhill to the tower.)

The Traverse to Avalon Canyon Road. Backtrack to Old Stagecoach Road (Stage Road for short) and turn onto that street. In 0.1 mile at the junction, turn left onto Camino Del Monte. Follow the short workout upgrade, then enjoy a steep downgrade on a tree-lined street with impressive residences. At the next intersection, stay to the right (as with each succeeding intersection up to the Catalina Canyon Hotel) and proceed on Las Lomas Avenue. Pedal downhill past Marilla Avenue and turn right at East Whittley Avenue.

Just beyond, turn hard right onto Country Club Drive, follow the downhill on tree-lined roadway, and enjoy the view of the canyon area. At the Catalina Canyon Hotel, follow the road as it proceeds past the spur road to the right (also named Country Club Drive) and veers to the left (east). Follow the fun downhill past Picture Point (a golfer viewpoint/meeting point) and the Catalina Clubhouse, and free-wheel to Tremont Street (6.8). Turn right and, in a short distance, turn right again at Avalon Canyon Road.

Wrigley Memorial and Botanical Gardens. Follow the tree-lined uphill road past the north edge of the Catalina Island Golf Course; the 1.2-mile route to the Wrigley Memorial is on steady uphill varying from moderate to testy. This rural road passes the Sand Trap at Falls Canyon Road (lemonade, "firewater," and snacks), the Catalina Stables, and Bird Park Campground (water, restrooms), and heads past the southern edge of the golf course (7.4).

In 0.2 mile, pass the Avalon Canyon Campground (water, restrooms) and follow the steady workout grade to the pay entrance to the stately Wrigley Memorial. Bike riding is prohibited beyond this point. Note that every type of plant life indigenous to the area and a few imported varieties are all classified in the general area (7.9).

The Finale. Backtrack to Tremont Avenue and turn right, biking 0.2 mile to Clarissa Avenue (9.2). Turn left and continue through a residential area to the street's end at Crescent Avenue. Turn left for the Avalon Shopping Mall (no biking between Clarissa Avenue and Metropole Avenue). However, the reference route turns right, proceeds past the Cabrillo Crescent Picnic Area, and returns to the trip origin at Cabrillo Mole (9.7).

CONNECTING TRIPS: There are no current connector routes. Bicycling into the island interior beyond the gate above Old Stagecoach Road requires a permit, which can be obtained at the Catalina Conservancy Office.

ADDITIONAL TRIPS

Interstate Highway 5 viewed from Old Ridge Route Road

TRIP #51 - DOMINGUEZ HILLS

GENERAL LOCATION: Carson

LEVEL OF DIFFICULTY: Loop - easy
                              Distance - 3.5 miles
                              Elevation gain - essentially flat

HIGHLIGHTS: The major portion of the ride is a tour of the California State University at Dominguez Hills (CSUDH). The trip is broken into a tour of the campus periphery followed by a tour within the main campus complex. Particularly during weekends, this is a pleasant family riding area, well off the major roadways and with little traffic. There is an option to connect this ride with an excursion to well-stocked Victoria Park nearby.

TRAILHEAD: From the San Diego Freeway, take the Torrance Boulevard off-ramp to Figueroa Street and turn left (north). Drive 1.5 miles to Victoria Avenue and turn right, continuing 1.75 miles to the CSUDH east entrance area across from Birchknoll Drive. Park on the street, Monday through Saturday, or in the nearby campus lot on Sunday. From the San Diego Freeway, exit north at Avalon Boulevard and drive two miles to Victoria Avenue. Turn right (east) and continue one mile to the east entrance area.

Bring a light water supply. There are public water sources on campus and at Victoria Park.

TRIP DESCRIPTION: **Campus Periphery.** Bike to the east entrance and follow the on-campus frontage road west, paralleling Victoria Avenue. Continue to the edge of the westernmost parking area (0.45) and follow its periphery to the next intersecting street. A right (south) turn here leads by the Olympic Velodrome (0.7). Another turn east leads past LeCorte Hall, while a subsequent turn south takes cyclists by the tennis courts. Return east at road's end, pass the upper edge of the southernmost parking lot, and bike to an intersection with a sign noting that the "Physical Plant" is straight ahead (1.45).

Go straight and reach road's end in an area with at least 50 large greenhouses. Return to the prior intersection and turn right (north) (2.0). Staying on the campus edge at each turn leads bikers through some welcome tree cover and alongside the student housing area. The road curves and heads down to an intersection. Right (north) leads towards Victoria Avenue, while the main campus complex is straight ahead (2.6).

Main Campus. One of many possible rides might be to keep straight ahead, veer left to stay on the roadway, and turn right into the "Natural Sciences" complex. At the "T"-intersection, turn right, then turn left again at the Student Union Building (2.8). At the next "T"-intersection, turn right and bike to the frontage road that parallels Victoria Avenue (3.1). Following this road to the right (east) puts cyclists back at the start point in another 0.4 mile. There are numerous other routes, within the main campus, which can be used to explore other areas, as well as to extend the trip mileage.

Victoria Park. It is a short excursion to Victoria Park. An easy way to get there is to take the University Drive exit out of the south parking lot and turn west. Follow that road 0.6 mile to Avalon Boulevard, turn north, and bike a few hundred feet to 189th

Street. Turn west again and bike past Towne Avenue to the park periphery. There are several Class I paths which tour the park, making this segment ideal for all-age family biking. The park also boasts water and restrooms, grass, tree shade, picnic facilities, and children's play areas.

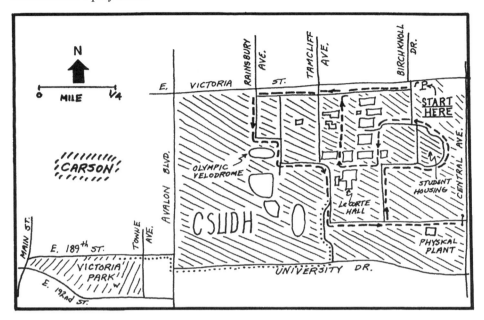

TRIP #51 - DOMINGUEZ HILLS

TRIP #52 - AGOURA HILLS LOOP

<u>**GENERAL LOCATION**</u>: Agoura Hills, Thousand Oaks

<u>**LEVEL OF DIFFICULTY**</u>: Loop - moderate
Distance - 8.7 miles
Elevation gain - periodic moderate grades

<u>**HIGHLIGHTS**</u>: This pleasant loop trip passes several nice parks on the way up to the base of the Conejo Ridge, cruises through some scenic "outback," coasts down Lindero Canyon Road, and returns through the heart of the impressive city of Agoura Hills. The route is generally lightly trafficked and mostly on a Class II bikeway; the Class X portion has a wide bike shoulder. This route also can be combined with the Westlake Village ride (Trip #53) and North Ranch Loop (Trip #54) to provide a myriad of neat bicycle route options.

<u>**TRAILHEAD**</u>: From the Ventura Freeway, exit north at Kanan Road. Drive 0.75 mile to Thousand Oaks Boulevard, turn right, and continue one-third mile to Argos Street.

TRIP #52 - AGOURA HILLS LOOP

Turn right again and follow that road a short distance to Chumash Park. This a nice grassy park with some shade, water, restrooms, playgrounds, and recreation fields.

   Bring a filled water bottle for hot days, although scattered public sources are available on all but the Lindero Canyon Road segment.

TRIP DESCRIPTION: Kanan Road. Bike 0.4 mile back to the intersection of Thousand Oaks Boulevard and Kanan Road. Turn right (north) on Kanan Road and pedal uphill on the Class II path. Pass a shopping center to the left and continue to the crest near Laro Drive (0.7). To the right is Sumac Park with water, restrooms, a picnic area, barbecues, and some shade.

   Continue through this residential area with a view of the hills directly ahead. Pedal on a mild uphill to Fountainwood Street, reach a flat, and continue on another moderate

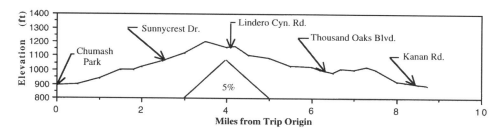

grade which peaks near Conifer Street (1.6). To the right is Mae Boyar Park with water, restrooms, tennis courts, a playground, and scattered shade.

Start uphill again through this residential area, reaching the top of the grade in 0.3 mile. In a short distance is Smoketree Avenue and a mild upgrade through a thinning residential area. The top of the grade is near Sunnycrest Drive, where the road begins to swing to the left (2.3). The curving roadway passes Medea Creek Park (which has a Class I walkway/bikeway that runs from Kanan Road a little over a mile south, including an entry from Sunnycrest Drive) and Oak Park High School, now heading west. The hills to the north below the Conejo Ridge are lightly developed in this area (2.7).

Bike downhill to the flat near Hollytree Drive where the marked bike path ends (the shoulder remains wide). A short diversion north on that street leads to Oak Canyon Community Park (pond, small manmade waterfalls, and the core of the park further up with restrooms, paved bike/walk paths, picnic tables, and children's playgrounds). Next there is a moderately steep upgrade which reaches a crest in a small flat area (3.3). Just beyond, the road rounds a bend and greets cyclists with a view into a valley of upscale residences. Next on the winding road is a short, moderate-to-steep uphill. The road continues through a light residential area, transits alongside Los Arcos Drive and the entry to Valley View Park (restrooms, sports fields, and unshaded picnic areas), and meets Lindero Canyon Road and a cluster of small shopping centers in a short distance (4.1).

Lindero Canyon Road. (This is the return payment for all that uphill.) Turn left (south) and continue on the Class II, wide-shouldered roadway past Lakeview Canyon Road (4.2). The road passes between a set of small hills, meets Rockfield Street (4.7), and then follows a mild upgrade through a lightly developed area. An easy downgrade follows, then the road flattens and reaches Hedgewall Drive (5.5). The path returns to a high-density residential area on a tree-lined street, reaching Thousand Oaks Boulevard and a group of shopping centers (6.2).

Thousand Oaks Boulevard. Turn left (east) on the Class II bikeway on a busier road through impressive Agoura Hills. Peek at the Santa Monica Mountains to the south and then follow a mild downgrade past the first of several shopping complexes. Continue on rolling hills past Lake Lindero Drive (6.5) (Lake Lindero itself is half a mile to the south) and return to a residential setting.

Bike through another high-density residential area past Reyes Adobe Road (7.0) and follow a 0.3-mile moderate upgrade to a crest with a nice view into the hills to the east. Just south on Forest Cove Lane is Forest Cove Park with restrooms, athletic fields, scattered shade, and children's playgrounds. Coast downhill past Grey Rock Road (8.0); there are residence-sprinkled hills to the north and housing tracts on the opposite side

Medea Creek Park

of the street. Continue the roller-coaster ride through more high-density residential areas until the route flattens near Kanan Road (8.3). Pedal east past this junction to Argos Street and return to Chumash Park (8.7).

CONNECTING TRIPS: 1) Continuation with the North Ranch Loop (Trip #54) - there are several options, but one of the most pleasant is to bike the extended loop comprised of Kanan Road, Westlake Boulevard, and Thousand Oaks Boulevard; 2) connection with the Westlake Village ride (Trip #53) - at the intersection of Lindero Canyon Road and Thousand Oaks Boulevard, continue south on the former roadway.

TRIP #53 - WESTLAKE VILLAGE

GENERAL LOCATION: Westlake Village, Thousand Oaks

LEVEL OF DIFFICULTY: Loop - easy
                         Distance - 9.2 miles
                         Elevation gain - periodic moderate grades

HIGHLIGHTS: This easy-going Class I/II trip is centered around Westlake Lake. The tour begins in a cleverly laid out residential neighborhood, travels across the Ventura Freeway through a pleasant and massive business and shopping complex, and proceeds along the southern boundary of lovely Westlake Lake. The return segment is through less-developed areas with a few light rolling hills. There are several marked diversion routes through the Westlake Village area.

TRAILHEAD: From the Ventura Freeway, exit northbound on Westlake Boulevard and continue 0.5 mile to Cascade Avenue, which is the next left turn beyond Thousand Oaks Boulevard. Turn left (west) and proceed down Cascade Avenue to its terminus across from a school and Russell Park.

Only a light water supply is needed. Fill up at the trip origin or at other water spots noted in the trip map.

TRIP DESCRIPTION: **Southbound - Westlake Lake.** Leave the cul-de-sac and turn left on Cascade Avenue, pedaling 0.4 miles to N. Westlake Boulevard. Turn right (south) and follow the Class II bikepath across Thousand Oaks Boulevard (0.7). Stop and enjoy one of the many vistas into the surrounding hills, with a particularly nice view into the Santa Monica Mountains to the south. In a quarter mile, the path crosses the Ventura Freeway and enters an area of extended and delightful business and shopping complexes. The locale transitions into residential and remains so, up to our left turn at Triunfo Canyon Road (2.1). Note that there is a mixed Class II/Class X diversion route up to Lake Eleanor or Lake Sherwood by continuing on S. Westlake Boulevard.

Pedal another 0.4 mile on an unmarked thoroughfare with a wide shoulder (this entire section rides like a Class II bikeway) to a bridge with a clear view of Westlake Lake. This is a popular "high altitude" duck feeding spot. Continue cruising Triunfo Canyon Road, with periodic peeks down the lanes into the lake, until reaching Golden Leaf Drive (3.5). This is the open end of the lake, with a fine view of the center island and the many small boats, and with a tree-covered rest area, to boot. In 0.2 mile, pass "tennis court city" and make a sharp left turn on S. Lindero Canyon Road.

Northbound - Less-Developed Country. Bike over a bridge which crosses Triunfo Canyon Creek and pass Ridgeford Drive (or turn onto that roadway for a challenging Class X uphill) (4.0). Pedal 0.1 mile to the top of a knoll where there is an excellent view of the lake's south end. At Lakeview Canyon Road (4.6), the marked Class II path resumes. Cyclists can divert left at Watergate Road to reach the private entrance to the island at the lake's center. However, the designated route cruises ahead

Westlake Lake from Triunfo Canyon Road

TRIP #53 - WESTLAKE VILLAGE

for 0.9 mile to Agoura Road. For this trip segment, the bikeway is along a tree-lined roadway. The road is bordered by the walls of the surrounding residential tracts to the west and hillside homes to the east.

In 0.2 mile beyond Agoura Road, the route crosses back over the freeway and proceeds on a moderate upgrade, reaching Via Colinas and the open fields of the Valley Oaks Memorial Park Cemetery. The upgrade continues to Thousand Oaks Boulevard where there is a shopping cluster (6.6).

Westbound - Rolling Hills. However, our route heads west on the Class II bikeway and continues another 0.3 mile uphill through lightly developed territory. Now begins the roller coaster! First there is a free-wheeling downhill to Via Colinas (7.3), followed by a 0.3-mile upgrade. At the top of the grade is the trip's premier view south into the Santa Monica Mountains. After a 0.2-mile downhill, the roadway narrows and the path shifts onto the sidewalk as posted (Class I) (7.7).

In another 0.2 mile, the bike route passes just below the Westlake High School baseball fields (there is a drinking fountain near the middle of the complex) and soon reaches Lakeview Canyon Road (8.2). In 0.3 mile on the sidewalk route, reach N. Westlake Boulevard. Turn right (north), proceed to Cascade Avenue, and return to the trip origin (9.2).

CONNECTING TRIPS: 1) Connection with the Agoura Hills Loop (Trip #52) - at Lindero Canyon Road and Thousand Oaks Boulevard, turn east onto the latter road; 2) connection with the North Ranch Loop (Trip #54) - at Cascade Avenue and Westlake Boulevard, turn north on the latter road.

TRIP #54 - NORTH RANCH LOOP

GENERAL LOCATION: Thousand Oaks, Westlake Village

LEVEL OF DIFFICULTY: Loop - moderate
Distance - 10.9 miles
Elevation gain - periodic moderate upgrades

HIGHLIGHTS: This fine rural loop is mostly on lightly traveled roads. Much of the route is on a Class II path or Class X with a wide shoulder. The tour highlights include a visit to the classy North Ranch residential area, a long but mild runout on Lindero Canyon Road (paid for with the prior uphill pumping), and a ride by the northern periphery of Westlake Village. This path can be linked with the Agoura Hills Loop (Trip #52) and the Westlake Village ride (Trip #53), sufficient to keep bikers going for a healthy chunk of the day.

TRAILHEAD: From the Ventura Freeway, exit northbound on Westlake Boulevard and drive 0.5 mile to Cascade Avenue, which is the next left turn beyond Thousand Oaks Boulevard. Turn left (west) and proceed down Cascade Avenue to its terminus across from Russell Park.

Bring a filled water bottle. There are limited on-route water sources as noted on the trip map.

TRIP DESCRIPTION: **Westlake Boulevard.** Leave the parking area and bike up Cascade Avenue to Westlake Boulevard. Turn left (north) and coast a mild downgrade on a road that is tree-lined at the center median. Continue on the marked Class II path through an area with residential pockets on the left and hills to the right. Pass Hillcrest Drive (0.4) and bike through less-developed territory which is bordered by hills. Bike

TRIP #54 - NORTH RANCH LOOP

on a light downgrade past Skelton Canyon Circle and meet Deepwood Drive a short distance beyond (1.1).

Pump a 0.3-mile upgrade, enjoy a short downgrade with a canyon view, and pass Valley Spring Drive (1.7). The marked bike lane ends here, although the wide shoulder continues. Begin another uphill in an area with plush homes to the east and take in a scenic view of North Ranch. In a short distance, reach Kanan Road (2.4).

Kanan Road. Turn right (east) and bike on the Class II road with a wide bike shoulder. Just off Upper Ranch Road to the right is North Ranch Park with a water fountain, open fields, a children's playground, and a patch of tree cover. The street skirts the northern perimeter of stately North Ranch, with the rolling hills of the Conejo Ridge on the opposite (north) side of Kanan Road. In 0.2 mile, bike a short upgrade which levels near Rayburn Street. Follow a half-mile upgrade alongside the North Ranch Golf Course, which "gets serious" about 0.2 mile before reaching a crest near Dawn Meadow Court (3.5).

Cycle along the eastern edge of the golf course (4.1), pass Windy Mountain Avenue, and follow the downhill past South Rim Street (4.4). There are residences on both sides of the road here and an occasional hawk for bird-watchers. The road levels near Falling Star Avenue (4.7) and, in 0.2 mile, continues to the mall-clustered junction at Lindero Canyon Road.

Lindero Canyon Road. Turn right (south) and ride on the Class II, wide-shouldered road past Lakeview Canyon Road (5.0). The road passes between a set of

Kanan Road in North Ranch area

small hills, transits Rockfield Street (5.5), and then follows a mild upgrade through a lightly developed area. A mild downgrade follows, then Lindero Canyon Road flattens and reaches Hedgewall Drive (6.3). The path returns to a higher-density residential area on a tree-lined street, and reaches Thousand Oaks Boulevard and another group of shopping centers (7.1).

Pass the shopping center at this intersection and follow the downgrade past the open fields of the Valley Oaks Memorial Park Cemetery. Continue a moderate downhill across Via Colinas (7.6) and reach the Ventura Freeway in 0.3 mile. Bike another 0.3 mile and arrive at Agoura Road.

Closing the Loop. Turn right on Class II Agoura Road and bike alongside the Westlake Village Golf Club (right) and the northern periphery of the Westlake Village residential area. (Just south at Greengate Court is Bennett Park with water, restrooms, a children's playground, and widely scattered tree shade.) In 0.3 mile, the street crosses Lakeview Canyon Road, then cruises along the southern edge of Westlake Plaza. At the end of this shopping center, turn right (north) at Westlake Boulevard (9.6) and pump uphill on Class II road over the Ventura Freeway (10.0). Bike through an open area 0.3 mile to Thousand Oaks Boulevard, then 0.2 mile to Cascade Avenue. Turn left (west) and return to the parking area (10.9).

CONNECTING TRIPS: 1) Continuation with the Agoura Hills Loop (Trip #52) - from the intersection of Westlake Boulevard and Thousand Oaks Boulevard, bike west on the latter street; 2) connection with the Westlake Village ride (Trip #53) - bike south on Lindero Canyon Road from the intersection of that street with Agoura Road. Also, at the Agoura Road/Westlake Boulevard intersection, head south on Westlake Boulevard.

TRIP #55 - CHATSWORTH-NORTHRIDGE-GRANADA HILLS LOOP

GENERAL LOCATION: Chatsworth, Northridge, Granada Hills

LEVEL OF DIFFICULTY: Loop - moderate
Distance - 28.4 miles
Elevation gain - periodic moderate grades

HIGHLIGHTS: An interesting loop that tours both city and country, this predominately Class X route is definitely for experienced bike riders only. Much of the trip is on lightly traveled roadway with plenty of biking room. However, there are heavy traffic areas and, for those segments, traffic route options are provided. So why take this trip? This tour originates from lovely Chatsworth Park North, explores the pleasant countryside on the western perimeter of the Chatsworth Reservoir, cruises by the campus of the California State University, Northridge (CSUN), and traverses the foothills below the Santa Susana Mountains before returning to the trip origin. There are numerous mountain views. The Chatsworth Reservoir segment is country bike riding at its best! There are plentiful parks along the route for rest-stopping and water bottle filling.

Several alternatives to the basic route are also provided. Their focus is to limit the amount of cycling on the busiest streets, to reduce route length, and/or to visit scenic side streets.

TRAILHEAD: From the Ronald Reagan Freeway, exit south on Topanga Canyon Boulevard. Drive past Stoney Point Park and turn right (west) on Chatsworth Street, 1.25 miles from the freeway exit. Continue to parking just below the road's end at Chatsworth Park North. From the San Diego Freeway, exit west on the Ronald Reagan Freeway and continue about eight miles to Topanga Canyon Boulevard. Proceed as described above. From the Ventura Freeway east of the San Diego Freeway, turn north on the San Diego Freeway and proceed as described above. Another option from the Ventura Freeway is to exit north at Topanga Canyon Boulevard and drive about seven miles to Chatsworth Street. Turn left (west) and find parking near road's end.

Bring a filled water bottle on hot days. Water is generally plentiful at parks and some commercial centers, but there are areas such as the west side of Chatsworth Reservoir where none was found.

TRIP DESCRIPTION: **Chatsworth Park North.** Follow the bikeway/walkway around the rustic, shaded park and investigate the rocky outcroppings before leaving. Then follow the path around the restroom and ride into the southern edge of the parking area. Continue just beyond to the origin of Valley Circle Boulevard. Follow Valley Circle Boulevard along the Santa Susana Wash 0.4 mile to Devonshire Street.

A right turn here leads to Chatsworth Park South (see Trip #39). However, our reference route continues 0.6 mile to Baden Avenue and, on the way, passes the woodsy, pastoral Oakwood Cemetery. Angle left at Baden Avenue and follow the rural route half a mile through small rolling hills to a dead end at Plummer Street (1.5).

Chatsworth Reservoir/Western Loop. The next 2.75 miles of roadway is biker's heaven! The street is a little narrow, but the countryside scenery is terrific. Turn right (west) and follow the short Class I bikepath segment on Plummer Street, which gives way to Class X biking. Follow the mildly winding street through a series of rolling hills. In 0.4 mile, the roadway mysteriously becomes Valley Circle Boulevard again, passing alongside the reservoir marshlands, as well as Chatsworth Oaks Park (a lovely shaded park with grasslands, barbecue facilities, a playground, hiking trails, and nice rock formations, but no water) (2.1).

The route stays on rolling terrain through a quaint rural residential area, passing the Log Cabin Mercantile and reaching Box Canyon Road (3.0). There is a fine panorama westward into a residential area built high into the foothills. Here Valley Circle Boulevard veers to the south through more rolling hills and meanders alongside the reservoir's west edge. In another 0.3 mile, Woolsey Canyon Road is passed. Our roadway has hills to the right and the reservoir to the left. The area begins to return to residential near Chatlake Drive (3.7). The path follows a nifty downhill, and there is a complete return to civilization (including a shopping center) at Roscoe Boulevard (4.4).

Southwest Trip Segment. Turn left (east) on Roscoe Boulevard, pedal past March Avenue, and skirt Orcutt Ranch Park (shade, water). The road widens in this residential area, opening up to a view of the Verdugo Mountains and the San Gabriel Mountains to the east (5.0). After going 0.8 mile on Roscoe Boulevard, turn right (south) on Woodlake Avenue, pass a shopping center, and turn left at Saticoy Street (5.8).

TRIP #55 - CHATSWORTH-NORTHRIDGE-GRANADA HILLS LOOP

(Route alternative: Bikers willing to bypass Orcutt Ranch Park can take a more scenic option on March Avenue, as noted on the map.) Bike on the more restricted path in heavier traffic through a mixed residential/commercial area to Topanga Canyon Boulevard (7.4). Turn left (north) and bike through a commercial area on the heavily traveled roadway for 0.6 mile to Strathern Street. A turn east leads along Lanark Park; there's water near the baseball diamond, shade, picnic areas, and playgrounds.

Cruise a short distance to Owensmouth Avenue and turn left, bike another short segment, and turn right (east) back onto Roscoe Boulevard (8.4). Follow this busy, cramped path through a heavy commercial area, cross Brown's Creek, and pedal 0.2 mile past Mason Avenue to Oso Avenue. Turn left (north), then turn right shortly at Chase Street and cycle alongside the Winnetka Recreation Center (water fountain behind the baseball diamond, recreation fields) (10.2). Continue another half mile to Corbin Avenue, turn left, and pedal through heavy traffic past several markets.

California State University, Northridge. Bike to Nordhoff Street (the east connecting segment of Nordhoff Street is north of the railroad tracks) and turn right (east) (11.8). Cross Vanalden Avenue (the turnoff to Vanalden Park) (12.5) and pass Wilbur Avenue. Pass Reseda Boulevard (13.1) and, in 0.7 mile, cruise in front of the CSUN campus. (Route alternative: The tour length can be reduced 10 miles by turning north on Wilbur Avenue and biking to Rinaldi Street.) There are several nice rest spots and bike paths on campus (see Trip #58). However, the reference route follows a beeline on Nordhoff Street past Dearborn Park at Amestoy Avenue (water, restrooms, sports courts, playground, light shade) (15.1) and turns left in 0.3 mile at Balboa Boulevard.

Western Segment. Balboa Boulevard is big and busy! Bike through a commercial area up a short but steep grade, pass Lassen Street (16.5), and reach San Jose Street (17.2). A short 0.2-mile pedal east (right) and a left at Petit Avenue lead to Granada Hills Recreation Center (water, tennis, recreation fields). Continue to Chatsworth Street, turn left, and return to Balboa Boulevard. Bike north past San Fernando Mission Boulevard, over the Ronald Reagan Freeway, and reach Rinaldi Street (19.5). (Reduced traffic alternate: From Vanalden Avenue [12.5], bike 0.3 mile on Nordhoff Street to Class II Wilbur Avenue. Turn left and pedal 0.5 mile to Class III Plummer Street. Turn right [east] and follow that road 3.4 miles [which includes a traverse of the CSUN campus] to Woodley Avenue. Turn left on that Class II roadway and continue 2.5 miles to Rinaldi Street. Then bike west on that street. This safer alternate makes access to Granada Hills Recreation Center less convenient and also adds two miles to the reference trip.)

The Northern (Foothill) Segment. Turn left (west) onto Class II Rinaldi Street and bike through a pleasant residential neighborhood on a series of moderate upgrades, reaching a flat at Zelzah Avenue (21.3). Just beyond, there is a view into Aliso Creek Canyon with the Santa Susana Mountains as a backdrop. The route passes just south and below Porter Ranch and continues on additional mild upgrades to Wilbur Avenue (22.6). Just beyond, there is a workout upgrade which tops out near Porter Valley Drive, the entry to the local country club.

In 0.3 mile, turn left (south) at a shopping center at Tampa Avenue (23.2). There are some excellent views into Limekiln Canyon (see Trip #57) and the southernmost portion of Limekiln Canyon Park along this segment, as well as mountain vistas to the east and back north. Coast downhill past Chatsworth Street (23.9) and turn right (west) on Devonshire Street. Pedal an upgrade on this wide tree-lined street with more mountain views in this area. Just past Corbin Avenue (25.1), the road narrows and the locale becomes more rural.

In 0.6 mile, reach Mason Avenue and a shopping center. Turn right and bike on a steady, moderate upgrade 0.2 mile to Mason Recreation Center, a grassy, tree-lined park with water, restrooms, and athletic fields (26.2). Just beyond, turn left (west) on Chatsworth Street into an affluent neighborhood with horse paths along the roadway. Cross over Brown's Creek (27.6), pass Canoga Avenue and a group of horse stables, and then bike into an area near Owensmouth Avenue with a straight-on view of Stoney Point and its park. The route crosses Topanga Canyon Boulevard and continues 0.3 mile further to the starting point (28.4).

CONNECTING TRIPS: 1) Connection with the Sepulveda Bike Basin ride (Trip #38) - at Woodley Avenue and Victory Boulevard, bike north 3.25 miles to Nordhoff Street; 2) connection with the Chatsworth Tour/Brown's Creek Bikeway (Trip #39) - at the intersection of Valley Circle Boulevard and Lassen Street, turn east on Lassen Street; 3) connection with the Santa Susana Pass ride (Trip #56) - at Chatsworth Street and Topanga Canyon Boulevard, turn north and bike about half a mile to Santa Susana Pass Road; 4) connection with the Limekiln Canyon Trail (Trip #57) - from the intersection of Devonshire Street and Tunney Avenue, turn north on Tunney Avenue and continue a couple of hundred yards to the Limekiln Canyon Trail marker; 5) connection with the California State University, Northridge Campus tour (Trip #58) - at the intersection of Nordhoff Street and Lindley Avenue, turn north into the campus; 6) connection with the Woodland Hills-Tarzana Loop (Trip #59) - from the intersection of Shoup Avenue and Saticoy Street, turn south on Shoup Avenue and drive to Victory Boulevard.

TRIP #56 - SANTA SUSANA PASS

GENERAL LOCATION: Chatsworth, Simi Valley

LEVEL OF DIFFICULTY: One way - strenuous; up and back - strenuous to very strenuous
Distance - 4.1 miles (one way)
Elevation gain - steady steep grade to the summit

HIGHLIGHTS: The ride up to Santa Susana Pass, though short, is a real heart pumper. The tour follows Santa Susana Pass Road through a multitude of interesting rock formations in the Simi Hills. The views back into Chatsworth and those of the western mountains from the pass are well worth the effort. The trip can be extended to include a scenic downhill coast into the Simi Valley. However, if you haven't arranged a car shuttle, plan on an equally strenuous ride back up to the pass for the return to the Stoney Point Park trailhead. For cyclists with the time and interest, we suggest a short tour of the base of Stoney Point monolith at the trip's end.

TRAILHEAD: From the Ronald Reagan Freeway, exit south at Topanga Canyon Boulevard and drive one-fourth mile to the Stoney Point Park area. There is parking on the east side of the road.
    Bring a couple of filled water bottles for rides on hot days, particularly if you are doing an up-and-back into Simi Valley. The only water source for the described trip is at Santa Susana Park, which has restrooms, grass, tree shade, and picnic tables.

TRIP DESCRIPTION: **The Uphill.** Bike north 0.1 mile to Santa Susana Pass Road and turn left, enjoying a brief downhill. A modest climb leads through some interesting

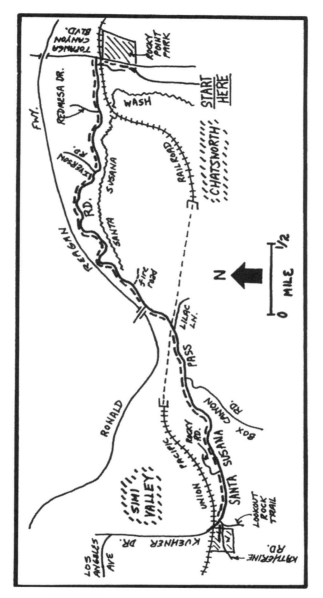

TRIP #56 - SANTA SUSANA PASS

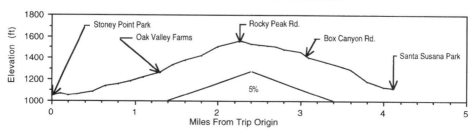

rock formations on a mild grade and passes Red Mesa Drive. The Union Pacific tracks can be seen below and to the left. The grade stiffens and the route passes the eastern entry to the Church at Rocky Peak. The road shifts to two lanes (0.8) and winds upward to a point just below the Ronald Reagan Freeway, then shifts east to parallel that thoroughfare.

Just past Oak Valley Farms (1.3), the roadway returns to a single lane. More of the Simi Hills rock formations appear at a distance on the left, and there are superb over-the-shoulder views back to Chatsworth and Stoney Point. The winding route takes a sharp turn left and climbs to a flat, passing a fire road entry on the left (2.1). Scenic westward views greet bikers as the contour flattens before reaching Rocky Peak Road at the summit (2.3). Rocky Peak Park (no facilities) and the Rocky Peak Fire Road entry are across the freeway.

The Downhill. Santa Susana Pass Road crosses over the unseen Union Pacific railroad tunnel near Lilac Lane and coasts past Box Canyon Road (3.1). The road continues to pull away from the freeway as cyclists are treated to mixed views of the Simi Hills, the Santa Susana Mountains, and eventually, Simi Valley. Further downhill, there are views into Twilight Canyon, where the Union Pacific tracks reappear out of the mountains. The route flattens, opens to two lanes, and passes picturesque Hideout Willies and several other interesting, venerable establishments. Just before reaching a sharp northward road bend is Katherine Road (3.9). (If you cross the railroad tracks, you've gone too far.) Turn left and bike another 0.2 mile to Santa Susana Park.

CONNECTING TRIPS: 1) Connection with the Chatsworth-Northridge-Granada Hills Loop (Trip #55) - from the parking area, bike south one-half mile on Topanga Canyon Boulevard to Chatsworth Street and turn right; 2) connection with the Chatsworth Tour/ Brown's Creek Bikeway (Trip #39) - follow the same directions as above, proceeding one-third mile to Brown's Canyon Wash.

Santa Susana Pass Road near Iverson Road

TRIP #57 - LIMEKILN CANYON TRAIL

GENERAL LOCATION: Porter Ranch

LEVEL OF DIFFICULTY: Loop - easy
Distance - 3.8 miles
Elevation gain - periodic light upgrades;
single short but steep upgrade

HIGHLIGHTS: A delightful outdoor excursion in the middle of suburbia, this is a pleasant ride through Limekiln Canyon, alongside Limekiln Creek and through lush bottomland. It is a nice family ride which does have a couple of short "workout" upgrades. The lower 1.2 miles of the trail is paved, while the upper 0.6 mile is graded gravel (bikeable with both thin- and balloon-tire bikes). The graded gravel roadway passes through the most naturally scenic part of the trip and provides a physical creek-crossing to boot!

TRAILHEAD: Exit the Ronald Reagan Freeway south at Tampa Avenue and drive about 1.25 miles to Tunney Avenue. Turn right (southwest) and continue 0.1 mile to Calvin Avenue. Turn left and find parking in the residential area, subject to local traffic laws.
     Only a very light water supply is needed for this trip.

TRIP DESCRIPTION: **Lower Trail.** Bike a short distance to Tunney Avenue, cross the street, and find the Limekiln Canyon Trail marker a few hundred feet south.

Limekiln Canyon north of the tunnel

TRIP #57 - LIMEKILN CANYON TRAIL

Continue up a short but steep upgrade to the spillway which straddles Limekiln Creek (0.2). From this point, enjoy one of many outstanding views into the Santa Susana Mountains to the north. The meandering Class I trail continues through the canyon, with the creekbed to the right and homes on the bluffs above, then reaches a short but steep upgrade just before Chatsworth Street (0.6).

Upper Trail (asphalt). Cross Chatsworth Street and follow a short and steep downhill back into the creekbed. Bike another half mile through the lush canyon bottom on a mild upgrade before passing under the Ronald Reagan Freeway. In 0.1 mile, the trail splits, with the left fork heading up the left bank and the poorly maintained right fork paralleling our middle fork route (1.2).

Upper Trail (graded gravel). In another 0.1 mile, the trail shifts from asphalt to gravel and proceeds through a 100-foot tunnel; there is scattered gravel and some glass in the dark tunnel (a chance to walk your bike…hint, hint!). From this point, the trail is on graded gravel, well suited for "balloon"-tire bikes and reasonable for "thin"-tire bikes. Proceed right (east) to the improved trail segment and bike through the lush canyon bottomland with its many trees and running creek. Cross on a small bridge over the creek and bike another quarter mile past a small picnic area.

Cross the shallow creek and follow a moderate upgrade to another more modest crossing (1.8). Pump a steeper upgrade to a flat where there is a particularly nice view of the local mountains through the tree cover. In a short distance, reach a turnaround loop where the reference trip ends. Those with balloon-tire bikes can ford the deeper creek on the spur trail to the right and continue northward.

Return Route. Proceed back almost to the tunnel, then take the trail to the left as it proceeds uphill to Rinaldi Street (2.6). To the west, there is a series of walking/cross-country bike trails; however, our reference route proceeds east 0.1 mile to Tampa Avenue and turns right (south). Bike on the Class X roadway over the freeway (2.9), freewheel another 0.5 mile downhill past Chatsworth Street, turn right on Tunney Avenue, and return to the starting point (3.8).

CONNECTING TRIPS: Continuation with the Chatsworth-Northridge-Granada Hills Loop (Trip #55) - from the trip origin, continue south on Tunney Avenue and turn right on Devonshire Street.

TRIP #58 - CALIFORNIA STATE UNIVERSITY, NORTHRIDGE CAMPUS

GENERAL LOCATION: Northridge

LEVEL OF DIFFICULTY: Loop - easy
Distance - 3.0 miles
Elevation gain - flat

HIGHLIGHTS: This free-form trip is a definite family favorite for weekends or vacation periods. The described route roams the campus periphery, but can also include numerous adventures throughout the picturesque central campus. All routes are unmarked, but traffic is light and there is a great deal of biking room. There are optional routes through adjoining (lightly trafficked) residential areas that can easily extend the total cruise to 4 or 5 miles, depending on the biker's imagination.

TRAILHEAD: From the Ronald Reagan Freeway, exit south at Reseda Boulevard and drive 2.75 miles to Nordhoff Street. Turn left (east) and continue about 0.5 mile to Lindley Avenue. Turn left onto the campus, left again into the parking area, and continue to the information sign in front of the Drama/Fine Arts Building.

TRIP DESCRIPTION: **North Leg.** Ride east to Lindley Avenue and turn left (north). Cycle past the Student Union Building (0.3), Plummer Street, and the fence opening just beyond. Next, cruise past the Fitness Center (0.7), recreation fields, a baseball field (with a water fountain), and the track and field stadium. Just off to the west are quiet residential streets with generous biking room, a possible later diversion. However, our route continues another 0.2 mile to Lassen Street (1.1).

Cross busy Lassen Street at the intersection and continue to the CSUN North Campus Annex. In 0.3 mile is Lemarsh Street; turn left (west) for a diversion to Northridge

NOTE: PARKING SHOWN ASSUMES CLASSES NOT IN SESSION

TRIP #58 - CALIFORNIA STATE UNIVERSITY, NORTHRIDGE CAMPUS

Recreation Center. In 0.2 mile, on our main route on Lindley Avenue, there is a newly constructed medical facility, the northernmost point of the route (1.7). On the return leg, cyclists can take a 0.3-mile diversion trip west on Lemarsh Street to Northridge Recreation Center. The center has grassy grounds and tree shade, as well as restrooms and water within the recreation facility itself.

South Leg. Return to Plummer Street and turn right (west) (2.8). Cruise 0.2 mile to Etiwanda Avenue and turn left (south) into the parking area. Follow winding Etiwanda Avenue to Prairie Street and turn right, continuing to Darby Avenue (3.6). Turn left and, in a short distance, turn back into the parking area. Free-wheel through the lot to Nordhoff Street and turn left (east), returning to the starting point in 0.2 mile (4.1).

CONNECTING TRIPS: 1) Continuation with the Chatsworth-Northridge-Granada Hills Loop (Trip #55) - from the trip origin, continue east on Nordhoff Street; 2) connection with the Limekiln Canyon Trail (Trip #57) - from the northernmost point of the trip, turn west on Plummer Street and continue 1.75 miles to Tunney Avenue.

TRIP #59 - WOODLAND HILLS-TARZANA LOOP

GENERAL LOCATION: Woodland Hills, Tarzana

LEVEL OF DIFFICULTY: Loop - moderate
Distance - 22.5 miles
Elevation gain - periodic moderate grades;
single steep grade in MacFarlane Drive area

HIGHLIGHTS: This interesting loop ride has both a city face and a country face. The flat northern segment traverses an urban-light commercial area for several miles before reaching the highly developed Promenade Mall/Topanga Plaza area. Once across the Ventura Freeway, the trip returns to a more rural setting amongst the foothills of the Santa Monica Mountains. This southern segment crosses the hillside community west of Topanga Canyon Boulevard (with some testy hill climbing if you choose) and then tours the elegant rural segment along Wells Drive. The beautifully treed and manicured Wells Drive "country lane" segment is the trip highlight.

TRAILHEAD: Exit the Ventura Freeway north at Balboa Boulevard and continue a short distance to Burbank Boulevard. Turn left (west) and drive 0.5 mile to Louise Avenue. Turn right (north) and proceed 0.6 mile to road's end. Turn left at Oxnard Street and find parking under a shade tree.

Bring a filled water bottle. There are strategically placed water sources along the route, but there is a long waterless stretch along the southern segment.

TRIP DESCRIPTION: **Oxnard and Topham Streets.** Bike west (away from Balboa Park) along Oxnard Street on the Class I Sepulveda Bike Basin path. Pedal on flat roadway (the trail is relatively flat on the entire segment north of the Ventura Freeway) past Louise Avenue (0.1) to White Oak Avenue (0.7). Across the street, the route becomes Class X. Continue on this road or bike one block north and turn left (west) on Bessemer Street. This alternate soon becomes a parallel path named Topham Street which is on the other side of the railroad tracks. (There is less traffic on this 1.5-mile alternate which ends at Wilbur Avenue.)

Just past Etiwanda Avenue (1.4), the path enters a light industrial area, crosses Reseda Boulevard (1.7), and proceeds to Wilbur Avenue where the surroundings return to residential (2.2). The street, which becomes Topham Street after it bends northwest, ends in 1.5 miles beyond Wilbur Avenue at Victory Boulevard.

Pierce College and Shopping Plazas. Turn left (west) at Victory Boulevard and pass the small Larson (baseball) Field. There is water alongside the dugout and shade, reached by turning right at Winnetka Avenue (4.3). The bikeway passes the Pierce College athletic fields, the entrance to the college at Mason Avenue (4.8), and the Pierce College Farm (open agricultural fields) before reaching De Soto Avenue. This is the beginning of a large commercial district (5.3). In a quarter mile, there is a little shopping center with several potential munchie stops. The traffic gets very heavy in this area, so try using the sidewalk for the next 0.5 mile. The route passes between the Promenade Mall (south) and Topanga Plaza, reaching Topanga Canyon Boulevard

TRIP #59 - WOODLAND HILLS-TARZANA LOOP

and a return to a residential setting just beyond (6.4). Continue to Shoup Avenue and turn left (south).

Ventura Freeway Crossing. Bike down tree-lined Shoup Avenue, passing Oxnard Street (7.5). In a quarter mile, reach the Woodland Hills Recreation Center. This is the best rest stop on the trip, with trees, water, and a pleasant foothill backdrop. Cross Burbank Boulevard and, in just 0.1 mile, turn right (west) on Berdon Street (8.2);

Detail Map for "**Ventura Freeway Crossing**" and "**Hill Country**"

in this quiet residential area, there is a three-mile marked Class III loop. Bike a short distance and turn left (south) on Capistrano Avenue, right on Clarendon Street, left on Sale Avenue, and right again on Mariano Street (most of this bikeway is marked) (8.5). Continue across busy Fallbrook Avenue (8.8) and, in 0.5 mile, reach Woodlake Avenue. Turn left (south), bike 0.3 mile to Ventura Boulevard (note that there is a gas station here), and follow that roadway to its end at Valley Circle Boulevard (10.0).

Bike over the Ventura Freeway to the massive shopping area on Mulholland Drive (10.6). Fill up with water in this area, as there are only limited sources for the remainder of the trip. A short diversion to the west leads to the Leonis Adobe and Plummer House. Just south from that area is Park Granada Boulevard, the roadway to the plush residential area surrounding Lake Calabasas.

Hill Country. Follow Avenue San Luis (the small street which parallels the freeway) up a short grade to Crespi Street (11.0). Just beyond, there is a small pedestrian bridge across the freeway. Continue on mildly rolling terrain past Fallbrook Avenue (11.5) to Shoup Avenue (12.2), where Avenue San Luis curves to the right and intersects MacFarlane Drive in 0.1 mile.

Now comes the decision point! Turn hard right and start the steep climb up MacFarlane Drive (it gets steeper!) or remain on more moderate Avenue San Luis. The former route offers some nice vistas of the surrounding hills and a short but stout workout. The route continues on a very steep upgrade to Llano Drive (12.8), bears left on that street, winds another quarter mile uphill, and then begins a very steep, winding downgrade to Clavel Court (13.6). Turn left, then left again at De La Osa Street, and cycle 0.1 mile to San Feliciano Drive. (The less challenging route goes 0.3 mile on

Avenue San Luis to San Feliciano Drive, then turns right [south] onto mildly rolling hills in a pleasant residential area, proceeding to Dumetz Road.)

The bikeway turns left (east) on Dumetz Road and heads through a tree-lined residential area, passing Topanga Canyon Boulevard and a small shopping center (14.1). Next there is a 0.75-mile series of rolling hills with a crest at Escobedo Drive, near the Woodland Hills Country Club entrance. Continue to Serrania Avenue, where the road bends sharply to the right (south), then curves and resumes its westward track, becoming Wells Drive. Just beyond Serrania Avenue is the like-named park with water, restrooms, grassy knolls, and children's play areas. This is the last convenient public water source that we found for the trip's remainder.

Wells Drive. Nearby is the Victorian Westchester County Private Estates (15.7) and, to the right, the entry to Serrania Park. However, our tour stays on Wells Drive and continues through moderately rolling hills in a well-groomed residential area. The top of the last grade is at Del Moreno Drive (16.2). Follow the steep downgrade past Winnetka Avenue, where the roadway narrows and passes through a pleasant grove of trees and continued awesome residential setting (16.7). In 0.4 mile at Corbin Avenue, the roadway crests, heads downhill for 0.3 mile, winds uphill again, and reaches Tampa Avenue (17.7).

Just beyond, there is a junction with Casa Drive where Wells Drive winds to the left. The relatively flat remainder of the trip starts by passing a small school recreation area with water fountains (probably locked on weekends) at Crebs Avenue (18.5), and the back side recreation fields of Gaspar De Portolá Junior High School. Wells Drive ends shortly at Avenida Hacienda (19.0). Turn right (south) and continue a short distance to Tarzana Drive (passing the El Caballero Country Club), turn right again at narrow Nestle Avenue, and then left at Valley Vista Boulevard (19.7).

Wells Drive near Kelvin Avenue

The Return Link. This area returns to a classy tree-covered residential setting with the roadway passing White Oak Avenue (20.2), then following a curve up a moderate grade past several gated properties. The roadway, now named Rancho Street, continues to Louise Avenue (20.9). Turn left (north) onto the light downgrade, passing more elegant estates. Bike across Ventura Boulevard (21.3), then on a light downhill over the Ventura Freeway (22.1), and return to Oxnard Street and the trip origin in 0.4 mile.

CONNECTING TRIPS: 1) Continuation with the Sepulveda Bike Basin ride (Trip #38) - from the trip origin, bike west to the end of Oxnard Street to Balboa Park; 2) connection with the Chatsworth-Northridge-Granada Hills Loop (Trip #55) - at Shoup Avenue, bike 1.5 miles north to Saticoy Street.

TRIP #60 - HANSEN DAM RECREATION AREA

GENERAL LOCATION: Pacoima, San Fernando

LEVEL OF DIFFICULTY: **Dam ride:** up and back - easy
    Distance - 4.5 miles
    Elevation gain - single short,
      moderate climb to dam

    Bottomlands ride: loop - moderate
      (modest off-road biking skills required)
    Distance - 4.1 miles
    Elevation gain - periodic moderate grades

HIGHLIGHTS: The primary ride featured is on top of the Hansen Dam itself. A short Class I trail climbs to the levee entry, followed by a flat, 3.4-mile (up and back) segment on the levee's paved surface. The views of the bottomland behind the dam and the more-distant mountain vistas are inspiring.

A second tour explores the Hansen Dam Recreation Area bottomlands and is best done with a fat-tire bike. It focuses on the western side of the bottomlands, exploring both the area just behind the dam and the areas below the bluffs of the Hansen Dam Aquatic Center and near the Fenton Avenue sports recreation area. There are numerous spurs off the described route for further exploration and the chance for riders to test their sand-riding skills. Also provided is a short diversion trip off the bottomlands tour, which leads to the Hansen Dam Aquatic Center.

TRAILHEAD: From the Foothill Freeway, exit south at Foothill Boulevard (Osborne Street to the north). Drive one mile to the connecting Osborne Street segment, turn left, and continue a quarter mile to Dronfield Avenue. Turn left and drive directly into the upper parking area. From the Ronald Reagan Freeway, continue east to the freeway

TRIP #60 - HANSEN DAM RECREATION AREA

terminus. Follow the transition route to the westbound Foothill Freeway and take the first exit south on Foothill Boulevard. Continue as described above. From the Golden State Freeway, exit northeast on Osborne Street. Drive 2.25 miles to Dronfield Avenue and turn right (east).

Bring a light water supply. The trip is short and the picnic areas have water.

ROUTE DESCRIBED FOLLOWS
NUMBERED SEQUENCE AS
SHOWN ON THIS MAP

•NUMEROUS SPUR TRAILS NOT
SHOWN
• SOME TRAILS AROUND HANSEN
LAKE ARE INACCESSIBLE
IN HIGH WATER

TRIP DESCRIPTION: **Dam Levee Ride.** A pleasant adult or family trip is the easy ride atop the dam. The levee is accessible by using a paved trail which starts at the southwestern end of the upper parking lot. The paved trail climbs and parallels Osborne Street just before reaching the parking lot at the levee edge. (This lot is an alternate, easier point of entry.) Pass through the open gate and bike directly onto the levee. The bottomlands behind the dam are below and to the left, while the Hansen Dam Golf Course is to the right. The route passes over the spillway at about one mile and reaches a closed fence and turnaround at 1.7 miles. The full ride is about 4.5 miles. (Note that the levee is a good vantage point from which to plan a bottomlands tour.)

Bottomlands Tour: Southern Recreation Area. Within the upper parking area, bike southeast of the Dronfield Avenue entry (toward the dam) to the entry road (① in the detail map) which heads towards the bottomlands. At the downgrade's end, within the paved lower parking lot, turn right (south at ②) and proceed past some grassy play fields and a picnic area (0.2). Pass around a locked gate and onto a compacted dirt trail which heads directly toward the dam.

Bike a short distance to a "reference junction" (③); take the path southeast toward the dam spillway. In 0.2 mile of winding through the trees and passing many spur trails, there is a "T"-junction in an open area. Left leads to the low-water point (Hansen Lake). Our route goes right and reaches the base of the dam in a short distance (0.4). In low water, bikers can turn left and follow a mixed-dirt trail across the spillway entry and along the entire dam base. This is for fat-tire cyclists who love to challenge sand.

The reference tour goes right along the base through mixed compacted/loose dirt and reaches another junction (④). Continue along the dam base and bike almost to the western dam edge. Follow the path toward the southwestern edge of the upper parking lot and take the first major junction to the right (1.1) (⑤). A 0.2-mile stint on paved path returns cyclists to the "reference junction" (1.3). Next, repeat the incoming route, then bike to the northern edge of the lower parking lot and follow the packed-dirt horse trail to the northeast (1.9).

Northern Recreation Area. Bike on the horse path past a couple of spurs and follow a short upgrade to another "reference" junction (⑥). Stay right and pass over a wash, then pass through an open gate (2.1). This route leads cyclists alongside the bluffs below the Hansen Dam Aquatic Center. Follow the wide trail through a mix of hard- and loose-pack and pump 0.2 mile to a "T"-junction (⑦). Right leads to a small rise above Hansen Lake, while the reference route heads left. This wide, hard-pack trail works over to a large recreation area off Fenton Avenue (⑧) (2.9). There are soccer fields plus picnic facilities, scattered tree cover, and restrooms at the north end of the complex.

This is our suggested turnaround point, although experienced and adventurous cyclists with fat-tire bikes can explore the eastern side and make a full loop of the area behind Hansen Dam. A myriad of sandy trails and two major wash crossings are in store for cyclists who opt for this adventure. (Note, however, that we saw few bicycle-tire tracks beyond the recreation area.)

The Return Segment. Backtrack to the reference junction (⑥), turn right (northwest), and bike a steep grade on a mixed-pack dirt surface. In about 100 feet, there is another trail fork (3.8). Right and steeply uphill is Stonehurst Avenue and the road entry to the aquatic area. Our route left cruises on a shelf which provides some interesting bottomland views. The trail passes through an open gate and follows the

Bottomlands area below Aquatic Center

next major fork right. A short climb leads back to the upper parking area and an easy glide back to the start point (4.1).

Diversion Trip to the Hansen Dam Aquatic Center. From junction (⑨), climb a 30- to 40-foot rise and bike a couple of hundred yards to Stonehurst Avenue. Turn right and pedal through the open gate on paved road. In 0.2 mile, there is a junction within a large parking area. Going right takes bikers to a bluff which overlooks the bottomlands area. Heading left leads to the Aquatic center with its pool and small man-made lake, complete with self-propelled paddlewheel boats. There are distant views into the Sunland and Tujunga areas from here.

CONNECTING TRIPS: Continue on Osborne Street 0.7 mile past Roger Jessup Park. (The park has grass, shade, picnic areas, water, and restrooms.) The path becomes Class III at this juncture. Bike another 2.8 miles (under the Golden State Freeway) to Woodman Avenue. There is a six-mile Class III bike ride south on this street.

TRIP #61 - EL CARISO REGIONAL PARK

GENERAL LOCATION: San Fernando

LEVEL OF DIFFICULTY: Loop - easy
                                Distance - 2.2 miles
                                Elevation gain - single moderate upgrade

HIGHLIGHTS: This dandy little Class I loop trip has some big offerings, particularly as a family bike outing. The route is flat with the exception of one 30-foot downgrade-upgrade. The loop provides two miles of variety, including recreation fields, a golf-course, Class X spurs into the Pacoima Canyon Wash, scenic view points, and a well-laid-out park. Bikers can extend the trip mileage by doing the loop several times or by selecting from among many route options within the park.

There is an option to leave the park and bike 1.25 miles on lightly trafficked Class X surface streets to Veteran's Memorial Park. (The route there involves some testy hill climbing.) This exceptional locale is slightly more hilly, but is a delight for family outings in one of Los Angeles County's most gorgeous and scenic park settings.

TRAILHEAD: From the Foothill Freeway, exit north on Hubbard Street and drive one mile to Garrick Avenue. Turn right into the park. Hubbard Street is roughly 3.5 miles east of the Golden State Freeway/Foothill Freeway fusion point and two miles north-west of the Ronald Reagan Freeway fusion point.

Water is plentiful. Bring a light water supply if the trip is to be extended to Veteran's Memorial Park.

TRIP DESCRIPTION: From the parking area near the park's swimming pool, bike southwest towards the tennis courts on the Class I path. Just beyond the courts, turn left and bike alongside the parking area. In a short distance, pass the Snack and Pro Shop (apparently not open in the winter) (0.2). Cruise through this pleasant and

TRIP #61 - EL CARISO REGIONAL PARK

well-manicured park between the baseball diamonds and then veer southeast through a parking area. A short pedal leads to the El Cariso Golf Course Club House (0.4).

Pass the clubhouse and cycle through the parking area on Rajah Street. In this area, bikers get a glimpse of a small lake within the golf course, as well as a view of the golfers "at work." At Eldridge Avenue, turn left (southeast) and hug the golf course periphery on the quality Class I path. Along this entire 0.4-mile stretch, there are opportunities to watch the hackers, whackers, and an occasional veteran golfer.

Hug the edge of the golf course and turn left at Harding Street, passing through a small motorized vehicle barrier. In 0.1 mile, the path reaches its most southeasterly point. There is a view of the Pacoima Canyon Wash and flood control dam here (for bikers with fat-tire bikes, this is a jumping-off point to explore the wash) (1.0). Just beyond, the path whips downhill to the floor of the wash; from this area, some of the off-road vehicle play areas in both the wash and the hills are visible.

Bike a short, moderately steep upgrade to a vantage point with an unobstructed view of the nearby mountains. We watched a hang-glider working the mountain drafts from here (1.3). In 0.2 mile, the path crosses Gridley Street, returns to the park, and passes through the main picnic area (water, restrooms, picnic tables, barbecues, scattered shade trees). There are numerous paths through the park interior here; our described path keeps to the right on the park periphery paralleling Simshaw Avenue. The route passes alongside a group of residences (1.8), crosses a park roadway, and winds its way parallel to Hubbard Street before reaching the trip starting point (2.2).

CONNECTING TRIPS: There is an option to bike a short distance to explore Veteran's Memorial Park. Follow Hubbard Street 0.75 mile to Shablow Avenue, turn left, and continue a quarter-plus mile steeply uphill to Sayre Street. Turn right for entry. The park has bikeways/walkways threading most of its interior, plus both sheltered and open picnic facilities, grassy rolling knolls, varied and prolific tree cover, restrooms, Los Angeles Mission College structures, and numerous viewpoints to the valley below. Families might opt to drive directly to the park and spend the day wandering around its intertwining, paved paths.

Middle Area of Veteran's Memorial Park

TRIP #62 - GLENDALE BIKEWAY

GENERAL LOCATION: Glendale, La Crescenta

LEVEL OF DIFFICULTY: One way - moderate; up and back - moderate
Distance - 9.6 miles (one way)
Elevation gain - periodic moderate grades

HIGHLIGHTS: This rewarding tour skirts the Verdugo Mountains, following the foothills from Brand Park in Glendale around to Crescenta Valley Park in La Crescenta.
The route includes several excellent parks, provides some scenic views, and is a varied
and entertaining ride. When ridden in the direction as described, the return leg from La
Crescenta provides a mild but continuous 4-5 mile downhill runout. (Does that say
something about the initial leg of this trip?) Though predominately Class X, the quality
of roadway, amount of traffic, and available bike shoulder make this ride similar to a
quality Class III route.

TRAILHEAD: From the Golden State Freeway, exit east at Western Avenue. Drive
toward the Verdugo Mountains foothills about 1.5 miles to Mountain Street. Turn right
and, in a few hundred feet, turn left into Brand Park. From the Ventura Freeway, transition north onto the Golden State Freeway and proceed as stated above. From the
Glendale Freeway, transition west onto the Ventura Freeway and then transition north
in about 2.5 miles onto the Golden State Freeway.
    There are strategically located water sources at the parks along the route. Howev-
er, bring a filled water bottle for an up-and-back trip in the summer.

TRIP DESCRIPTION: **Glendale Foothills.** Tour Brand Park's grounds before
departing, leaving some time to visit the classic and stately Brand Park Library. Once
outside the park, turn left onto Mountain Street and bike 0.4 mile through a quiet and
stately residential area to the point where the roadway veers right and becomes Highland Avenue. At the next intersection, turn left onto Cumberland Road and bike another
half mile through lightly rolling hills to the street's terminus at Valley View Road (1.2).
Note that any turn toward the foothills in this general area can lead to some challenging
uphill adventures for interested bikers!
    Turn right (south) and follow the steep downhill another half mile to Stocker Street.
There are scattered views across to the Santa Monica Mountains in this segment. Follow Stocker Street east across busy Central Avenue (2.1) and return to a residential area
and a mild upgrade in a short distance. At the end of Stocker Street, turn left (north) at

TRIP #62 - GLENDALE BIKEWAY

Rossmoyne Avenue (2.9) and bike another short upgrade to Mountain Street. Turn right and follow the curving road past compact, but delightful, Nibley Park; the road veers right and crosses the bridge over the Verdugo Wash (3.7).

Verdugo Road. Just beyond the wash, cross Mountain Street and ride into the parking lot behind the Glendale Civic Auditorium. In 0.2 mile, there is a pedestrian walkway (with a ramp entrance on the north side) over Verdugo Road. (Note also that just beyond and to the left there is a walkway which leads over the Verdugo Wash to large, well-equipped, Verdugo Park.) Follow the ramp (nice view from here) across to the Glendale College Campus, turn left in the parking lot, and pedal to Verdugo Road (4.3).

There is no such thing as a free ride! Follow Verdugo Road on a steady, slight upgrade that will continue several miles into La Crescenta. Pass a small eatery and market, follow the valley floor past Crestmont Court (4.7) and Wabasso Way (5.0), and reach the top of this grade at Glorietta Avenue (5.7). Pass Glorietta Park and ride about a quarter mile further to Sparr Boulevard just before the point where Verdugo Road and Canada Boulevard fuse.

La Crescenta Area. Turn right (east) at Sparr Boulevard, pedal uphill through a residential area to Glencoe Way (6.7), and turn left. Bike across Verdugo Road and pass a small shopping center. Cruise to Downing Avenue (6.9) and turn right (north); follow this road as it jogs right at Arlington Avenue and proceeds on a workout grade to Broadview Drive. Turn left onto a welcome flat and bike 0.3 mile to Roselawn Avenue (Rosemont Avenue to the north) (7.7).

Follow another workout uphill past Honolulu Avenue. (There are eateries to the right on Honolulu Avenue.) At Montrose Avenue, turn left (8.2). Cross that busy but flat roadway through a light commercial and residential area across Pennsylvania Avenue. Veer left onto Honolulu Avenue and pedal to Crescenta Valley Park near New York Avenue (9.6). The most naturally scenic area and best rest stop is at the northern end of the park; lift your bike over the entrance barrier to reach that fenced-in park area.

CONNECTING TRIPS: 1) Connection with the Burbank Bikeway (Trip #36) - from the trip origin, bike west on Mountain Street about one mile to Providencia Avenue; 2) connection with the Verdugo Mountains Loop (Trip #63) - at the trip terminus, cycle east on Honolulu Avenue past Crescenta Valley Park.

Brand Park Library

TRIP #63 - VERDUGO MOUNTAINS LOOP

__GENERAL LOCATION__: La Crescenta, La Tuna Canyon,
Burbank, Glendale

__LEVEL OF DIFFICULTY__: Loop - moderate to strenuous
Distance - 23.9 miles
Elevation gain - periodic moderate grades;
single steep upgrade in the La Crescenta area

__HIGHLIGHTS__: This grand looper takes a tour around the base of the Verdugo Mountains and includes a canyon visit to boot! The route starts at Crescenta Valley Park, drops down into La Tuna Canyon, and returns via Glenoaks Boulevard to the foothills of Burbank (see Trip #36) and Glendale (see Trip #62). The scenic views throughout various sections of this trip are outstanding. Much of the trip is on quality Class X roadways; the exception is that the descent into La Tuna Canyon is on a steep, winding downhill with limited shoulder for biking.

__TRAILHEAD__: From the Foothill Freeway, exit south at Pennsylvania Avenue and turn right (west) in a quarter mile at Honolulu Avenue. Motor about half a mile to the Crescenta Valley Park entrance at Dunsmore Avenue.

Bring a full bottle or two of water for this trip. Do not try this trip in the reverse direction unless you are a strong uphill biker! The ride out of La Tuna Canyon into La Crescenta is very difficult and the trip rating changes to "strenuous."

__TRIP DESCRIPTION__: __Honolulu Avenue.__ From the park, turn left (west) on Honolulu Avenue and bike uphill to Boston Avenue (0.3), cross under the Foothill Freeway, and begin a steeper uphill just beyond. The route flattens and climbs again before reaching a split in 0.6 mile from Boston Avenue. Honolulu Avenue ends. To the right is Tujunga Canyon Boulevard; our route is to the left on La Tuna Canyon Road.

__La Tuna Canyon Road.__ Cruise past the Verdugo Hills Golf Course and sweat out a very steep upgrade alongside the freeway, reaching a flat in 0.8 mile. Pass under the freeway (2.1) and begin a steep, winding descent into the canyon. The road continues through the narrowing canyon past a few isolated residences (3.9), reaching a flattening grade in another 0.3 mile.

Parallel the La Tuna Canyon Wash, passing a small dam/debris basin and a light residential area. Within a mile, there is a rustic area complete with several mini-ranches. The flat roadway passes Old Buckboard Lane (5.8) and enters an area where the canyon widens significantly. Within the next mile, the highway returns to civilization, passing more residences in the Wheatland Avenue area and a gas station and other commercial enterprises at Sunland Boulevard (6.8). There are plenty of rest and fuel-up/water stops in this area. Turn left (south) and bike 0.2 mile further to Glenoaks Boulevard.

__Burbank Foothills.__ Turn left (southeast) on flat Glenoaks Boulevard and ride through a light commercial/residential area past Nettleton Street (7.5), Lanark Street (8.2), and Hollywood Way (8.8). In 0.3 mile, turn left on Cabrini Drive and pedal 0.2

TRIP #63 - VERDUGO MOUNTAINS LOOP

mile uphill to Scott Road. Turn right and, in a short distance, pass through the motorized vehicle barricade. Pedal past Brace Canyon Park (9.9), then proceed to Kenneth Road and turn left. Now follow the Class III Burbank Bikeway route (Trip #36) to the northeasternmost point at Sunset Canyon Drive and Providencia Avenue (13.2).

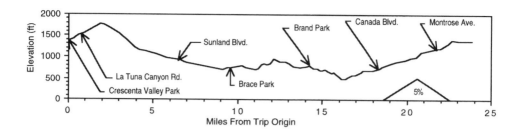

Glendale Foothills to La Crescenta. Continue another mile on Sunset Canyon Drive/Mountain Street to the entrance to Brand Park. Follow the directions of the Glendale Bikeway route (Trip #55) and return to the trip origin at Crescenta Valley Park. The total trip length is 23.9 miles.

CONNECTING TRIPS: 1) Continuation with the Glendale Bikeway (Trip #62) - the Verdugo Mountains Loop includes the Glendale Bikeway trip; 2) connection with the Burbank Bikeway (Trip #36) - from Sunset Canyon Drive and Providencia Avenue, turn south (downhill) on the latter street.

TRIP #64 - DUARTE BIKEWAY

GENERAL LOCATION: Duarte

LEVEL OF DIFFICULTY: Loop - easy
Distance - 5.0 miles
Elevation gain - essentially flat

HIGHLIGHTS: This easy-going ride tours some of the quieter streets in Duarte, passes several inviting parks, and finishes with a 1.7-mile Class I straight-away on the Duarte Bikeway. There are frequent views into the residential-spotted foothills and of the nearby San Gabriel Mountains along the way.

TRAILHEAD: Follow the San Gabriel River Freeway north to its end at Huntington Drive, where the freeway becomes Mount Olive Drive. Drive north one-fourth mile to Royal Oaks Drive and turn right, proceeding one-half mile to the Royal Oaks Park western entry at Vineyard Avenue. From the Foothill Freeway, transition north onto the San Gabriel Freeway and follow the directions given above. The grassy park is equipped with tree shade, restrooms, numerous sports courts, and a children's play area.

Bring a light water supply. This is a short ride and several water sources are available.

TRIP #64 - DUARTE BIKEWAY

TRIP DESCRIPTION: **Southbound and Westbound.** Bike east a short distance to Las Lomas Road and turn south. Bike on a wide roadway through a residential neighborhood. In about 0.5 mile, at the next street beyond Huntington Drive, is Maynard Drive. Turn right and bike to Crestfield Drive, then turn left. Make another right on Central Avenue (1.1). This route takes cyclists on the periphery of a large fenced maintenance and storage complex at the terminus of Las Lomas Road.

Pedal on Central Avenue, a lightly used freeway frontage road, and pass the Otis Gordon Sports Park (portable restroom, sports fields, children's play area) before reaching Mount Olive Drive. Cycle another 0.8 mile to Highland Avenue and Northview Park (playing fields), taking in the San Gabriel Mountains and scattered foothill residences just to the north. Beyond is Duarte High School, then the southern tip of the Duarte Sports Park (water, restrooms, tree shade, playing fields, courts), just before reaching Buena Vista Street (2.6).

Northbound and Eastbound. Turn right and pedal toward the mountains, on a busier street with a wide bikeway. At Huntington Drive, there is a small commercial complex, and 0.3 mile further is Royal Oaks Drive (3.2). Across the street, sandwiched between Royal Oaks Drive and Orange Avenue, is the pleasant, tree-lined, Class I Duarte Bikeway. Bike east on the wide bike/walk path, enjoying the local flora and an occasional view of the San Gabriels. The 1.7-mile path crosses under the petite Mount Olive Drive bridge and then works its way to the Vineyard Avenue terminus (5.0).

CONNECTING TRIPS: Connection with the San Gabriel River tour (Trip #22E) - from Las Lomas Road and Huntington Drive, bike east one-fourth mile on the latter road and look for the entry on the river's east side.

TRIP #65 - SAN DIMAS CANYON ROAD

GENERAL LOCATION: San Dimas

LEVEL OF DIFFICULTY: Up and back - moderate to strenuous
Distance - 8.9 miles
Elevation gain - variable moderate-to-steep grade

HIGHLIGHTS: This short canyon ride takes cyclists from the city streets into the foothills of the San Gabriel Mountains. The roadway is narrow and has many blind curves on the upper stretches, although the auto traffic is low speed and sparse. From San Dimas proper, the route climbs modestly past San Dimas Canyon Park, then steepens as it follows San Dimas Creek up into the Angeles National Forest. The uppermost stretches wind along the canyon's east side above the San Dimas Reservoir, then the road drops down to the rustic San Dimas Fire Station. The paved road ends at a locked gate just beyond; auto traffic beyond the gate is restricted to cabin owners and fat-tire bikers.

TRAILHEAD: From California Highway 210 westbound (the western extension of the Foothill Freeway in San Dimas), exit at N. San Dimas Avenue and turn north. At the next major thoroughfare (Baseline Road), turn (right) east and continue 0.75 mile, crossing San Dimas Canyon Road. Park in this residential area and under one of the tall trees. From the east on Highway 210, take the Foothill Boulevard off-ramp and turn right. Drive one-half mile and turn left (south) at San Dimas Canyon Road. In a few hundred feet, find parking near the W. Baseline Road intersection.

The above start point allows a full rural tour of San Dimas Canyon Road, which starts just above Foothill Boulevard. An alternate is to start at San Dimas Canyon Park, which is about one-third mile above Foothill Boulevard. The park has tree shade, grass, restrooms, picnic facilities, and recreation fields.

Bring a filled water bottle for the climb on hot summer days. The only public water source is at San Dimas Canyon Park.

TRIP DESCRIPTION: **Up to Golden Hills Road.** Bike across Foothill Boulevard and stare into the local foothills. (Surprise, surprise!) A sign immediately suggests that cyclists on this Class III route use the sidewalk, which disappears a short distance up the road. In 0.3-plus miles, reach Sycamore Canyon Road and alluring San Dimas Canyon Park. Beyond, the modest climb continues on a tree-lined road past Fernridge Drive (0.8) and passes alongside the San Dimas Canyon Golf Course. The San Dimas Wash is on the right. A short downhill is followed by a bridge crossing over San Dimas Creek (1.8). In 0.2 mile, the road narrows further and Golden Hills Road comes up on the right. This is the last residential entry of the uphill ride.

On to (Paved) Road's End. The narrow road follows the canyon with San Dimas Creek's abundant greenery to the left. Near (2.4), the overhanging tree shade graces the road and, in 0.3 mile, San Dimas Canyon Road enters the Angeles National Forest. Just beyond and to the left, there is a group of Forest Service structures, followed by the first glimpse of the San Dimas Reservoir dam. A set of steep "U"-bends leads up to a more open, exposed area with clearer views of the dam. A flat gives way

TRIP #65 - SAN DIMAS CANYON ROAD

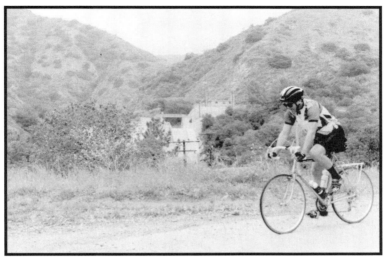

San Dimas Reservoir dam

to a sharp left and a view from above the dam and reservoir (3.2). The next 0.8 mile follows the winding contour of the east canyon wall on ever-narrowing road to the north end of the reservoir. (In this area, it is difficult for two cars to pass; however, a single slow-moving car and a biker work out well together.) At about (4.1), the road begins downhill and returns to forested environs, passing the San Dimas Fire Station in 0.2 mile. At 4.4-plus miles, reach the end of the city-maintained road and a gated access restricted to cabin owners.

If you have a fat-tire bike, continue onward should your heart desire. Otherwise, all that remains is a short climb and a great runout back to the start point!

CONNECTING TRIPS: Connection with the Baseline Road tour (Trip #45) - at the intersection of San Dimas Canyon Road and Baseline Road, follow the latter road east.

TRIP #66 - THOMPSON CREEK TRAIL

GENERAL LOCATION: Claremont

LEVEL OF DIFFICULTY: Up and back - easy
Distance - 4.7 miles
Elevation gain - mild steady grade eastbound

HIGHLIGHTS: This trail is a hidden treasure, even to many local area residents. The 2.3-plus-mile route follows Thompson Creek for most of its journey. The well-designed, well-maintained trail passes under a varied, light tree canopy for about three quarters of its length, then transitions into open space for the trip's remainder. Along the way are water fountains, sitting benches, and pastoral Higginbotham Park with a restroom and a unique children's playground. Thompson Creek Trail is a light but scenic workout for adults and families alike.

TRIP #66 - THOMPSON CREEK TRAIL

TRAILHEAD: From Baseline Road, turn north on N. Towne Avenue and drive several hundred feet to a parking area. This is a private entry, normally left open to the public; however, property owners do have the right to deny access. Starting near the trail's western end allows cyclists to do all the climbing on the outgoing leg, resulting in a nice coast back to the parking area on the return. There is a public parking area at the east end, which is at the intersection of Mills Avenue and Mount Baldy Road. To get there from Baseline Road, turn north at Mills Avenue and drive a little over one mile to the point where Mount Baldy Road originates and veers right. Continue a couple of hundred feet on Mills Avenue to the parking area.

Well-placed water fountains are available on the trail west of Indian Hill Boulevard. The trail is open from 6 a.m. to 10 p.m.

TRIP DESCRIPTION: **Towne Avenue to Pomello Drive.** Join the trail along the concrete channel which is Thompson's Creek and head eastbound. The trailside tree cover, foothills to the left, and trailside residences on the right are typical of this segment. In 0.4 mile, there is the first of many walk/bike/equestrian accesses from the residential area. (Equestrians use the dirt trail which parallels the walking/biking trail.) Nearby is the first of three water fountain/sitting bench combinations.

The trail crosses Mountain Avenue, the single trafficked street on the route, in another 0.1 mile. Just beyond (0.7) is a trailside restroom on the northern edge of Higginbotham Park; this grassy shaded park has picnic benches and a unique children's play area, complete with a miniature locomotive, a stagecoach, a southwestern adobe house, and other playtime amenities. At (1.0), near another water fountain/park bench, there is a trail fork. Stay to the left alongside the creek. The last water fountain is just before the trail intersection with the Pomello Drive terminus (1.6).

Pomello Drive to Trail's End. The trail stays alongside the creek but now enters a broad, treeless open space. The climb steepens and heads more northeasterly as the wall of the Thompson Creek Reservoir comes into view. The trail pulls away from Thompson Creek and passes under some power transmission lines near the top of the grade (2.1). In 0.1-plus mile is the trail exit and entry into a large parking area along Mills Avenue.

The Return. Coast back to Towne Avenue, maintaining a safe pace with the foot traffic in mind. To see the entire trail, continue another 0.1 mile to trail's end at Foothill Boulevard, then retrace the path back to the parking area (4.7).

TRIP #67 - CANYON COUNTRY TOUR

GENERAL LOCATION: Bouquet Canyon, Saugus, Santa Clarita, Forrest Park

LEVEL OF DIFFICULTY: Loop - strenuous
Distance - 20.3 miles
Elevation gain - steep grades on Sand Canyon Road
and Vasquez Canyon Road

HIGHLIGHTS: This tour is a canyon lover's delight, visiting Bouquet, Soledad, Sand, and Vasquez canyons in a single loop. The journey starts at comfy Bouquet Canyon Park and mostly coasts on Bouquet Canyon Road to the trip's elevation low point at the intersection with Soledad Canyon Road. The steady moderate climb on Soledad Canyon Road includes a 6.7-mile stretch of Class I path, much of which is alongside the Santa Clara River. A turn north leads to a heady summit climb on Sand Canyon Road, followed by another uphill workout on Vasquez Canyon Road. Views of the canyon floors and developed city areas, from these summits, are well worth the effort. Vasquez Canyon Road ends at Bouquet Canyon Road, where cyclists are treated to a refreshing downhill back to the start point. Note that some parts of the journey are on busy (parts of Bouquet Canyon Road and Soledad Canyon Road) or narrow (Sand Canyon Road and Vasquez Canyon Road) Class X road.

There is an option to take a shorter route using a bypass on Whites Canyon Road/ Plum Canyon Road. Cyclists are treated to a single steep, but scenic, 400-foot-plus climb on the bypass for this 12.8-mile alternative. In addition to reducing trip mileage, this alternative provides some of the better views into the southern Santa Clarita and Saugus areas.

TRIP #67 - CANYON COUNTRY TOUR

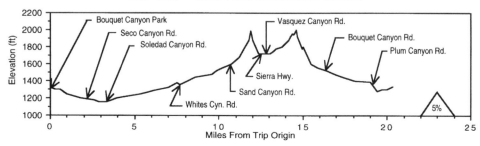

TRAILHEAD: From the Golden State Freeway, exit east at Valencia Boulevard and drive 2.5 miles to Bouquet Canyon Road. Turn left (northeast) and continue 2.75 miles to Urbandale Avenue. Turn left, drive one-third mile to Alaminos Drive, turn right, and go four blocks to Wellston Drive. Turn left and drive up to Bouquet Canyon Park at the end of the road. The park has limited shade, water, restrooms, playgrounds, recreational fields, tennis and basketball courts, and picnic facilities. There are also hiking trails and some mountain bike terrain nearby.

Bring a couple of water bottles for hot days. There are several public water facilities on Bouquet Canyon Road and Soledad Canyon Road; however, Sand Canyon Road and Vasquez Canyon Road are waterless.

TRIP DESCRIPTION: **Bouquet Canyon.** Retrace the incoming route to Bouquet Canyon Road and turn right onto a Class II roadway. Coast past Haskell Canyon Road and scope out the massive pipelines of the California Aqueduct in the hills to the left. The Class II path disappears at Alamogordo Road; across the street is Central Park, a massive sports and recreation facility that has restrooms, but little shade. On the continued downhill, the route passes one of many shopping centers at Seco Canyon Road (2.4). In another 0.8 mile, reach the trip's low point at the Soledad Canyon Road intersection after crossing the Santa Clara River.

Soledad Canyon. Turn left and traverse busy and fast-moving Soledad Canyon Road on a steady, 7.5-mile moderate upgrade to Sand Canyon Road. Our preferred option is to take the Class I bikeway/walkway (the Santa Clarita Trail) on the north side of the street. The initial couple of miles are (relatively) lightly developed, but do include the Saugus Speedway. The Class I path shifts to the south side at Golden Oak Road (6.7) and stays alongside Soledad Canyon Road to the next Santa Clara River crossing (7.4). At this juncture, cyclists can ride the streets or, better, stay on the bike path. The path swings away from Soledad Canyon Road, passing alongside a shopping complex, and follows the banks of the Santa Clara River.

The bikeway tracks east and passes under Whites Canyon Road (7.7), Sierra Highway (8.6), and the Antelope Valley Freeway (9.5) before reaching its terminus at an outlet just west of Deep Creek Drive (9.9). (There are also outlets to the first two overpassing streets, as well as one to Soledad Canyon Road just east of Sierra Highway.) Along this stretch, there are steady views of the wide riverbed. Once back on Soledad Canyon Road, it is another 0.8 mile to Sand Canyon Road on Class X roadway.

Sand Canyon and Vasquez Canyon. Turn left (north) and start a mild grade through rapidly thinning development and relatively barren landscape, which is typical of the two canyons. The grade steepens and the road narrows as it winds along the contour of the surrounding hills. In 1.3 miles is the summit, where there is a partial view of the lower Mint Canyon area. A swift 0.5-mile downgrade leads to Sierra Highway (12.6). A right turn and 0.3-mile flat lead to Vasquez Canyon Road.

Turn onto that road, pass over the Mint Canyon Wash, and cycle through a hill-dotted landscape with scattered small ranchos. A short flat gives way to a 1.1-mile climb to the tour's second scenic crest, where there is a view north into Vasquez Canyon. On the fast downhill, take some time to stop and admire the sculpted rock formations on the left. The route passes Lost Creek Road, on a moderate grade, and reaches Bouquet Canyon Road in another 0.6 mile (16.5).

The Bouquet Canyon Return. Turn right and pedal a satisfying downgrade through rural ranchland with the first treeside shade in quite a spell. The route reenters the signed Santa Clarita city limits, passes a small shopping center, where the Class II bikeway begins, and reaches Plum Canyon Road in another 0.3 mile (19.1). In 0.5 mile, reach Urbandale Avenue; a right turn leads to the backtrack route to Bouquet Canyon Park (20.3).

Whites Canyon/Plum Canyon Shortcut. A shorter (moderate-to-strenuous) loop involves staying on Soledad Canyon Road (as opposed to taking the Class I route junction along the Santa Clara River) and going 0.3 mile to Whites Canyon Road. Turn left onto a moderate grade which becomes a serious climb to a false summit in 1.3 miles. Pump past Steinway Street and reach the crest in another 0.3 mile. Take in both the city and canyon views before following a well-deserved 0.4-mile runout through a less-developed area on what is now Plum Canyon Road. Pass Rogers Drive (3.7) and cycle on flatter terrain 0.4 mile to Bouquet Canyon Road. Next go 2.6 miles, mostly downhill, to Urbandale Avenue and return to Bouquet Canyon Park. The total tour length with this option is 12.8 miles.

CONNECTING TRIPS: 1) Connection with the Valencia Loop (Trip #68) - at the intersection of Bouquet Canyon Road and Soledad Canyon Road, follow the latter road southwest 1.75 miles (the road name changes to Valencia Boulevard) to McBean Parkway; turn left and proceed a short distance to Del Monte Drive; 2) connection with the San Francisquito Canyon and Bouquet Canyons ride (Trip #69) - the trips share a common route on Bouquet Canyon Road below Vasquez Canyon Road.

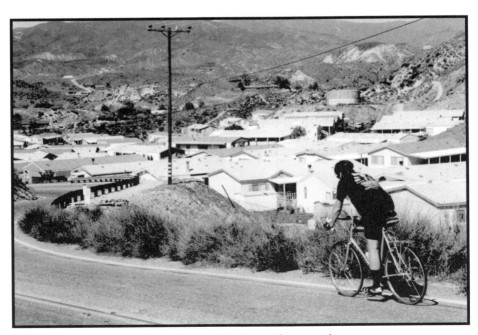

Sand Canyon Road near the summit

TRIP #68 - VALENCIA LOOP

__GENERAL LOCATION__: Valencia

__LEVEL OF DIFFICULTY__: Loop - easy
                         Distance - 7.8 miles
                         Elevation gain - periodic moderate grades

__HIGHLIGHTS__: This interesting tour travels both the main thoroughfares and residential "back waters" of Valencia. This predominantly Class X ride on wide city streets cruises through pleasant tree-lined sections of Orchard Village Road and McBean Parkway, then diverts to a quiet residential runout just west of the Santa Clara River. There is an option to add two excellent miles to the trip by touring scenic Old Orchard Park and the surrounding residential area.

In addition, just off the main route is the 3.5-mile Class I South Fork Trail which plies the South Fork of the Santa Clara River. Finally, there is a short excursion to William S. Hart Park, which has the Hart Mansion with its knockout vista point, the Saugus Train Station Museum, and some inviting natural grounds.

__TRAILHEAD__: From the Golden State Freeway, exit at Lyons Avenue and turn east. Drive about one mile (near Peachland Avenue on the south side of the road) and park along Lyons Avenue near Old Orchard Park. From the Antelope Valley Freeway, exit at San Fernando Road and drive northwest two miles to Lyons Avenue. Turn left (west) and drive about one mile to the park. Turn left on Avenida Rotella and left again into the small parking area. The park has trees, grass, restrooms, children's play areas, and athletic courts.

Bring a filled water bottle in the summer. There are gas stations and other commercial establishments along the route, although we found few convenient public water sources. Bring an automobile roadmap as a backup, should you miss any key roads in the southbound residential leg.

__TRIP DESCRIPTION__: __Old Orchard Park.__ Before starting the main loop, take time to investigate the cozy bikeways within Old Orchard Park (see map insert) and the pleasant surrounding residential area. This is some fine family biking which represents about two miles of Class I trailway. This is a grand example of intelligent community planning!

__Main Thoroughfares - Northbound.__ From near Avenida Rotella and Lyons Avenue, bike along Class X Lyons Avenue past Avenida Entrana (0.3) and continue to Wiley Canyon Road (gas station) (0.7). Turn right (north) and pedal a moderate upgrade on the Class II path through a residential neighborhood. In a short distance, follow the downgrade past Tournament Road onto a flat area near Avenida Cappela (1.3). In 0.4 mile, turn left on Orchard Village Road and follow that tree-lined Class X road on a steady and modest upgrade to Mill Valley Road (2.0).

In another 0.2 mile, reach McBean Parkway. Turn right on that Class X street, passing some commercial areas, and bike beneath the roadside tree cover past Avenida

TRIP #68 - VALENCIA LOOP

Navarre (2.5). In 0.2 mile, near a shopping center, there is a clear view north into the mountains. Just beyond is Arroyo Park Drive (2.9), and 0.4 mile further is Del Monte Drive. The area is relatively open and flat, and there is a sweeping panorama into the Santa Clarita Valley.

Residential Streets - Southbound. Turn right (east) on Del Monte Drive and begin an extended stretch of ride through a quiet residential community. There are scattered community recreation centers with pools, volleyball courts, and other goodies (maybe even drinking water!) in this area. Follow the road 0.8 mile through a wide curve and turn left at Estaban Drive (4.1). Cruise about 0.3 mile just past Carrizo Drive and turn left on John Russell Drive.

Follow that road a short distance and turn left again at Alicante Drive (4.6). Bike along the curved roadway to its end at grassy, open Almendra Park, then turn left at Alta Madera Drive. In short order, make a right at Avenida Velarte and a left at Via Dona Christa (5.5). Cycle through this residential area 0.5 mile to Via Telino, transit a walk-through fence, and follow Via Dona Christa as it turns right (west) and becomes Via Barra. In 0.2 mile at Via Pacifica, turn left and bike a short distance to Wiley Canyon Road (6.3).

Turn right, cruise 0.3 mile to Orchard Village Road, and turn left. At Avenida Ronada, one option is to enter the residential area and bike on the Class I bikepath back to the park. However, our reference route continues south 0.8 mile on Orchard Village Road and turns right (west) at Lyons Avenue (7.4). All that remains is a short 0.4-mile pedal back to Old Orchard Park (7.8).

South Fork Trail Excursion. At Estaban Drive, just beyond Sandalia Drive, there is an entry to South Fork Park. Other entries along the reference route are at Via Dona Christa just south of Via Flored and at Via Pacifica at its south end. From the Estaban Drive entry, the Class I path follows the west bank of the South Fork of the Santa Clara River 1.75 miles north and east to McBean Parkway and south 1.75 miles to Orchard Village Road. Bikers and walkers share this path, which supplies numerous river vista points and a variety of city views. (Additional trail entries are at McBean Parkway, Valencia Town Center, Valencia Boulevard, Magic Mountain Parkway, and Orchard Village Road.)

William S. Hart Park. From Orchard Village Road and Lyons Avenue, bike east one-third mile to Newhall Avenue and turn right. In one-half mile, just after the fusion with San Fernando Road, turn right at the marked entry to the park. The expansive lower grounds have the headquarters and visitor's center, as well as water, restrooms, barbecue facilities, grassy grounds, and abundant tree cover. The Mason Mansion, the park's highlight, is reached via a small, steep roadway (not open to bicycles) from the lower park. From the mansion area, there is a grand 360-degree view of the local environs. The Saugus Train Station Museum is at the park's southeastern edge along San Fernando Road. It offers a historic look at vehicles used for travel in bygone eras.

CONNECTING TRIPS: Connection with the Canyon Country Tour (Trip #67) - at the intersection of McBean Parkway and Del Monte Drive, continue north to Valencia Boulevard and turn right (east).

TRIP #69 - SAN FRANCISQUITO AND BOUQUET CANYONS

GENERAL LOCATION: Santa Clarita, Green Valley, Leona Valley,
                       Bouquet Canyon

LEVEL OF DIFFICULTY: **CANYONS LOOP** - very strenuous
                          Distance - 40.8 miles
                          Elevation gain - several steep-to-sheer grades

                          RIFT ZONE LOOP - strenuous to very strenuous
                          Distance - 22.8 miles
                          Elevation gain - several steep-to-sheer grades

HIGHLIGHTS: Two separate loop trips are provided.

The **CANYONS LOOP** follows San Francisquito Canyon Road, Spunky Canyon Road, and Bouquet Canyon Road in successive order and starts from Santa Clarita. After a mild pedaling stretch, the ride climbs almost 15 miles on the way to Spunky Canyon Road. Along the way are Powerhouses #1 and #2 and their mammoth hillside penstocks, part of the Los Angeles Aqueduct. Between the two are the remnants of the Saint Francis Dam, whose collapse resulted in the single-event, second greatest loss of life in California history. Spunky Canyon Road passes through pastoral Green Valley, climbs to a superb valley overlook, and flies down to the Bouquet Reservoir. The route shifts onto Bouquet Canyon Road, follows a last-gasp upgrade, and then works its way downhill through serene Bouquet Canyon before returning to the bustle of Santa Clarita. The total elevation gain on this tour is over 3000 feet!

The **RIFT ZONE LOOP** plies upper San Francisquito Canyon, Leona Valley, and upper Bouquet Canyon Road. The ride starts from the Green Valley area and climbs to an overlook of Leona Valley, on San Francisquito Canyon Road, then dives down to the valley and Elizabeth Lake Road. A tour of the rift zone and the town of Leona Valley follows, leading to the Bouquet Canyon junction. An easy-going valley ride gives way to a steep climb to an overlook of Bouquet Reservoir and a swift downhill to that body of water. Loop closure is via Spunky Canyon Road, which just reverses the route discussed in the loop above. This ride has an elevation gain of over 2000 feet.

An option for cyclists in excellent shape, seeking a greater challenge, is to continue past Spunky Canyon Road, do the three legs of the RIFT ZONE LOOP, and again bypass Spunky Canyon Road at the Bouquet Reservoir. The final leg is the Bouquet Canyon Road segment of the CANYONS LOOP. (Don't get us wrong; the two loops initially described are side splitters!) This little monster requires more than 3500 feet of hill-climbing over the 52.4 miles!

TRAILHEAD: From the Golden State Freeway, exit east at Valencia Boulevard and drive 2.5 miles to Bouquet Canyon Road. Turn left (northeast) and continue one mile to Seco Canyon Road. Turn left and motor one-third mile to Guadilamar Drive. Turn left again and enter the parking area of Santa Clarita Park. The park has tree shade, grass,

TRIP #69 - SAN FRANCISQUITO AND BOUQUET CANYONS

water, restrooms, picnic tables, sports fields, a children's playground, and a pool. From the Lancaster/Palmdale area, starting points might be Leona Valley, Elizabeth Lake off Elizabeth Lake Road, or Green Valley on Spunky Canyon Road. Elizabeth Lake itself is a good parking area, as is a spot near the diner or general store in Green Valley or Leona Valley. Note that starting from this direction "saves" the rugged uphill for late in the ride.

Bring a couple of filled water bottles or load up at the trailhead. There are few public sources directly on the upper part of the route. However, a service station, diner, and market are in Green Valley (partial loop) and Leona Valley (full loop), and numerous support facilities are in the lower Bouquet Canyon area (both loops). Keep in mind that the trip will be hot and dry in the summer. (Alternately, this can be a very cold ride in the winter!)

TRIP DESCRIPTION: **CANYONS LOOP. Santa Clarita to San Francisquito Powerhouse #2.** Turn left (north) on Seco Canyon Road and climb lazily for 0.8 mile to Copper Hill Drive, then turn left again. In 0.5 mile, turn right (north) at San Francisquito Canyon Road (which is Northpark Drive to the south). The route leaves the dense residential environs almost immediately on a short climb. The road works its way toward and drops near to the bed of the Santa Clara River, then begins a northerly journey on the east side of San Francisquito Canyon, passing Lady Linda Lane (on the left) (3.3). In a little over 1.5 miles, cross the Angeles National Forest boundary. (What is interesting is that the sparse tree cover to this point thins even further beyond the boundary.)

The two-lane winding road continues further into the narrowing canyon, passing the Drinkwater Flat 4X4 road (dirt) at (6.7). A few crossings over narrow bridges bring cyclists around a bend to view a massive group of penstocks (water conduits to us normal folk) coming down the hillsides to San Francisquito Powerhouse #2 (7.4). This structure is part of the Los Angeles Aqueduct. Just before reaching the powerhouse, there is an entry to the San Francisquito Ranger Station; stop and read about the 1928 Saint Francis Dam collapse, an event that resulted in the deaths of 400 people downstream. Another 1.5 miles upstream, there are large chunks of concrete and steel in the riverbed, the remnants of the old dam.

The Climb to Green Valley. Continue uphill through scattered tree cover, pass Dry Gulch Fire Road, and cycle by the San Francisquito Conservation Camp (11.8). In another 0.6 mile is the Bee Canyon Ranch turnoff, followed by a steepening grade that takes cyclists to a grand vista area below the penstocks of San Francisquito Powerhouse #1. At the junction with paved, private Pelton Street (13.9), general traffic stays to the left and cyclists follow a downright nasty switchback upgrade, pass dirt Clearwater Canyon Road, and transit near the penstocks themselves. The grade moderates and lets up near where the power transmission lines cross San Francisquito Canyon Road (15.0). A brief coast and renewed climb lead past South Portal Canyon and its namesake road, residences begin to reappear on what is now a flat, and riders meet Spunky Canyon Road (17.0).

Spunky Canyon Road. Turn right (east) on this road, pedaling through the tree-dotted town of Green Valley. A gas station, general store, and eatery are at Ensenada Road (17.9). (None appeared prone to offer restroom facilities except for paying customers.) Pedal to the outskirts of town and pass the Spunky Canyon Campground in

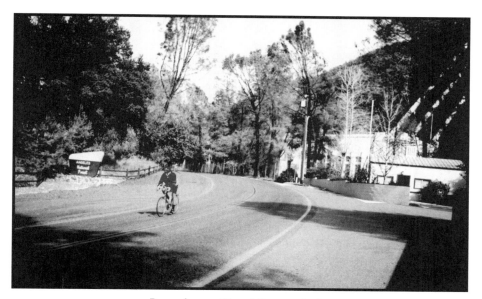

Powerhouse #2 and the penstocks

another 0.8 mile. (It has tree shade, porta-potties, and picnic facilities, but we found no water, as was true of the remaining campgrounds on the return leg.)

Shortly, a very steep climb begins which takes cyclists upward for another 1.5 miles, a segment with great over-the-shoulder views of Green Valley. Beyond the summit, there is an equally sinuous and steep downhill with excellent Bouquet Reservoir vistas. The road dumps out alongside the reservoir and winds its way eastward to Bouquet Canyon Road (23.4).

Bouquet Canyon Road and the Downhill. "It ain't over till it's over," because another steep 0.7-mile climb awaits. Beyond the summit are numerous Bouquet Reservoir views as the road bends around that reservoir's contour. The now tree-shaded road heads downhill alongside Bouquet Canyon Creek and passes the marked Bouquet Canyon Recreation Area and a collection of cabins (25.7). Del Sur Road and Big Oaks Lodge (29.0) come up, and bicyclists pass a dense mixed grove of trees with a palm tree immersed in the middle!

The road through the narrowing canyon leads past the Texas Canyon Ranger Station (32.1) and both Zuni and Los Cantiles campgrounds (with interesting rock formations nearby), reaching the Saugus Ranger Station at (32.7). In 0.5 mile, cross the Angeles National Forest boundary, then pass a few scattered ranches and Coarsegold and Lenny roads, and enter an area where the canyon widens. Passage by Vasquez Canyon Road (35.0) signals a return to a more developed area, with the Santa Clarita city limit reached in 1.7 miles. Just beyond, there is a small shopping center, as well as the beginning of a Class II bikeway, with Plum Canyon Road reached 0.3 mile later (38.0). Glide alongside the myriad of shopping plazas and reach Seco Canyon Road in 2.4 miles. All that is left is to pedal a mild upgrade back to Santa Clarita Park (40.8).

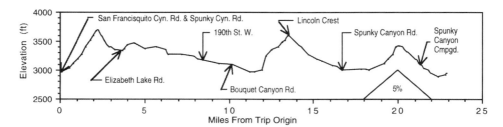

RIFT ZONE LOOP. San Francisquito Canyon Road. At Spunky Canyon Road, start a mild climb on San Francisquito Canyon Road, passing numerous residences on the right-hand side. Just above Calle Manzanita, on the left, is San Francisquito Campground (0.5), beyond which the residential development all but ends. The uphill steepens considerably and the road passes the Green Valley Ranger Station (1.5). The summit is reached in 0.7 mile, where there is an impressive view of the extended valley floor below. The exhilarating 0.9-mile downhill through a more barren landscape passes Leona Divide and Tule Divide fire roads before bottoming at Elizabeth Lake Road (3.1).

Elizabeth Lake Road. Turn right (southeast) and begin a modest uphill pedal on the rural road through narrow Leona Valley. Though no signs proclaim it, this road lies nearly atop the San Andreas Rift Zone! Cyclists pass a llama ranch early on and enjoy lightly rolling terrain on a general downhill which will continue all the way to Bouquet Canyon Road. At (8.5), reach 90th Street West and a stop sign, which signal the town of Leona Valley's civic hub. A market, a gas station, and a couple of eateries are nearby. Bike another 1.6 miles of this easy-going valley pedal to Bouquet Canyon Road.

Bouquet Canyon Road. Turn right (south) and cruise nearly two miles through a wide valley with agricultural fields, ranches, and scattered residences, together with occasional fruit and flower stands. Next there is a gut-busting 1.5-mile climb through a narrowing canyon alongside Bouquet Canyon Creek. At Lincoln Crest (13.6), the reward is a stunning view of the Bouquet Reservoir below. The winding highway plummets past the Leona Divide Fire Road toward the reservoir, then straightens appreciably and meets Spunky Canyon Road (16.7).

Spunky Canyon Road. This is just the reverse path on Spunky Canyon Road taken on the CANYONS LOOP. The lightly used road follows the contour of the reservoir for 1.6 miles before turning into the hills and beginning a sweat-it-out upgrade. Now, however, cyclists ride the outside edge over a steep drop-off for a distance before reaching the protective shelter of the Spunky Canyon side, where the road meshes into the hills. At the summit near the 20-mile point, Green Valley is spread out below and to the west. Crane to the east into the hillsides and look for the plush growth of the Spunky Saddle Plantation, a marvelous clustered growth of human-planted trees. A very steep and winding downhill levels near the Spunky Canyon Campground (21.1). An easy ride through verdant Green Valley with its surrounding peaks leads back to the ride start at San Francisquito Canyon Road (22.9).

CONNECTING TRIPS: 1) Connection with the Canyon Country tour (Trip #67) - the trips share a common route on Bouquet Canyon Road below Vasquez Canyon Road; 2) connection with the Old Ridge Route Road tour (Trip #70) - at Elizabeth Lake Road on the RIFT ZONE LOOP, turn west on that road and bike to Lake Hughes Road.

TRIPS #70A-#70C OLD RIDGE ROUTE ROAD

This is a three-part ride that forms a very strenuous 69-mile loop. Riding the full loop is reserved for veteran riders in superior condition. The loop ride involves tackling over 6500 feet of elevation gain! The Lake Hughes Road (initial) and Pine Canyon Road (middle) segments are on sometimes-narrow, winding roadway with light, but periodic, fast-moving traffic. The Old Ridge Route Road (last) segment, though paved, has a 20-mile non-maintained section and is best done on a mountain bike. If using a fat-tire road bike, bring a beefed-up tire patch kit as a precaution. The non-maintained segment is little-used and remote.

For the full loop, bring 3-4 water bottles to see you through the waterless stretches. Beyond Castaic, we found water only at tiny Lake Hughes, at a single small market. If not willing to rely on that water source, consider bringing 5-6 quarts of water.

TRIP #70A - LAKE HUGHES ROAD

<u>GENERAL LOCATION</u>: Castaic, Lake Hughes

<u>LEVEL OF DIFFICULTY</u>: One way - strenuous to very strenuous
                          Distance - 23.5 miles
                          Elevation gain - several long, moderate-to-steep grades

<u>HIGHLIGHTS</u>: This segment follows Lake Hughes Road from its origin in Castaic to its end at the small town of Lake Hughes. There is over 3000 feet of climb as the road works its way above Castaic Lake, plummets into the outlet of Elizabeth Lake Canyon, and follows that canyon as it winds its way 13 miles and 1300 feet to Lake Hughes. On the way, there are superb Castaic Lake vistas and sporadic looks beyond the canyon walls to other distant canyons which pepper this region. Auto traffic is light and the traffic speed is low on the (generally) sinuous portions of the route; however, some drivers do push it in the straighter sections of roadway, requiring that cyclists stay vigilant and ready to hug the road shoulder.

<u>TRAILHEAD</u>: From the Golden State Freeway in Castaic, exit east at Lake Hughes Road. Park at Castaic Lake, then turn left at the next intersection, Castaic Road. Several hundred feet up the road is the Castaic Center mall, with plenty of parking. An option is to start from the Castaic Lake Recreation Area, which is on Lake Hughes Road about half a mile from the Castaic Road intersection.
    Bring 2-3 water bottles to see you through the waterless stretch between Castaic and Lake Hughes. Note that there is a ranger station near the midpoint, should cyclists need emergency assistance.

<u>TRIP DESCRIPTION</u>: **Castaic to Warm Springs Road.** Return to Lake Hughes Road and turn east, passing Old Ridge Route Road (the full-loop outlet) and Castaic Lagoon and the Castaic Lake Recreation Area just beyond (0.5). In 0.4 mile, start a steep climb above Castaic Lake. There are numerous lake vistas on the way up, which continue up to the Elizabeth Lake Canyon inlet. Pass the marked "Main Launch Ramp" (2.3) and continue climbing through sage-brush-covered hillsides, reaching the Angeles National Forest boundary in 0.8 mile. A short downhill gives way to a two-mile climb, which crests, then drops to the Dry Gulch Road junction (7.1).
    Lake Hughes Road climbs again for a mile, pulling back towards Castaic Lake, then begins a well-deserved downhill. Two miles into the downgrade, the N. Castaic Reservoir Road junction is reached (10.1), shortly after a distinct entry into Elizabeth Lake Canyon. The road follows the canyon contour back uphill to a crest (11.6), then transits a relatively flat area, passing Ruby Canyon Road and reaching Warm Springs Road in 0.6 mile (13.2). There is a ranger station here, private camp facilities, and other local amenities, all off the main road.
    Warm Springs Road to Lake Hughes. Lake Hughes Road follows the winding canyon on a sustained uphill for the next ten-plus miles. For most of the way, the road is not far above creekbed level. The route passes seasonal campgrounds at (14.8)

Lake Hughes Road above Castaic Lake

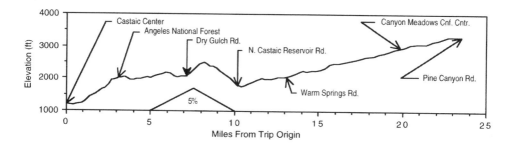

and (19.6) and enters a forested zone. In another 0.3 mile is the private Canyon Meadows Baptist Conference Center, followed by the Forestry Nursery (Lake Hughes Unit) (20.0) and a couple more private campgrounds. In another 1.7 miles starts a series of small roadside ranches and the outskirts of the tiny community of Lake Hughes. At 23.5 is the junction with Pine Canyon Road, complete with a small market and roadside tavern. (Note that tree-surrounded Lake Hughes itself can be reached with a quarter-mile diversion east on Elizabeth Lake Road and a turn right [south] at Norblett Drive.)

CONNECTING TRIPS: 1) Continuation with the Pine Canyon Road tour (Trip #70B) - turn left (west) at Pine Canyon Road at the Lake Hughes Road northern terminus; 2) continuation with the Old Ridge Route Road ride (Trip #70C) - turn left (north) at Old Ridge Route Road in Castaic; 3) connection with the San Francisquito and Bouquet Canyons tour (Trip #69) - at the Lake Hughes Road terminus, turn east onto Elizabeth Lake Road (Pine Canyon Road to the west).

TRIP #70B - PINE CANYON ROAD

<u>GENERAL LOCATION</u>: Lake Hughes, Sandberg

<u>LEVEL OF DIFFICULTY</u>: One way - strenuous
Distance - 17.2 miles
Elevation gain - periodic moderate-to-steep grades

<u>HIGHLIGHTS</u>: The Pine Canyon Road segment is a 17-mile countryside ride through tree-bedecked rolling hills, much of it straddling the San Andreas Rift Zone. There is close to 2000 feet elevation gain with several sustained moderate-to-steep grades. The first 9.3-mile portion is on a countryside lane with scattered residences and sporadic, fast-moving traffic. The remainder of the trip (beyond Three Points Road) is very lightly traveled and is more typified as having well-separated ranches. If your joy is solitude and a countryside setting, the latter portion of the ride is road biking at its best.

<u>TRAILHEAD</u>: From the Lancaster/Palmdale area, take the Antelope Valley Freeway and turn off westbound at Elizabeth Lake Road (County Highway N2), then drive 14 miles to the Lake Hughes Road intersection. (Note that the road name changes to Pine Canyon Road just beyond.) Turn south onto Lake Hughes Road and find parking near the market or tavern. From the Golden State Freeway, exit east at Lancaster Road (State Highway 138) and drive 21 miles to Three Points Road. Turn right and continue five miles as the road veers left and merges into Pine Canyon Road. In another 9.5 miles, reach Lake Hughes Road. Park as described above.
   Bring a couple of water bottles to see you through this "dry" route on hot days. If the plan is for an up-and-back tour in the heat, add water to suit your needs.

<u>TRIP DESCRIPTION</u>: **Lake Hughes to Three Points Road.** Start on this two-lane country road under a scattered tree canopy. Relish the thought that, unlike the Lake Hughes Road portion, this is typical of most of this segment. Start a 4.5-mile moderate climb that peaks, then drops to Kings Canyon Road. Along the way are scattered residences and a creekbed alongside the road. Near the summit are a private church grounds and a wedding chapel at Tweedy Lane (6.1).
   A refreshing downhill that ends just beyond Kings Canyon Road is followed by a modest 1.7-mile climb. The road then passes scattered residential pockets on a long, blow-it-out downhill that bottoms at Three Points Road (9.3).
   Three Points Road to Old Ridge Route Road. Cyclists that blink will wind up heading north on Three Points Road, since a hard left is required to stay on Pine Canyon Road. A modest climb takes cyclists beyond the scattered residential pockets, past Seccombe Road (10.4), and into an area dotted by small ranches. This area of rolling hills is well-treed, both away from and alongside this winding road. After a nice downhill, pass Rancho Corona del Valle, one of the larger ranches in the area (14.8). The ride finale is a steady 1.6-mile upgrade which leads to the Pine Canyon Road terminus at Old Ridge Route Road (17.2). (The skinnied-down track across Old Ridge Route Road is a private drive used by Sandberg residents.)

Pine Canyon Road near Sandberg

CONNECTING TRIPS: 1) Continuation with the Lake Hughes Road tour (Trip #70A) - turn south at the trip origin at Lake Hughes Road; 2) continuation with the Old Ridge Route Road ride (Trip #70C) - turn left (south) at Old Ridge Route Road at the terminus of this ride.

TRIP #70C - OLD RIDGE ROUTE ROAD

GENERAL LOCATION: Sandberg, Castaic

LEVEL OF DIFFICULTY: One way - strenuous (north to south); very strenuous
(south to north)
Distance - 28.0 miles
Elevation gain - periodic moderate to steep grades
(north to south); periodic steep-to-sheer grades
(south to north)

HIGHLIGHTS: Being both on-road and off-road cycling book authors, we think this ride is a charmer for both groups! Much of the ride is on paved, but non-maintained, Forest Service Road 8N04. It is doable with any fat-tire bike that has good tire tread, but is best done on mountain bike tires. There is little road traffic north of Templin Highway (read that as few vehicle nuisances, but also that it is remote) and the route transits high-desert scrub with minimal tree cover.

The north-to-south ride described has nearly 4000 feet of drop, yet still offers some challenging climbs (1500 feet total) with some mixed perspectives of the great, relatively undeveloped outdoors, together with the downlooking vistas of the bustle of Interstate Highway 5. There are remnants of the grand days of the Old Ridge Route Road, including the old Tumble Inn, together with many looks at the stratified geology and plant life of this high-desert arena. The varied canyon, Castaic Lake, and even developed town of Castaic vistas along the way are awesome. The peace and quiet of the natural northern trip section and the rewarding downhill blowout on the more-developed southern section give this ride the best of both worlds!

TRAILHEAD: From the Golden State Freeway, exit at Lancaster Road (State Highway 138) and drive east 8.5 miles to County Highway N2. Look for the sign noting "Old Ridge Route Road." Turn right (south) and climb two miles to the Pine Canyon Road junction. From the Lancaster/Palmdale area, take Avenue "D" westbound, continuing as it becomes Lancaster Road. At six miles west of 300th Street West, turn left (south) at Highway N2 and follow the directions above.

Bring a couple of water bottles to see you through this waterless and remote segment; bring more on hot days. Ensure that your tire patch kit and repair tools are packed, otherwise it could be a long walk out!

Old Ridge Route Road above Fisher Springs Road

TRIP DESCRIPTION: **Trailhead to Reservoir Hill.** Climb one-half mile on paved road to a flat where the maintained road ends. The surface transitions to a mix of broken asphalt and concrete with scattered seams of dirt and then returns to a modest climb above Liebre Gulch (to the west). At (1.6) is a level, where there is a distant peek at Pyramid Lake. The first downhill leads past a marked turnoff (Forest Service Road 7N23) to Bear Canyon and Sawmill Mountain campgrounds (3.1). Shortly, there is a shift to an eastern exposure, one of a myriad of view changes that will occur on this ridge ride.

A mild uphill leads past a rock wall and the site of the old Tumble Inn (4.4), followed by some ups and downs and a passage through a narrowing slide area (6.4). A downhill takes cyclists on the first of several passes below transmission lines to the start of an extended saddle (7.1). A tough 1.4-mile, 400-foot climb leads to a crest below the Reservoir Hill summit, where there is a majestic view into Cienaga Canyon to the east (9.1). This is the most challenging upgrade for the north-south Old Ridge Route Road transit.

Reservoir Hill to Templin Highway. The road quality improves somewhat on the downhill as bicyclists pass a road closure gate and reach another saddle, where there is a brief first glimpse of Interstate Highway 5 (10.8). Soon there is a passage through another slide area and a nice winding downhill with open Highway 5 vistas, followed by a transit under a pipeline-supporting suspension bridge (12.3).

Beyond a low saddle, there is a climb past Forest Service Road 6N43, and the first Castaic Lake vistas are just beyond the summit (16.8). A refreshing downhill takes cyclists on a sweeping turn to a southeast heading and over the Angeles Tunnel of the West Branch of the California Aqueduct (18.0). The road continues past a roadside ranch with trailer homes in the lower reaches in another 0.5 mile. From here to trip's end, the ride is on quality asphalt roadway. A one-mile climb leads to a flat and an exposed area with steep drops above Castaic Lake's upper bay. Just beyond is the first stop sign and the junction with paved Templin Highway (20.2).

Templin Highway to Castaic. Bike straight ahead on a short steep climb to a flat (diverting either direction on Templin Highway will require a steep return to this junction) and follow the winding road past an out-of-place trailer home situated on a lake overlook (21.3). What follows is a refreshing 6.3-mile, 1800-foot runout to Lake Hughes Road in Castaic. The road passes a small cluster of homesites and dives down toward and parallels Highway 5 from above. There is a minuscule climb at (24.5), followed by more downhill and an entry into a residential pocket above Castaic Lagoon in about two miles. The trip's second stop sign looms at (26.7), followed by the Lake Hughes Road intersection (27.6). A right turn (west) and a second right at Castaic Road return cyclists to the Castaic Center shopping complex (28.0).

CONNECTING TRIPS: 1) Continuation with the Lake Hughes Road tour (Trip #70A) - turn east on Lake Hughes Road in Castaic; 2) continuation with the Pine Canyon Road ride (Trip #70B) - at the trip origin, take Pine Canyon Road east.

TRIP #71 - CALIFORNIA AQUEDUCT

GENERAL LOCATION: Llano, Baldy Mesa, Hesperia

LEVEL OF DIFFICULTY: One way - moderate; up and back - moderate to strenuous
(difficulty rating is dependent on weather conditions)
Distance - 27.5 miles
Elevation gain - essentially flat

HIGHLIGHTS: This tour is a desert rat's dream. There are grand mountain views in the distance and relatively undeveloped desert landscape up close, throughout the entire tour of over 27 miles. Those who revel in peace and solitude will find that the route is lightly used for most of the year. The nearby flora and fauna are generally undisturbed, i.e., left to be enjoyed by those quietly passing through.

TRAILHEAD: From State Highway 138 west of Pearblossom and near Llano, turn south on 165th Street and drive two miles to the California Aqueduct. Park on the east side of the street, away from the entrance area. There is a portable restroom here. Another option is to start from Hesperia near the intersection of Amargosa Road and the aqueduct. From U.S. Highway 395, turn west at Main Street/Phelan Road and turn right (north) at Key Pointe Avenue. Drive to a "T"-intersection and turn right on Amargosa Road, following that frontage road a quarter mile to the aqueduct.

TRIP #71 - CALIFORNIA AQUEDUCT

The route is waterless, exposed, and relatively remote, although there are scattered residences off some roadways which cross the aqueduct. Bring 2-3 water bottles on hot days as a contingency, or bike this route in the <u>cool</u> of winter. (It does snow at this 4000-foot elevation!) Temperatures of over 100 degrees F are not uncommon in the May-October period, and high winds are a staple in this high-desert area. In addition to the normal repair tools and tire patch kit, bring some sunscreen – there is no tree cover and minimal shade from any source. Sunglasses are a must! Finally, stay out of the aqueduct! The walls are steep and can be slippery, making it extremely difficult to get back out.

TRIP DESCRIPTION: Start by reading the sign at the entry gate, which reads, *Walk-in Fishing Only, No Bicycles, No Vehicles*, then observe the *Bike Trail* sign further in. (Oh, well!) Slip through the walker/biker entry on the north side and cycle on a rough asphalt surface, characteristic of the entire tour. The route is flat with a few little ups and downs. To the right (south) are the San Gabriel Mountains with Mount Baldy and sister peaks prominently on display in the distance and a chain of foothills in the fore-ground.

Observe the yucca trees and mixed desert scrub to the north. Both the mountain vistas and high-desert landscape are characteristic of the scenery on the entire tour. Also, plan on visits from numerous crows, a few hawks, and other of nature's desert creatures. We saw a couple of large dogs (or possibly coyotes) from a distance, on the far eastern segment, actually working their way out of the water.

On the ride east, there are unmarked road crossings (both paved and unpaved) requiring cyclists to dismount, pass through an entry gate, cross the road, and reenter

California Aqueduct west of Oasis Road

through the gate on the opposite side before resuming the tour. Luckily these distractions are well spaced and can serve as welcome breaks for the "backside." Street names are stenciled on the sides of the overpasses which face the aqueduct. Major cross streets are Largo Vista Road (4.3), Highway 138 (6.5), Oasis Road (11.3), Sheep Creek Road (15.9), Johnson Road (17.3), Caughlin Road (21.4), Duncan Road (22.5), and Baldy Mesa Road (23.7).

The mountain panorama changes slowly as bikers find themselves nearly north of the Cajon Summit on the eastern segment of the trip. The San Bernardino Mountains are to the southeast. The ever-plentiful yuccas seem to come in every shape and size. There are pockets of residences near some of the road crossings, becoming more prevalent in the Baldy Mesa locale. Near trip's end, bicyclists stare directly at the high-speed traffic of U.S. Highway 395 and soon reach Amargosa Road (26.2).

CONNECTING TRIPS: Connection with the aqueduct segment eastbound out of Hesperia: cycle from the trip end point south to the Key Pointe Road/Phelan Road intersection and turn left (east) onto the latter roadway. Bike 1.5 miles on what becomes Main Street to the aqueduct crossing and look for the marked entry on the east side. The trail follows some modest ups and downs, then essentially flattens for the remainder of the ride, which ends in 6.6 miles at Ranchero Road. Intervening cross streets are Maple Avenue (3.9), Mesquite Street (4.3), and Cottonwood Avenue (5.2).

INDEX TO LANDMARKS AND ATTRACTIONS
BY TRIP NUMBER

SUNBELT PUBLICATIONS

"Adventures in the Natural History and Cultural Heritage of the Californias"
Series Editor—Lowell Lindsay

SUNBELT'S OUTDOOR RECREATION BOOKLIST

Anza-Borrego A to Z: People, Places, and Things	Diana Lindsay
Anza-Borrego Desert Region (Wilderness Press)	L. and D. Lindsay
Baja Legends: Historic Characters, Events, Locations	Greg Niemann
Campgrounds of Los Angeles and Orange Counties	Jeff Tyler
Campgrounds of San Diego County	Jeff Tyler
Campgrounds of Santa Barbara and Ventura Counties	Jeff Tyler
Cycling Los Angeles	D. and S. Brundige
Cycling Orange County	D. and S. Brundige
Cycling San Diego	Copp and Schad
Fire, Chaparral, and Survival in Southern California	Richard Halsey
Leave Only Paw Prints: Dog Hikes, San Diego County	Donna Lawrence
Mission Trails Regional Park Trail Map	Casey Cook
More Adventures with Kids in San Diego	Botello, Paxton
Orange County Place Names A to Z	Phil Brigandi
Orange County Day Journeys and Picnics	Linda Pyle
Pacific Peaks and Picnics: Day Journeys in San Diego County	Linda Pyle
Palm Springs Legends: Creation of a Desert Oasis	Greg Niemann
Peaks, Palms, and Picnics: Day Journeys in Coachella Valley	Linda Pyle
San Diego Architecture Guide (SDAF)	Dirk Sutro
San Diego County Place Names A to Z	Leland Fetzer
San Diego Legends: Historic Characters, Events, Locations	Jack Innis
San Diego Mountain Bike Guide	Daniel Greenstadt
Weekend Driver San Diego	Jack Brandais

Incorporated in 1988 with roots in publishing since 1973, **Sunbelt** produces and distributes natural science and outdoor guidebooks, regional histories and reference books, plus pictorials and stories that celebrate the land and its people.

Our publishing program focuses on the Californias which are today three states in two nations sharing one Pacific shore. Sunbelt books help to discover and conserve the natural and historical heritage of unique regions on the frontiers of adventure and learning. Our books guide readers into distinctive communities and special places, both natural and manmade.

We carry hundreds of books on southern California!
Visit us online at:
www.sunbeltbooks.com